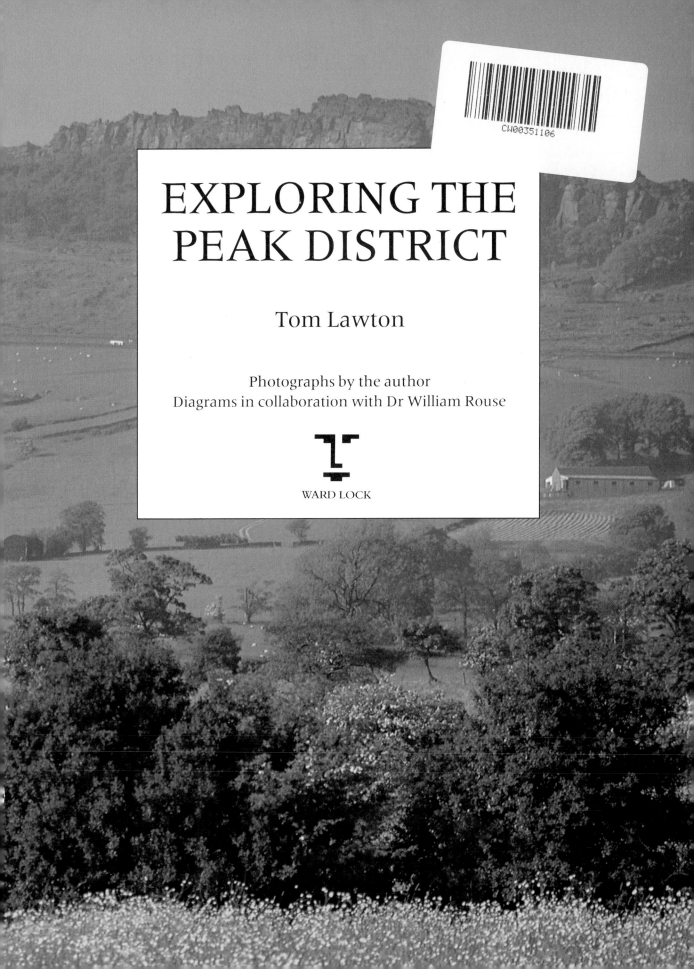

EXPLORING THE PEAK DISTRICT

Tom Lawton

Photographs by the author
Diagrams in collaboration with Dr William Rouse

WARD LOCK

A WARD LOCK BOOK

Paperback first published in the UK 1997
by Ward Lock, Wellington House, 125 Strand, London WC2R 0BB

A Cassell Imprint

A British Library Cataloguing in Publication Data block for this book may
be obtained from the British Library

ISBN 0 7063 7635 8
Typeset by Litho Link Ltd, Welshpool, Powys, Wales
Printed and bound in Slovenia by DELO TISKARNA by
arrangement with KOROTAN LJUBLJANA

Cover photograph (front and this page): *Kinder Scout viewed across Kinder Reservoir.*
Back: *The view westwards from Curbar Edge.*
Photographs courtesy Tom Lawton.

Page 1: *The Roaches, observed from Middle Hulme.*
Page 4: *Tissington Spires, Dove Dale.*

CONTENTS

PREFACE

When the suggestion was first put to me that my second guide book in this innovative *Exploring* series should cover the Peak District, it initially generated a mixture of emotions ranging from delight to apprehension. Let me hasten to explain.

First, the delight. I was born in the shadows of the Peak at Lake Hospital, Ashton-under-Lyne. Later, whilst a pupil at Audenshaw Grammar School, I discovered the immense pleasure and satisfaction of hill-walking with like-minded school chums. We often trekked over that part of the Peak which was accessible by public transport, relying on ancient motor buses and puffer trains to bring us to our starting points. The area we covered included the challenging Saddleworth Moors, the hills around Glossop and Hayfield, mighty Kinder Scout and the delightful valley of Edale. The 'walking bug' has remained with me ever since those early, formative years; it has invaded my mind and my physique with a sense of relaxation, well-being, pleasure, and physical and mental satisfaction. Furthermore, it attracts the most congenial company. I have, therefore, much to thank the Peak District for.

Secondly, the apprehension. In recent years I have spent much time walking amongst the Lakeland Fells and also in the spectacular Alps of Austria, Switzerland and Italy. Because of this, I wondered whether returning to the Peak of my youth might be an anti-climax and might fail to rekindle the old magic. Also, this was to be an illustrated book and I needed plenty of photogenic landscapes.

The apprehension was unjustified. My first return exploration into the Peak District was a walk with two stalwarts who were in serious training for a 40-mile marathon and were nearing their own 'Peak' of physical fitness. Our inspired route was from Hayfield, up William Clough, along the Snake Path, across Kinder to above Edale, then along the edges and so back to Hayfield — one of the more strenuous walking routes included in this book.

The walk was superb. We chose a good day weather-wise; the route was through challenging, remote and rugged terrain, with continuously arresting views and fascinating millstone grit rock configurations. All this, even crossing the peat hags, I enjoyed immensely. I returned home, weary but highly contented, from a pleasurable walking route as physically and mentally demanding as any I would care to undertake, anywhere. I had also captured some rewarding photos and had experienced a joyous return to the slopes of my youth. From then on, the researching, recording and classifying of information for this second volume of circular walks quickly developed into a labour of love.

Like *Exploring the Lakeland Fells*, this collection of illustrated walking routes is intended to provide further purpose to seasoned walkers who are already generally familiar with the Peak District, and also to provide encouragement to those who have yet to experience the thrill and satisfaction of venturing on foot across these wide-ranging moorlands, up the craggy tors, along seemingly endless gritstone edges and through majestic limestone gorges. Take care in undertaking these explorations; go well equipped with maps, compass, a torch and adequate food and drink; let somebody know where you are going; enjoy yourself to the full and always return from your walk with the feeling of being jolly glad that you did it and ready for 'the off' again.

T.L.

Author's Acknowledgments

It is a pleasure to record my gratitude to the many kind people who have contributed to the completion of this book. They have given generously of their precious time and expertise and I am fortunate to have access to such valuable assistance. To all those concerned, please accept my warm appreciation and sincere thanks for your efforts.

Some of these collaborators deserve a more specific mention. My special thanks are due to my friends and walking companions of long standing, Bob Carter, Eddie Fidler and Bill Rouse. In particular Bill made his usual, immaculate contribution to the design and production of the computer diagrams, whilst Bob and Eddie meticulously checked my draft manuscript and audited, most professionally, the proof stages of the book. Another colleague, Ian Morris, kept my computer systems running and upgraded with the best,

Below: *National Trust workmen renovating the summit of Mam Tor*

state-of-the-art, electronic technology. Many thanks, Ian, especially for the almost 24 hour round-the-clock service placed at my disposal.

I also express my appreciation to the knowledgeable Rangers of the Peak National Park for checking through the text of all thirty routes and for their expert guidance and helpful, constructive suggestions. This was arranged through Roland Smith, Head of Information Services, and I am also indebted to Roly for other information which he so expertly and willingly provided.

Once again I talked to many fellow walking enthusiasts whilst out and about and these pleasant exchanges of views and experiences between people who share a common bond stimulated my endeavours and gave further purpose and direction to my work.

Finally, may I express my thanks and gratitude to my wife Bridget and also to my two daughters Katrina and Helen, who accepted unreasonable competition for my time and attention during the compilation of this book and who always provided agreeable support for my efforts and demands.

Approximately 14 per cent of the Peak District is owned and managed by the National Trust, in particular, much of the moorland of Kinder, Bleaklow and Derwent, and many farms in the High Peak, Dovedale, Ilam, and Longshaw. The Trust is actively involved in footpath and erosion repairs on many parts of the moors. The National Trust is a charity and relies heavily on public support to fund its extensive conservation activities. The Trust is currently spending around £1.5 million per annum on landscape maintenance in the Peak District. If you would like to support the National Trust's work in caring for the Peak District, they can be contacted at:

The Peak District Appeal
The National Trust
Clumber Park Stableyard
Worksop
Notts S80 3BE
Telephone (01909) 486411

USING THE BOOK

This book, the second in the 'Exploring' series of walking guides, closely follows the successful format used in the first, *Exploring the Lakeland Fells*. This presentation has been further refined and it has been adapted, where necessary, to relate more specifically to the different geography and contrasting geology of the Peak. A number of enhancements have also been incorporated.

In the present guide details are provided, where such possibilities exist, of **alternative starting points** for each walking route and all the walks have been allocated a **grading** which indicates their perceived ease or difficulty. In addition the **route maps** now show forest plantations and areas of woodland.

The main objective of the book is to provide a collection of interesting walking routes which comprehensively cover the varying landscapes of the high moorlands of the Dark Peak and the contrasting limestone features of the White Peak. The walks are presented clearly and concisely with diagrams and photographs to provide an authoritative and appealing collection of routes. The text describes these routes in detail, and points out features of interest that can be seen along the way.

convenient rectangular formats adopted by Ordnance Survey for their two Outdoor Leisure Maps of this region, but instead it is related to the main geological structures of the two segments. Therefore, the **Dark Peak** is that surface area covered with millstone and sandstone grits and shales, whilst the **White Peak** has surface rocks of carboniferous limestone.

There is one main area of difference between the Ordnance Survey and this book. The long protruding spurs of grits extending south and terminating in the Roaches on the western flank of the limestone region and in Baslow Edge on the eastern flank are included in this book as part of the Dark Peak. In the Ordnance Survey publications they appear in the rectangles contained in Outdoor Leisure Map 24 which covers the area of the White Peak.

In total the 30 walking routes cover over 470 km (over 290 miles) and the cumulative height climbed is approaching 12 800 m (nearly 42 000 feet), which is about one and a half times the height of Mount Everest. The range of pertinent features of the 30 walks are summarized in the following table.

Arrangement and composition

In all, 30 walking routes are covered and these have been divided into 16 walks in the Dark Peak and 14 in the White Peak. For both of these areas, the first walks presented are located in the north of the region; the remainder of the routes broadly track from west to east through the area and finish with those in the south. The challenge of the routes ranges widely, from walks graded as easy/straightforward to those classified as difficult/severe. All the walks start from a conveniently located car park or lay-by and details of these and of other facilities available there, such as toilets, picnic areas and information centres, are provided.

For the purpose of this book, the differentiation between Dark and White Peak does not follow the

FEATURE	FROM	TO
Grading	Easy/straight-forward	Difficult/severe
Time allowance hours	4.0	9.5
Distance (excluding height) kilometres miles	10.4 6.5	28.7 17.9
Total height gained metres feet	30 100	960 3150
Principal height metres feet	235 770	633 2075

Grading

It is almost impossible to allow for all the factors that might contribute to a universal grading system. The variables include generalities such as weather conditions and the seasonal differences in hours of daylight, and also more personal criteria.

However, there are a number of physical features which, when combined, are likely to determine the ease or difficulty of a walk, and for the purposes of this guide these include:

- Length

- Total height gained

- Steepness and difficulty of slopes (both up and down)

- Spacing of these gradients

- Whether some elementary scrambling is necessary

- Overall roughness of terrain

- Drainage and the extent of waterlogged areas

- The crossing of peat hags

- The degree of exposure to the elements

- The state of the footpaths

- The extent and quality of signposting, way-markers, cairns etc.

A qualitative judgement has been made of each of these and, based on this assessment, each walk has been allocated into one of three categories:

- **Easy/straightforward**
  Distance usually significantly below 15 km (10 miles). No sustained long or severe slopes. Climbing well spaced out. No dangerous exposure or difficult terrain. Minimum waterlogged ground and no peat hags. Route finding presents few problems and the way is adequately signed. Paths are, for the most part, good and certain. Suitable for family groups and usually with plenty of general interest.

- **Moderate**
  Walk suitable for all reasonably fit walkers who wish to follow a route which could occupy up to a full day. A combination of some features which are more exacting than those on which the previous category is based, such as perhaps some demanding climbing, together with a longer route, sections of which are not as clearly defined as might be expected.

- **Difficult/severe**
  Route includes several features which in total make the walk a challenging one, even for experienced and fit participants. These walks will be either relatively long or will contain steep gradients, or even both. Sections of the terrain covered will quite often be rough, waterlogged, treacherous and/or exposed. Paths may not exist in places and route signing will sometimes be incomplete. All strenuous routes across the difficult terrain of the Dark Peak's exposed, high moorlands have been allocated to this category.

Routes which straddle two categories have been appropriately bracketed. Additionally, the allocated category may be either down- or up-graded by selecting one of the suggested escape or extension variants provided for each of the 30 main walking routes described.

Diagrams

There is a diagram for each route giving a map and a cross-sectional relief of the walk. These have been computer-generated and are based upon grid-reference points down-loaded from Ordnance Survey Maps – The Outdoor Leisure Series 1:25000, 4 cm to 1 km (2½ inches to 1 mile).

The **relief cross-section** is mathematically accurate with the map. This relief is wrapped out from the starting location and accurately follows the exact line of the route.

Camera symbols locate the position and direction of take of each of the photographs that illustrate the walks and are additional aids to route

THE PEAK DISTRICT NATIONAL PARK

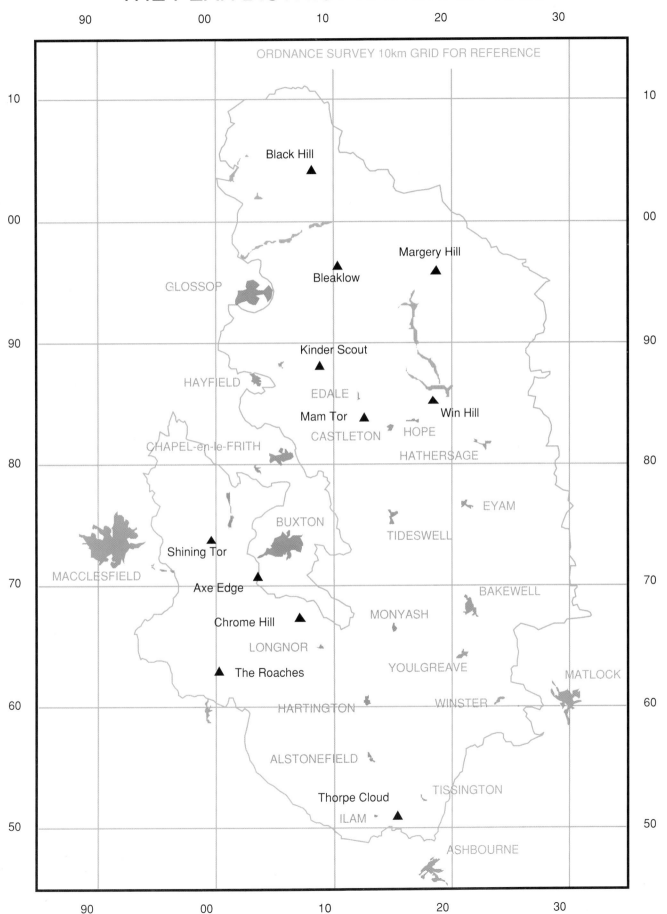

finding. Each photograph has been allocated a distinctive number, identical to that given in the photograph caption. The first part of the number indicates the route, whilst the second part refers to the sequence of the photograph within each route. Photographs taken along the route are indicated by the camera symbol pointing either along or away from the line of the walk, whereas photographs taken of the route from other locations are identified by the camera symbol pointing inwards from the edge of the map.

Summary tables

Pertinent statistics of the walk are provided in the summary table at the start of the description of each of the 30 routes. This summary contains information on **starting location**, **public transport** and **alternative starting points**; it gives an **overview** of the route including features of interest; it details the state of the **footpaths** and the adequacy of signs etc., the allocated **grading**, the **time** to be allowed for completing the walk, the **distance** covered, the **total height** gained and the **principal heights** scaled.

Estimates of **walking time** include allowances for stops including lunch. The estimates have been calculated by allowing 1 hour to walk each 2½ miles, plus an allowance of a further 1 hour for each 2000 feet climbed, plus 1 hour for lunch and all other stops, and a final adjustment of up to ± ½ hour per walk, depending upon additonal factors, such as difficulty of route finding, state of the paths, type of terrain etc. You can adjust these basic estimates to suit your own walking speeds.

Photographs

The photographs were taken throughout the four seasons. The camera used to take them was a Canon EOS 650 using a standard 50 mm lens and a 35–135 mm zoom lens, in each case with polarizing filters. Fujichrome 100 colour slide film has been used exclusively.

Abbreviations

The minimum number of abbreviations has been used, and only to avoid constant repetition. These are listed below.

L	left	cm	centimetre(s)
R	right	ft	foot/feet
		in	inch(es)
N	north	km	kilometre(s)
NNE	north north east	m	metre(s)
NE	north east	mm	millimetre(s)
ENE	east north east	yd	yard(s)
E	east		
ESE	east south east	G-stile	gap stile
SE	south east		(squeezer stile)
SSE	south south east	K-gate	kissing gate
S	south	L-stile	ladder stile
SSW	south south west	MR	map reference
SW	south west	OLM	Outdoor Leisure
WSW	west south west		Map
W	west	OS	Ordnance
WNW	west north west		Survey
NW	north west	P-stile	post-stile
NNW	north north west	s-stile	step-stile
		w-stile	wall-stile

Geological terms and dialect

BLUE JOHN	variety of fluorite, containing purple, yellow or colourless bands
BOOTH	herdsman's shelter or cow-shed
CLOUGH	stream valley; narrow ravine
COL	a sharp-edged or saddle-shaped pass
CULVERT	a drain or covered channel
EDGE	steep cliff
GINNEL	a narrow passageway between buildings
GRIT	coarse-grained sandy sediment, ill defined
GROUGH/HAG	a natural channel or fissure in a peat moor; a deep drainage ditch in a peat bog

HAUSE	summit of narrow pass, col
KNOLL	small, rounded hill
LIMESTONE	a sedimentary rock composed almost entirely of calcium carbonate, mainly as calcite
MILLSTONE GRIT	a coarse-grained carboniferous sandstone used for the manufacture of millstones
PIKE	pointed summit
RINDLE	a stream which only flows in wet weather
SANDSTONE	a sedimentary rock of sand and/or silt bound together by a cement, often calcite or silica
SHALE	a fine-grained sedimentary rock formed mainly of compacted clay
SINKHOLE	an area, especially in limestone, where a surface stream sinks underground
SLOUGH	a hole where water collects; a hollow filled with mud or bog
SQUEEZER STILE	stile containing a narrow gap
TOADSTONE	a Derbyshire name for decomposed, basaltic, volcanic rocks
TOR	a core of unweathered, harder rocks standing above a surrounding area of weathered rock
TOWER	tall, squarish structure of unweathered rock, usually located on or near the steep slopes of rocky gorges
WELL	a spring or stream

Miscellaneous

MAPS AND COMPASS

Use the Ordnance Survey Outdoor Leisure Maps and a reliable compass at all times when you are walking in the Peak. Be sure that you know how to use this combination correctly.

COMPASS BEARINGS

All compass bearings are to the nearest 22½ degree point, e.g. (N), (NNE), (NE) etc. This is considered to be sufficiently accurate over the relatively small distances travelled between the taking of successive readings. Get into the habit of taking frequent compass bearings, particularly when the visibility is poor and/or you are not sure of your exact position.

DYNAMICS

The human-constructed features of the Peak are constantly changing, fences appear and disappear, K-gates replace L-stiles and vice versa, additional waymarker signs appear, some signs get removed and so on. Therefore, should you come across isolated differences along the route from those described, presume that these have occurred since the book went to press and proceed with confidence to the next certain feature described.

RECORDED HEIGHTS OF HILLS

The heights of the major hills have been given in both metric and imperial measurements. The metric heights have been extracted from the most up-to-date Ordnance Survey maps. The imperial equivalents have been calculated from these using a conversion factor of 0.3048 m=1 ft. These equivalents have been rounded off to the nearest 5 ft.

SPELLING

Sometimes there is more than one version of the spelling of place names. In such instances the spelling which appears on the OS OLMs has been used, unless otherwise indicated.

ORDNANCE SURVEY MAPS

The Ordnance Survey maps are excellent but not infallible. On the rare occasions where there are differences between the route descriptions and the paths shown (or not shown, as the case may be) on the OS maps, rely on the route descriptions.

Route 1: DOVE STONE RESERVOIR, ASHWAY ROCKS and CHEW RESERVOIR

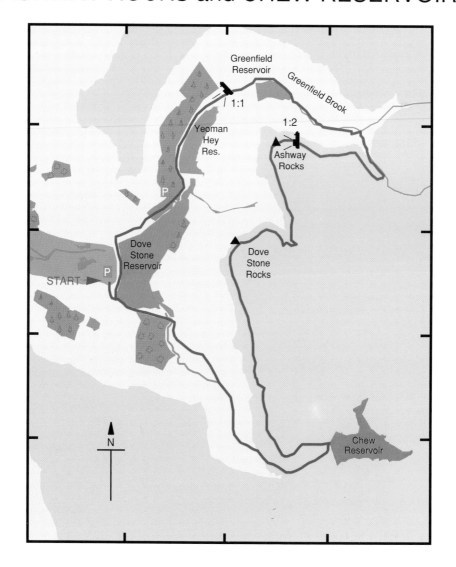

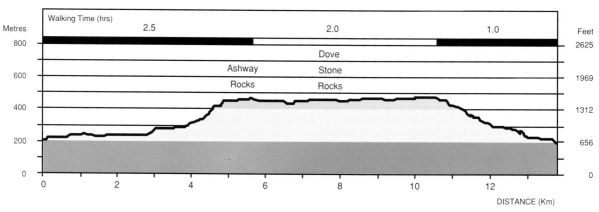

1

THE DARK PEAK

ROUTE 1

Dove Stone Reservoir, Ashway Rocks and Chew Reservoir

•

STARTING LOCATION
Car park at Dove Stone Reservoir.
OLM 1: MR 013036.
Extensive car parking facilities, including
  Information Centre/Ranger Service and toilets.

ALTERNATIVE STARTING POINT
Nearby car park at Binn Green (MR 018045).

PUBLIC TRANSPORT
Bus routes 903 and 904.

OVERVIEW/INTEREST
Tremendous variety of scenery through wild, remote
  terrain.
Mixture includes reservoirs, cloughs and extensive
  millstone grit edges.
Series of fantastic rock formations.
Good views of both open and enclosed landscapes.
Sailing on Dove Stone Reservoir.
Challenging route, one best undertaken on a fine,
  dry day when the ground is firm underfoot.

FOOTPATHS
In the vicinity of the reservoirs the paths and signs
  are first class.
Edge pathways quite good; otherwise the route is
  challenging with some minor scrambling.
Ground covering a mixture of firm rock and clinging
  peat.

GRADING
Moderate/severe.

TIME ALLOWANCE
5½ hours.

STATISTICS

DISTANCE

Excluding Height	13.8 km	(8.6 miles)
TOTAL HEIGHT GAINED	360 m	(1180 ft)
PRINCIPAL HEIGHTS		
Highest Point (edge path)	480 m	(1575 ft)
Chew Reservoir	474 m	(1555 ft)

The way to Raven Stones   *Allow 2½ hours*

The car park occupies a superb setting just beneath the towering embankment of the westward reaches of Dove Stone Reservoir. The surrounding countryside is wild and magnificent. Millstone grit edges abound with rock formations jutting out along rims and piercing the skyline with an assortment of shapes. The gentler contours of the escarpment culminating at Dick Hill dominate the view to the N. This is just the country for well prepared walkers to tramp over.

Leave the car park at its upper end and walk along the minor road towards the sailing club. Turn immediately L to cross the embankment of the dam by means of the wide path heading N. Open views abound and the harsh, rugged landscapes are pleasantly softened by groups of trees, in which Scots pines and larches predominate. At the N end of the embankment a K-gate provides access to an elevated, macadam roadway cum pathway leading further round the reservoir to the NE. From here, the spectacular, shattered edges of Great Dove Stone Rocks, rising steeply from the

13

1:1 Peering down Yeoman Hey Reservoir

far side of the waters, may be located high above to your R in the SE.

The path round this part of the complex reservoir system has been thoughtfully designed to accommodate wheelchairs so that immobile people can also enjoy this spot. Continue up rising ground along the broad way stretching to the NE to skirt a plantation of densely packed Scots pines to your L. This leads past some waterworks sluice channels on the other side of your way. Turn R down the more substantial macadam roadway ahead and then bear L to reach the second, upper reservoir of Yeoman Hey at its retaining dam. A commemorative stone in the wall here informs you: 'This stone was laid by HM The King of Tonga 1981.' Further away, Ashway Rocks sweep up on your R (ENE).

Progress N, veering NE round the westward side of the narrowing Yeoman Hey Reservoir. Always keep to the broad track hugging the side of the reservoir on your R as higher, more barren, treeless slopes appear ahead, shutting out views beyond. Further on, the path passes through another conifer plantation before bearing R towards the retaining embankment of Greenfield Reservoir, the highest catchment of the series. From here, the views back down the valley over the narrow reservoirs are delightful. In stark contrast, the stepped edges of Raven Stones appear for the first time, distinguishable high above the valley in the SE.

For some distance now you share the way with the concrete connecting channels of the reservoirs as your direction changes to due E, aimed at the extensive high ground of Saddleworth Moor looming up ahead. The water channel is crossed before your path snakes round to the R, closely following the irregular, stone-lined slopes of the man-made reservoir basin. After this, proceed with confidence along the narrow causeway. This unusual feature leads to the upper termination of the reservoirs where they are fed by the catchment waters of Greenfield Brook.

The channel to your L is re-crossed and the wide track leads further into the narrowing valley beside the peaty stream. Along here is a sighting high above of the perpendicular rock columns of the Trinnacle. These three spectacular ramparts belong to the Raven Stones structure which you will visit later on. Then a solitary, much weathered hawthorn tree is passed on your R. The valley becomes progressively more enclosed as the slopes steepen and become strewn with gritstone boulders and shattered rock fragments. The stream is crossed once more in a wild, remote and desolate setting.

Some distance ahead, the rising valley system divides and your continuation way is up the R-hand fork of Birchen Clough. There is no actual public right of way along this clough but walkers regularly use this route-of-convenience and you are now walking in 'open country'. The entrance to the side valley is reached by veering sharp R and then turning L to pass round a wired-off deep culvert running into a wide-bore water tunnel down below. The underground aqueduct feeds Dove Stone Reservoir at the end of its 1 km (0.6 miles) underground journey S. In crossing this feature there is a revealing view to your L up inhospitable Holme and Rimmon Pit Cloughs with tangled rock falls littering their steep slopes. At the end of the wire fence, now to your L, cross the fast-flowing stream with care and then enter Birchen Clough following a narrow, grassy footpath. Your direction of travel changes to SSE from MR 038049.

Large rock slabs are almost immediately encountered, impeding your direct progress up the clough. There are several acceptable ways across these and there are more alternatives further up the narrow valley. Based on experimentation with different routes, the one advocated is to work your way above the first series of large boulders to cross a dilapidated stone wall and thereafter to climb up the clough near to the stream bed, making whatever use you can of the indistinct and intermittent stretches of pathway. In dry weather the actual stream bed sometimes provides the easiest route over certain sections. Some minor scrambling will be necessary but, with care (particularly when treading near slippery, submerged rocks), the climb provides interest and excitement rather than undue risk.

After following the stream for some distance you will reach some relatively high waterfalls. Cross the stream again at a convenient spot below these falls and climb up the severe slopes on the far side, following a faint path which gains height above the basin of the clough. After the inital steep rise, the way levels off above and along the course of the stream, now some distance below. Your way then travels further uphill maintaining its relative position to the stream. Be vigilant along here because the path is narrow and there is a nasty, exposed drop to your L. There are more places along here where it is sensible to deploy elementary scrambling techniques but fortunately the rock pitches are small and there are plenty of conveniently positioned, secure foot and hand holds. Along this meandering stretch your predominant direction is SSE.

Further up, the valley starts to widen out as glimpses of the flatter, higher terrain towards the head of the clough are revealed. This marks the boundary rim of the moorlands which stretch for miles to the SW. Change direction here by veering R to ascend the steep, pathless hillside, climbing SW along a route of your own choice across rough, tufted grasses. Further up, when heather-clad ground is reached, bear R still gaining height by climbing westwards. This upwards diagonal connects with a narrow path cum sheep track further on. Veer further R along this way, now walking NW towards and above the interesting millstone grit edges rearing up ahead. Your path becomes better defined as you approach these outcrops. Other paths merge with yours and this consolidated way leads to the weathered grit boulders, bluffs and columns of Raven Stones. There are some spectacular views down into the valley from between the huge rock structures, including the Trinnacle, that make perfect foreground frames for those with a camera.

15

The way to Chew Reservoir   *Allow 2 hours*

From the Raven Stones the continuation route is along an obvious path which winds westwards along the extensive millstone grit rim. This section presents many more photogenic views from the craggy edge. Further along the edge there is a choice of ways and the one recommended is by way of the branch path to the R that continues nearest to the edge. This provides continuous views over the precipitous rim, although there is some slight penalty to pay for this further along when you have to climb back to higher ground over to your L. Continue walking by the edge, following the path but on no account surrendering any height. To achieve this, veer to the L at the next promontory and then make use of a shallow, dried-up, enclosed depression of sand and rock. Further on, the path veers L away from the edge to cross a small, flattish stretch of boggy moorland before it forces you to climb to another section of the rocky edge above and to the ESE. This is attained by means of veering R along an indistinct path which then travels upwards to reach another intermediary edge above to your L. From here the climbing of a steeper slope composed of loose, scattered rock takes you to the highest edge once more. In completing these manoeuvres you have walked in a wide semi-circle around the spur of Ashway Rocks.

Continue along the edge path. A short distance further on you will reach the Ashway Memorial Cross at MR 030045. The intricately carved stone cross is in memory of James Platt, Member of Parliament for Oldham, who was fatally injured at this spot in 1857 whilst out shooting grouse. Beyond this monument keep to your present elevation round the edges, walking s. The next section is hard going over frequent stretches of oozing, clinging peat. The edge path eventually winds down to and then across the deep clough which drains Ashway Moss above. Cross this

1:2 Mountain Rescue teams in position at Ashway Rocks

watercourse by veering R and using a natural bridge some way up the indent, above a small waterfall.

Further on, a narrower clough is crossed on a more direct and steeper line. Beyond this second watercourse follow a wide sandy path, still keeping close to the contortions of the rocky edge on your R. From hereabouts, in good weather, the monument located on Alderman's Hill may be spotted to the NW. Further on, the path passes the distinctive rock that houses the memorial plaque to Brian Toase and Tom Morton, who died whilst descending the second Sella Tower in the Italian Dolomites.

Then the mighty chasm of Chew Valley comes into view far away on the R. After this sighting it is only a short distance to a ruined stone building built into the rock face. This is Bramley's Cot and it still provides some protection from the elements. From this abandoned construction a dry and sandy path leads further S towards Chew Valley. The way winds tortuously round every nook and cranny along the indented edge, crossing several minor cloughs along the way before sweeping round to the L to reach the grass-covered embankment of the reservoir. However, before this a boggy, peat-lined channel, situated some distance away from the edge, has to be negotiated. Climb up to the retaining wall of the reservoir and you are standing at the highest man-made stretch of water in England. This is at an elevation of 474 m (1555 ft). Another feature at this location is the sighting of the Holme Moss TV transmitter, far away across the water to the ENE.

The way back to Dove Stone Reservoir

Allow 1 hour

Although Dove Stone Reservoir is still some 3 km (1.9 miles) to the NW, way below in the valley, the return to it can be achieved relatively quickly along the fine approach road to Chew Reservoir. From the parapet, turn R and follow the grassy track that leads diagonally down below the dam to reach the surfaced road ahead. Turn R and descend down the wide, deep valley. The road

almost immediately passes close to flooded, abandoned quarry workings which contain some interesting exposed gritstone faces. On the other side, Chew Brook has cut a deep, V-shaped valley to the S. Slopes strewn with shattered rock rise steeply beyond on the far side.

Although progress down here is fast and only temporarily arrested by the occasional stile, there is ample time to admire the interesting views both back along the twisting valley and of the several groupings of rock formations lining the edge of the valley, high up at the top of the steep slopes beyond the stream. Of these, the configuration named Wimberry Stones is one of the most impressive. Much further down trees re-appear: sparse groupings of deciduous species, with thicker, more extensive conifer plantations further down the sweeping hillsides. Keep to the road which will lead you back to the SE tip of Dove Stone Reservoir, passing the clubhouse facilities of the sailing fraternity en route.

Alternative routes

ESCAPES

Shorter walks should be confined to exploring the reservoir system at that level, by keeping to the excellent low-level pathways which skirt these pleasant, sheltered waters.

EXTENSIONS

This is a circular walk and opportunities for alternative routes are extremely limited once the high ground above Birchen Clough has been attained.

There are no really sensible major extensions which do not necessitate penetrating the very difficult moorland terrain lying to the N of Chew Reservoir. Even then, this will be at the expense of missing much of the scenery visible along the extensive main edge route. Such demanding diversions are not recommended.

One modest extension is on the way down Chew Valley: cross the brook at MR 025024 and thereafter use the longer, pleasanter footpaths extending to the S of Dove Stones Reservoir to return by a broad loop back to the car park.

17

Route 2: CROWDEN, BLACK HILL and LADDOW ROCKS

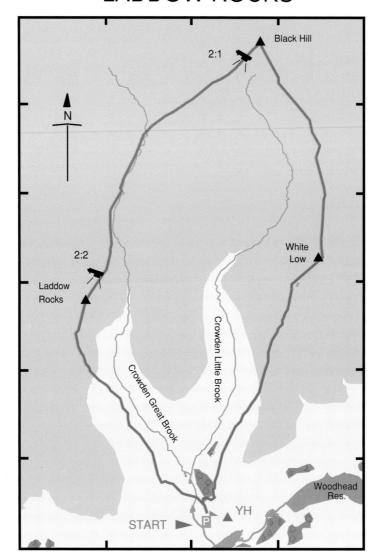

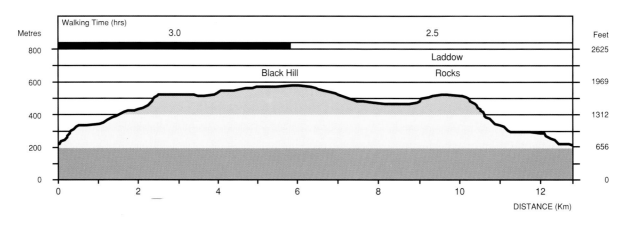

ROUTE 2

Crowden, Black Hill and Laddow Rocks

●

STARTING LOCATION
Car park at Crowden.
OLM 1: MR 073993.
Well appointed small car park, holds about 20 cars.
Popular starting venue so get there early.
Toilets.

PUBLIC TRANSPORT
National Express Coach 350.

OVERVIEW/INTEREST
Challenging route across high, exposed moorlands.
Extensive areas of rough, waterlogged ground.
Many peat hags and boggy areas to contend with.
Vast, open landscapes and wide valley systems.
Impressive panoramic views.
Fantastic pitches of Laddow Rocks.
Section along Pennine Way.
Save this one for a fine, sunny day with the ground
     firm underfoot.

FOOTPATHS
Considering the difficult terrain, the paths are
     reasonable.

They do have a tendency to become obscure or
     submerged in several areas. (Compass and map are
     essential).
Signs and directional indicators, particularly cairns,
     relatively reassuring.
Holme Moss television mast (blinking lights) is quite
     helpful.

GRADING
Difficult/severe.

TIME ALLOWANCE
5½ hours.

STATISTICS

DISTANCE

Excluding Height	12.8 km	(7.9 miles)
TOTAL HEIGHT GAINED	430 m	(1410 ft)
PRINCIPAL HEIGHTS		
White Low	530 m	(1740 ft)
Tooleyshaw Moor	541 m	(1775 ft)
Black Hill	582 m	(1910 ft)
Laddow Rocks	502 m	(1645 ft)

The way to Black Hill   *Allow 3 hours*

This exacting and strenuous route should be saved for a fine, sunny day when the going underfoot is firm. Late summer, particularly after prolonged dry weather, is quite a good time but ideal conditions are on cold, dry days in the winter months, particularly after severe overnight frost.

The small car park is located just off the main A628 (T) road. The Longdendale Valley reservoirs nestle below to the s, whilst challenging high moorland terrain containing steep-sided hillocks, wide valleys and impressive gritstone edges beckon to the N. Walk N towards these: leave the car park up the path signed to toilets and on reaching these turn R along the lane. The lane leads northwards past a camp site. Cross another lane at right angles and pass over a stile beside a gate. From here, walk along the lane which is signed to open country and to Crowden Outdoor Centre. Within 100 m (110 yd) bear R, to continue slightly uphill with a stone wall on your R.

A short distance further on, the wall is crossed by means of a L-stile. From here, there are compelling views ahead and to your L up the wide, twin valleys of Crowden Great and Little Brooks. These are separated by the higher, rounded moorlands of Bareholme Moss. Height is agreeably gained as the path winds uphill. When the way bends L, bear R to climb more steeply up the hillside, following a rougher path. This is again signed to open country. The way then traverses to your L and further on a solitary oak tree above sparse Brockholes Wood is passed. Following a short, sharp climb up a rough slope, the route levels off to pass some extensive quarry spoils.

Your direction of travel is now NNE. A short distance further on, another path merges at an acute angle from the R. Open country is then reached; from here, continue northwards along the obvious path heading directly towards more remote and higher moorland terrain. Ahead, and just beyond a distinctive stone pillar over to the L, be viligant to veer R along a continuation path which climbs gradually uphill to the NE.

Your way continues above the valley, cut by Crowden Little Brook, uphill to the NE. The long, pleasant gradient leads up to the higher moorland of Hey Moss. Further on, the path narrows and becomes less distinct, as it is invaded by clumps of tufted grass and then crosses the heather delineation line. The first exposed patches of wet, waterlogged peat are soon encountered and this is a gentle taste of what lies ahead. Then a small stone cairn is passed. Beyond this, the higher ground leading to Westend Moss rises to your R in the NNE. Beyond this, there is another, more flattened cairn; beyond this, the way continues to traverse N, before swinging R to climb more steeply to the ENE up the extensive rounded hillside. For a time the path becomes less certain and there is more than one way across the intervening moorland, before several well-trodden routes converge into a better established path which then leads with greater clarity, further uphill. More cairns are passed and ahead the higher slopes leading to Westend Moss are reached.

When you penetrate the more eroded ground, keep over to the L to cross the exposed peaty patches by the easiest route possible. Towards the top, the path bears further L to assume a NNE bearing in its final approach to the flatter ground of Westend Moss. At this point, in clearer weather, the high television mast located at Holme Moss appears. You then head NNE towards White Low. Further on, a small bog pool is passed to your R. This is marked on the OLM and is located at MR 082018. A wide expanse of fairly level ground then has to be crossed and your main bearing over this is towards the TV mast, heading NE. There are more nasty hags to circumvent, but fortunately several drainage channels head your way and present acceptable through routes. As further

progress is made, the deep valley separating the higher ground you are treading over from that on which the TV mast is standing becomes increasingly better defined. This impressive valley, over to your R, has been carved out by Heyden Brook. Ahead, your continuation path northwards towards White Low is now clearly revealed for some distance to come.

Another cairn is reached and then the way passes between grouse butts. The route now leads northwards across expansive rough and exposed moorland. In gaining further height, a point is reached where, in the clearest of weather, long, flat, bluish ridges may be discerned on the far horizon to your rear. These are the outlines of distant Bleaklow with Kinder pleateau behind. Then for some distance use may be made of the sandy bed of a stream and relatively fast and easy progress may be accomplished through this section.

A series of guiding cairns appear. These are reassuring, particularly in wet, misty conditions, as your direction of progress subtly varies to first NNW and then NW, by progressively veering to your L as Tooleyshaw Moss is crossed. Fortunately, in this exposed area the path becomes relatively clearly defined. More cairns follow, guiding you further NNW as the moorland becomes a real challenge to cross. In all but the driest and firmest of conditions, significant deviations from your direct line (between NW and NNW) are inevitable, so constantly check your overall direction of travel.

If you have adhered strictly to this basic route description, you will now sight a trig point ahead. This marks the top of Black Hill and signifies that the worst terrain and most difficult part of the route finding has been successfully accomplished. Well done! On reaching the rectangular pillar, you are standing at MR 078047. This is at 582 m (1910 ft) and is the highest elevation of the entire route and also the most northerly point you will reach. The harsh terrain surrounding the trig point is relatively flat; interesting, long-distance views from this high point are somewhat obscured. You have now made your intended rendezvous with the Pennine Way at the targeted spot.

2:1 Approaching Black Hill from Grains Moss

The way back to the car park at Crowden

Allow 2½ hours

Be careful to depart to the sw from the trig point in order to commence your return journey along part of the Pennine Way footpath. This path is a right mixture, very clear at times with guiding cairns, punctuated by several less well-defined sections. Therefore, you must exercise constant vigilance until you reach an obvious narrow path some considerable distance further down. The worst is then over and from here you will be following a much better established route with guiding cairns to assist your direction finding. More wide, open landscapes appear and you pass

through this somewhat daunting region keeping steadfastly to a sw bearing, surrendering marginal height in the process. The peaty path of sorts then leads down the gentle slopes of Dun Hill into the commencement of Meadowgrain Clough. This is a fairly insignificant watercourse hereabouts but lower down it develops into the huge valley complex cut by Crowden Great Brook.

Lower down, the slopes steepen and your rate of descent increases as these are negotiated. Then a particularly large, conically shaped cairn is passed providing an easily recognizable landmark. Beyond this, the path crosses to the L of the clough for some distance before reverting (and from here on remaining) to the R of the swelling watercourse. Your heading hereabouts is wsw. Then, in clear weather, you see a vast, wide depression ahead and you steer across this formidable moorland between wsw and ssw, continuing to surrender height. More sheltered ground is reached as the path begins to snake to your L and in so doing it once again becomes better defined.

Beyond some waterlogged ground, the way leads across Little Clough, the shallow slopes of which provide some protection for a short stop for refreshments if you feel the need. From here, the path heads ssw above and to the R of the main watercourse. The path continues to vary in both certainty and quality but it never strays far away from the meanders of the stream to its L. At a point where the sweep of the stream has cut into a small cliff on the right, the watercourse has to be crossed and then re-crossed in order to progress further down the clough.

After this, more side cloughs, containing infant watercourses flowing down exposed bedding planes of millstone grit, are crossed. Then the main stream falls more rapidly into the enlarging valley as your continuation way veers R maintaining greater height. Your heading along this section is ssw. Fortunately, the path now becomes clearer and more obvious, traversing round the slopes ahead, initially along a fairly level course and then climbing gradually to increase the height between you and the valley bottom, now some appreciable distance below. Watch every step along the exposed edge ahead as you tread along the narrow, slippery path which leads above the extensive boulders and rock pitches which form the impressive cliffs of Laddow Rocks. There are some challenging climbing routes up these. In your final approach to the edge, some eroded ground has to be avoided and the re-directed path climbs above this round to the R and then up a short and narrow, rocky gully.

Once the final traverse to the ridge has been accomplished there are competing choices between inspecting the configurations of Laddow Rocks, which afford many glimpses down their vertical pitches into the valley far below, the wild landscapes from which you have just descended and the route ahead leading down into the vast

spaces occupied by the lower reaches of Crowden Brook before its submergence into the depths of Torside Reservoir in Longendale. At Laddow Rocks there is an optional path leading down to a climber's cave, but if you decide to explore this, retrace your steps the short distance back upwards to regain the safety of the path along the edge before continuing.

Eventually, the ground ahead descends into the valley and a good, rocky path leads sse down the slopes. Another watercourse is crossed, this one named Oakenclough Brook, and past this the descent steepens appreciably down an obvious way. A cairn and another erosion control marker are reached and beyond these there is a steeper section and the path drops down this to the L to cross a swiftly flowing stream. The sides of this clough are smothered in heathers. Lower down, when the path divides, select the lower branch to the R which immediately passes along the L flank of a mini hanging valley. Then, quite surprisingly, a large, isolated holly bush is passed. From this, an obvious way leads further down the valley, descending another steep section immediately ahead. Eventually, beyond a stream, a small fenced-off clump of mixed larch and beech trees is passed on your L. Just beyond these, veer L down the lower path at a fork ahead. From here, the way leads to the grounds of the Outdoor Centre. Veer R to do this, avoiding a path off to the L which then crosses the stream by means of an elaborate stepped dam.

To enter the grounds of the Crowden Outdoor Centre, turn sharp L and use the stile and stone bridging to cross a deep drainage channel. Walk past the buildings and cross Crowden Brook by means of the vehicular bridge. Over this, veer R along the surfaced lane and then retrace your outwards steps back to the car park a short distance below.

Alternative routes

ESCAPES
Apart from retracing your footsteps at any point before reaching Black Hill, there is one feasible short-circuit: from the vicinity of either Westend

Moss or White Low, head w across the rough, uncharted moorland to connect with the firm valley path leading down along Crowden Little Brook. The pathless crossing of the intervening moorland is about 1 km (0.6 miles) and it may be helpful to follow the course of the stream, Whitelow Slack, from just w of the summit area of White Low to its merger into Crowden Little Brook lower down.

EXTENSIONS

No extensions are advocated for this demanding circular route. For those who must, there is a footpath from the top of Laddow Rocks which leads NW to Chew Reservoir, the extreme easterly tip of which is no more than 1½ km (0.9 miles) away. This path branches off the Pennine Way footpath at MR 057013. If you decide to visit Chew Reservoir, return directly to your departure point from the Pennine Way path, retracing your outwards steps. A more ambitious circuit back, further w and then s, is really only suitable for those with the stamina of fell-runners.

2:2 Laddow Rocks near Crowden

Route 3: OLD GLOSSOP, SHELF STONES and BLEAKLOW HEAD

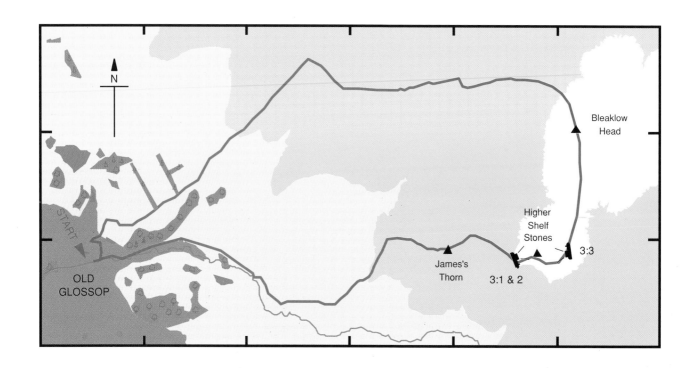

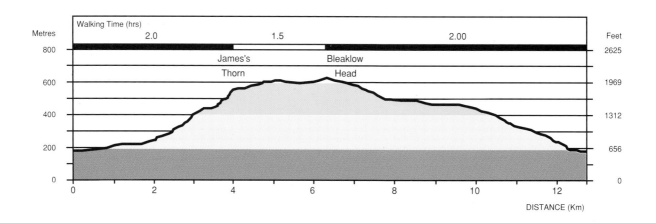

ROUTE 3

Old Glossop, Shelf Stones and Bleaklow Head

•

STARTING LOCATION
Adequate parking along Shepley Street, Old Glossop, particularly at weekends.
OLM 1: MR 045948.

PUBLIC TRANSPORT
Bus routes 214/215 and 239.

OVERVIEW/INTEREST
Exciting and extended initial series of climbs.
Several fascinating rock configurations visited.
Open views of vast moorland landscapes.
Poignant wreckage of crashed Superfortress.
Crossing of challenging peat hags and grouse moors.
Save this route for a fine sunny day following a prolonged dry spell.

FOOTPATHS
Good and obvious at start and finish.
Intermittent and obscure across Bleaklow.
Demanding sections of peat hags and waterlogged ground.

Unusual crossing of moorland utilizing high-level plank bridging.
Route finding an exacting task on occasions.

GRADING
Difficult/severe.

TIME ALLOWANCE
5½ hours.

STATISTICS

DISTANCE

Excluding Height	12.7 km	(7.9 miles)
TOTAL HEIGHT GAINED	470 m	(1540 ft)

PRINCIPAL HEIGHTS

Higher Shelf Stones	621 m	(2035 ft)
Hern Stones	609 m	(2000 ft)
Bleaklow Head	633 m	(2075 ft)

The way to James's Thorn   *Allow 2 hours*

Walk to the E end of Shepley Street and select the lane heading further E up the valley. You are soon treading through open country with the slopes of Moorside covered with Scots pines rising on your L and the vast, higher moorlands and gritstone ridges eventually culminating in the expanse of Bleaklow rising in progressive stages ahead. Ignore a path across a bridge off to your R and continue past a barn and then a row of renovated cottages. At this stage you are treading along the course of a former Roman Road now named Doctor's Gate path and along here the wooded slopes of Shire Hill, rising to your R, will soon be passed. Beyond the entrance to the Charlesworth Shooting Club, keep to the main Doctor's Gate path for the time being, by passing through a narrow gate adjacent to a much wider one, disregarding the L-stile over a wall on your L. Walk ESE up the grassy cart-track through ever widening terrain and pass over a stile positioned at another gate.

There is now a wide, flat valley floor to your R down which the gurgling stream of Shelf Brook meanders contentedly. Beyond the next stile and gate keep to the obvious signed footpath, though you will probably have to tread across patches of waterlogged ground. After this, cross a railed bridge over a tributary stream before veering L uphill away from the main track bridging Shelf Brook and leading to Mossy Lea Farm. You are still following the Doctor's Gate path. Another stile-cum-gate follows, near to which a sign reads: 'Doctor's Gate – Roman Road – To the Snake Inn and Alport Bridge.' Then keep to the R, bypassing a track off to the L as your way swings for a short distance more to the S and the gradient steepens. At this point the formidable shape ahead, across the now narrowing clough, is the craggy outline of Lordship Hill. The path sweeps L again, now beside a well-maintained dry-stone wall, and from here fine views are revealed, in favourable weather conditions, of the boulder-strewn features of Shelf Benches and James's Thorn, your next immediate objectives.

Near a barn further on at MR 064944 you eventually part company with the Doctor's Gate path by forking L along the lesser-used path eastwards which immediately penetrates higher ground. This is up a wide, grassy cart-track, at least to start with. Some distance on, bear R away from the protective wall to head directly uphill towards Shelf Benches to the NE. The route continues along an excellent grassy path. A dilapidated stone wall is then reached and at this feature veer L along the upper of two distinctive narrow paths, yours climbing eastwards to the R of the ridge above. From here on the high moorland landscapes are magnificent.

A diagonal path leads you to a cart-track that serves grouse butts. Bear L along this. When you reach the first stone butt, veer R through a convenient gap in the dilapidated stone retaining wall above and climb E along a narrow grassy path that leads towards the rocky outline above. Your path winds below and to the L of this distinctive helmet-like feature. Further up your well-drained, narrow path leads to and over the stony edge of the escarpment along an interesting diagonal approach. You have now reached Shelf Benches and the weathered rock configurations along this extensive edge deserve your passing attention.

From Shelf Benches there are various routes up to the higher rocks at James's Thorn, which rises less than 1 km away further E. The more obvious path leads eastwards across a shallow hause before climbing the slopes beyond in a more or less direct line to James's Thorn. (Always follow this more certain route in misty conditions.) A more interesting variant is to follow the ledges of Shelf Benches northwards before veering R across the

intervening rough moorland to connect with the previously indicated more direct route. On this second variant, although there are some intermittent paths to guide you, almost inevitably the exact route you decide to follow across this section will be unique to you. However, on no account venture beyond Wigan Clough and always keep to the R of the sunken stream flowing down this clough by climbing ESE before you reach this watercourse. On the way up most walkers will be fortunate enough to come across a small, sheltered tarn (which is an unusual occurrence in this landscape). It is not identified on the OLM.

From this oasis a final, steepish and on occasions quite slippery section leads to the more rounded slopes of peat and gritty sand that line the extruding spur of James's Thorn. The S tip of this spur provides particularly revealing views. The continuation of the Doctor's Gate route lies down below to the S, whilst far beyond the long, flattish ridges regress towards the distant skyline of the mighty Kinder plateau. Away to the E your next objective, the craggy outline of Lower Shelf Stones, beckons invitingly.

The way to Bleaklow Head   *Allow 1½ hours*

From James's Thorn continue walking NE up slightly rising terrain along the apex of the broad, rounded ridge. There is some taste of what is to come along here in the form of having to cross a series of peat hags but these are, uncharacteristically, relatively easy to negotiate or avoid. The way then bends progressively to your R between E and SE, following the higher, firmer ground. Further on the path becomes less distinct and a series of more demanding stretches of peat, some quite extensive, have to be crossed. Always retain or increase your elevation along this stretch. Then make directly for the outcrop of rocks ahead on the horizon. These form part of Lower Shelf Stones and are located at MR 086948. On arrival, veer R through the rocky buttresses, weaving your way S to the end of the promontory.

The weathered rock formations at Lower Shelf Stones are quite fantastic — an assortment of

3:1 Above: *the author busy taking notes at Lower Shelf Stones*

3:2 Below: *the approach to Higher Shelf Stones*

shapes and sizes, some grotesque, others alluring but each separate feature adding to the overall grandeur of this gritstone outcrop. Amongst more distant features, many of which should now be familiar to you, the trig point of Higher Shelf Stones may be observed in fine weather from this rocky perch. This lies to the E. Walk there in a sweeping semicircle to your R always keeping to the crumbling edge, falling away also to your R. This way to Higher Shelf Stones is round intervening peaty slopes.

At Higher Shelf Stones the sheltering rocks surrounding the trig point make a good haven for eating your lunch. New views from here include further revelations of the vast expanses of Kinder Scout and to its L the distinctive conical peak of Win Hill may be identified in the SE. Further E the long, flattish and seemingly endless profiles of the extensive Derwent Edges come into sight. To the NNE the barren, peaty moorlands rising to Bleaklow Head gain increasing prominence.

From the certain location of the trig point at MR 089948 head initially NE across the peat hags, keeping wherever possible to the more stable, sandy stone beds of interconnecting drainage channels. This bearing will take you directly to the scattered remains of a crashed aeroplane slowly

sinking into the peat. The fragments belong to a B29 Superfortress named 'Overexposed', belonging to the 16th Photographic Reconnaissance Squadron USAF. All 13 crew members perished at this bleak spot on 3rd November 1948 whilst the aircraft was descending to Burtonwood through thick cloud.

From this wreckage, continue making progress between NNE and NE across dreadful terrain which becomes more and more hostile as the bog intensifies and as you endeavour to plan a route ahead which takes advantage of any detected firmer ground. Further on, a dominant NNE bearing will eventually connect you with the Pennine Way in the vicinity of Hern Stones, a distinctive grouping of weathered rocks located at MR 092953. Considerable care needs to be exercised in making this demanding crossing where a compass bearing between N and NNE indicates your paramount direction of travel.

When you reach the Pennine Way the route improves with occasional marker posts together with countless footprints preserved in the peat bog indicating just how many unique routes have been pioneered across this morass. Yours will probably be added to this perpetually growing collection. The next objective is to reach the Wain Stones and these lie further up the moorland across more peat hags about ½ km (⅓ mile) due

N. Fortunately there are now many pairs of footprints to guide you; follow the concentrated ones as two prominent rocks on the horizon mark your correct direction of approach. The harsh terrain relents marginally on the final phase of the route to these boulders. The boulders have been named 'The Kiss' and the reason for this will become obvious as you approach them. Promiscuity up here in this harsh environment deserves its just rewards! Continue due N from here to cross Bleaklow Head some distance to the L of a large marker cairn situated at a slightly higher elevation. Quickly locate a renovated section of the Pennine Way now stretching downwards across further desolate moors.

Extensive renovations and improvements are currently being carried out along the Pennine Way footpath and you may be in for a pleasant surprise in finding other sections of the route better defined and easier to walk along.

The way back to Old Glossop *Allow 2 hours*

The path of sorts leading initially northwards from Bleaklow Head is down a well-defined, shallow channel over firmer, bilberry-covered ground.

3:3 A poignant reminder of the bravery of those who protected our freedom

This part of the route gradually weaves to the w as the underlying terrain progressively falls. The section of the way w is along Wildboar Grain. There are several acceptable descent routes along this clough and lower down on the r hand side of the stream you will find more improvements being carried out to the Pennine Way in the form of a wide pathway constructed from large stone paving-slabs.

The separate paths and other ways down merge at a confluence of the streams and cloughs lower down. This is at John Track Well located at MR 081965. Assuming you are faithfully following the directions provided, ford the streams at this point, climb up the opposite bank and continue walking downhill to the NNW, above and along the L side of the stream, now walking through a pleasant area of heather and bilberry. Further on, an erosion control sign is passed. The Pennine Way continues to descend NNW along the renovated flagged pathway towards Torside Clough. However, within a short distance your more adventurous route peels off, sharp L and to the w, along a narrow, peaty path by the remains of a dilapidated wire fence. This is at MR 081965.

The next part of the route is across extensive moorland to the L and above shooting butts. The correct path is obvious in this vicinity. Initially some ingenuity is again necessary for the safe negotiation of several boggy watercourses that cross your way forward. Further on, some judiciously positioned planks will aid your progress over further boggy areas and watercourses. After some distance the route veers R towards the rounded hill ahead as the direction of travel changes to NW. More improvised footbridges follow and you need to keep steadfastly to this intermittent line of planks. The way leads to a derelict, rectangular stone building situated at MR 066967, just below the summit of the sheltering hill. At this point Crowden, Holme Moss and Black Hill lie away to the N.

From here your route descends sw following a further orderly line of grouse butts and is down a narrow, grassy path towards Cock Hill. Do take appropriate care when crossing this section and comply with any temporary safety restrictions that may be in force from time to time. The route bypasses to the L the trig point you are approaching but a short detour will bring you to the top of Cock Hill off to your R. Continue to descend sw as you pass through an extensive area of disused quarry workings. Following this, the descent steepens as views of Glossop appear ahead with Cown Edge dominating the skyline above the straddling town. The path then crosses a wire fence containing some of the nasty barbed variety. Safely across this, veer immediately L to pass through a gap in a dry-stone wall before continuing to descend along your established sw diagonal.

The path leads to a walled way which marks the boundary of open country. Continue walking sw between the two retaining walls, crossing further stiles of several varieties on the way down. Beyond a restricting hawthorn bush, and across a final stile, a momentary change of direction to your R will bring you back to habitation at Charles Lane. From here turn acutely to the L along the next road to pass Starstone Villa, the first of several stone-built houses on your L. Beyond these, follow the road round to the R as it descends to lead you back to Shepley Street.

Alternative routes

ESCAPES

During the ascent to Higher Shelf Stones, simply turn about when you have had enough and make your way back along your approach route down into Old Glossop.

EXTENSIONS

This route is an isolated round, complete in itself. Although in terms of distance covered and height gained it is relatively short and seemingly undemanding, do not be fooled by these statistics for the way will test your resolve and it encompasses several stiff climbs and the crossing of significant areas of clinging bog. Therefore, no extensions are offered.

Route 4: GLOSSOP, COWN EDGE, WILLIAM CLOUGH and DOCTOR'S GATE

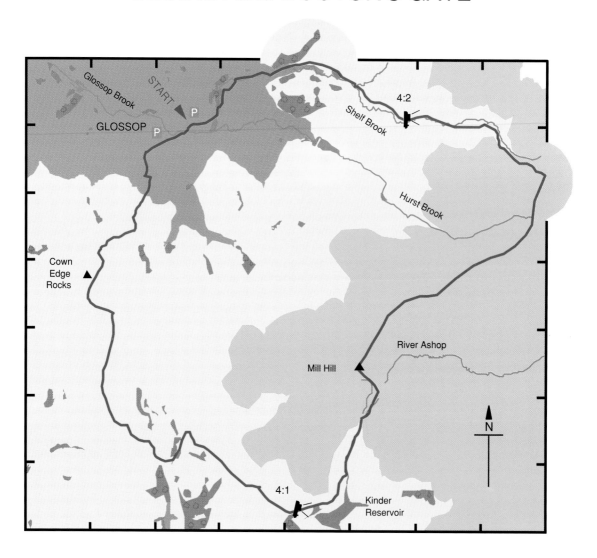

Glossop Brook

START

GLOSSOP

P

P

Shelf Brook

4:2

Hurst Brook

Cown
Edge
Rocks

River Ashop

Mill Hill

N

4:1

Kinder
Reservoir

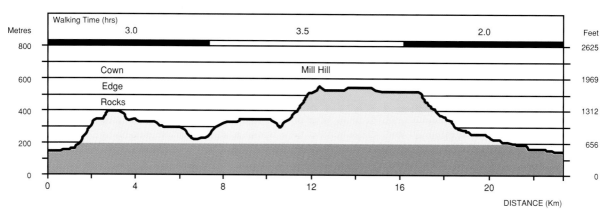

Walking Time (hrs)		
3.0	3.5	2.0

Metres

800

600

Cown

Mill Hill

Edge

Rocks

400

200

0

Feet

2625

1969

1312

656

0

0   4   8   12   16   20

DISTANCE (Km)

ROUTE 4

Glossop, Cown Edge, William Clough and Doctor's Gate

●

STARTING LOCATION
Central car park at Glossop.
OLM 1: MR 036940.
Large car park.

PUBLIC TRANSPORT
Principal town with extensive bus and train services.

OVERVIEW/INTEREST
Long, rugged and exacting route.
Fine elevated views.
Mixture of pleasant rounded hills and ridges at start, followed by crossing of vast, high, exposed moorland.
Uses part of Pennine Way footpath.
Return along Roman Road.

FOOTPATHS
A real assortment!
Pleasant and firm at start.
Interesting ways along recessed watercourses.
The first section of the high moorland crossing is arduous over nasty peat hags.
Further on excellent renovation of path by means of sunken paving slabs.
Route finding a challenge in places.

GRADING
Difficult/severe.

TIME ALLOWANCE
8½ hours.

STATISTICS
DISTANCE

Excluding Height	23.4 km	(14.5 miles)
TOTAL HEIGHT GAINED	570 m	(1870 ft)
PRINCIPAL HEIGHTS		
Cown Edge	400 m	(1310 ft)
Mill Hill	544 m	(1785 ft)

The way to the Glossop Road (A624) at Carr Meadow Farm
Allow 3 hours

The first objective is to escape the confines of Glossop. To do this walk back along the narrow entrance lane to the car park and cross the main A624 road. Continue diagonally to your L across the adjacent short-term car park, walking W and passing the telephone exchange on your L. Bear further L to proceed up Philip Howard Road, at the end of Market Street. Cross over the next road junction and continue along Princess Street turning R at its T-junction end. Cross over and select the next turning, marked by a telephone box, to your L. A narrow, cobbled path then leads downhill towards open country. An iron gate is passed and the next section of the path is known locally as 'the Chicken Run' for obvious reasons.

Veer L at the bottom of 'the Run', cross the busy road with care and proceed along the wide public footpath opposite. This leads uphill at a tangent to the L, away from Simmondley New Road. At this point the first views of the rounded, grassy slopes leading to Whiteley Nab appear ahead to your R, in the SW. The way leads through a gap in a hedge between two stone gateposts. Immediately after this turn sharp L before some distance further squeezing through a narrow G-stile next to an iron gate in the L-hand corner of the field. Then bear L along the lower, better-used of a choice of two paths. This narrow path leads to a lane which you turn R along, now walking towards a nursing home named 'Pennine Way'. Bear L round this establishment, heading uphill directly towards Whiteley Nab.

Further on, squeeze between iron posts and then pass through a gateway to reach more open country. Continue to climb SW up progressively

31

steepening, grassy slopes to reach and pass through a G-stile in a stone wall to your L. There is an obvious path from here, still leading relentlessly up the higher ground stretching away to the SW. Ahead, attractive heather-clad slopes will spur you on. When you reach more gently sloping ground, locate a small bog pool which will provide an enhanced foreground for landscape photographs of Glossop spreadeagled below amongst surrounding hills. Veer L from this spot to walk round the edge of a recently established plantation of sapling Scots pines, keeping these immediately on your R.

Along here the massive, darker slopes and edges of Kinder plateau come into view on your L to the SE, whilst over the next brow the craggy outline of Cown Edge Rocks (your next immediate objective) appears across the intervening slopes to the SW. Continue straight ahead to intersect and cross Monk's Road at MR 022922. The final approach to the road is often across extensive boggy ground and detours, to either the L or R of the worst patches, will almost inevitably prevent you from taking a direct line to the road which is crossed near an iron gate by means of stiles positioned on either side.

Over the road, continue climbing uphill, now along a narrow, stony path. This leads to higher ground up a diagonal to your L. Eventually, the gradient eases as your heather-strewn route continues SSW between fences. Soon you will be treading along a pleasant path which skirts the interesting millstone grit edge and passes the scars of several long abandoned quarry workings. Beyond another stile, bear L, making further progress southwards along the edge. Be vigilant now to keep to the main grassy track as it commences to descend, ignoring a narrow, rocky path off to the R which continues higher up along the edge.

Your way then leads sedately down to Rocks Farm, passing over a stile in the final approach. Turn L here and walk E down the lane by way of Higher Plainstead Farm towards Monk's Road. Just before reaching the road turn R to climb over a P-stile and then continue along the signed public footpath beyond. Cross the shallow depression to your L and proceed down the faint, grassy path along a diagonal to reach the far corner of the field ahead. Carefully mount the stepped stile, paying due regard to the loose stones at the top of the wall which now has to be crossed. Safely down, continue walking up the seldom-used lane opposite (ignoring the L-stile and footpath immediately off to your L), now proceeding due S from MR 023910.

The imposing entrance to Butcher's Piece Farm is passed and further on, where the lane bends R, cross the stile, dead ahead, over the stone wall. On the far side veer R following the clear, grassy path winding through heather as it leads marginally downhill to the SSW across the attractive grouse-inhabited slopes of Matley Moor. Keep to the distinctive path as it bends L to assume a SSE direction of travel. Further down, a G-stile provides entry to a walled lane which you turn L along, immediately negotiating a further stile before continuing to walk SSE along a sandy way.

After some squelchy patches and further obstacles, the route leads you to Matleymoor Farm. This is located at MR 024896. Turn L here, now walking slightly uphill to the E along a walled approach lane. Further on, veer to the R keeping to the lane and crossing over cattle grid immediately before reaching a gateway. Continue down the surfaced lane ahead.

Then disregard a footpath off to your R. Beyond this the buildings of Lanehead Farm are reached with their interesting arrangement of monuments of swans and horses' heads. A steepish descent follows, along the winding lane that leads down to Brookhouse Farm, passing Stet Barn Farm on the way. Past more delectable dwellings the busy A624 Glossop Road is reached at MR 033891. Cross over this with care, well away from the bend, and walk along this road heading towards Glossop for about ½ km (⅓ mile), exercising extreme caution with regard to fast oncoming traffic.

Pass by the inviting gateway on your R and continue up the main road to reach a signed zigzag bend at Carr Meadow Farm a short distance further on. Turn R here.

The way to the Snake Road (A57) at
MR 088929
Allow 3½ hours

Having abandoned the busy A624 traffic artery, the next section of your route is along the delightful public footpath and bridle road signed to 'Edale and Castleton via the foot of Kinder Scout'. From the road bear immediately to your R to cross the bridge in memory of Thomas Boulger (Peak District and Northern Counties Footpath Preservation Society 1921 to 1963) located at the entrance to Hollingworth Clough rising to the E. Continue along the obvious eroded path which climbs out of the clough, snaking up the heather moors into the vastness of open country away to the SE. Further on, as your route bears away from

the protection of a sheltering stone wall on your R, the distinctive pointed profiles of the twin peaks of Mount Famine and South Head appear in the distant SSE. The splendour of the wide-ranging views ahead continues to improve as the impressive boulder-strewn edges of Kinder come more prominently into focus in the ESE. The way continues to the L across the rounded, heather slopes as a white-painted shooting cabin appears across the moors on your L. A short distance further on a bridge is crossed which conveniently spans a nasty area of deep bog.

4:1 Approaching Kinder Reservoir with Kinder Scout beyond

Then at an altitude of some 332 m (1090 ft) your way connects with the well-trodden main path from Hayfield to the Snake Inn via William and Ashop Cloughs. Veer L along this route, initially heading ESE directly in line with Kinder Edge. Further along, bear L again passing a bridleway on the R which leads down to Hayfield. The attractively indented shape of Kinder Reservoir is revealed round the next bend, snugly filling the lower parts of several cloughs, their feeder streams swelling the catchment waters contained by the reservoir. Your narrowing way continues NE along White Brow, high above the reservoir, to converge on yet another diagonal route up from Hayfield. Then marginal height has to be surrendered before the steep slopes of William Clough, rising to the NNE, are engaged. Keep to the L-hand path during the final approach to this indentation.

The path up this confined valley is narrow, a little tricky in places but always fairly obvious; you just keep going up! You may like to keep yourself mentally alert as you climb up to the higher ground towards Ashop Head by counting how many times you have to cross the stream. My tally has been eight times without striving for any record. The steepest and most demanding bit is near the top, where you exit from the clough up severely eroded, steep slopes of packed earth and where it is relatively difficult to retain sound footholds. Flatter ground is then reached at the intersection of the Snake Path and the Pennine Way at MR 063902.

Leave the Snake Path at this junction by turning L and walking initially NNW along the Pennine Way. Unfortunately, extensive peat hags are quickly encountered as you continue towards still higher ground, your correct route pointed out by a marker post visible on the horizon towards the top of Mill Hill. Some ingenuity and a little patience is now called for in crossing the boggy intervening terrain before the temporary sanctuary of firmer sandy ground is reached towards the marker post. The path bears R at this landmark, directly to the NE, as open panoramic views reveal the vast slopes that curve up towards the serrated edges of Kinder. Further, demanding bog now has to be crossed and two muddy ways lead NE over the extensive waterlogged ground of the featureless high moorland of Glead Hill. This section will inevitably test your resolve. Along here keep the guiding marker posts continuously in sight, whichever of the two far from perfect ways you squelch along.

Eventually the Snake Road will be observed ahead on your L to the NE as your way continues eastwards along the line of marker posts and across rough, boggy ground over which progress is exasperatingly slow. Then the cavalry appears, in the form of a relatively luxurious paved path which is gradually being extended westwards.

The way back to Glossop   *Allow 2 hours*

Cross the busy highway, to the R of a bog pool on the far side. From here a good, wide gravel path leads NNE across undulating terrain after a P-stile has provided access to open country once again. About ½ km (⅓ mile) along this path the Roman Road of the Doctor's Gate footpath is reached. A nearby marker post confirms the location. This interchange is named 'Old Woman' on the OS OLM. Turn L down the Doctor's Gate path to commence the long descent towards Shelf Brook and thence into Glossop, now some 6 km (3.7 miles) away to the W. The lengthy plunge westwards is along a path which is an everchanging mixture of grass, stones, peat, bog and intermittent watercourses. Your circuitous route, high above the valley floor, is down an obvious path and beyond the void to your R there are several intriguing rock formations. These include, in order of approach, the configurations of Higher and Lower Shelf Stones, James's Thorn and Shelf Benches. Much further down the path reaches and crosses, by means of a bridge, Shelf Brook.

After this crossing the going becomes appreciably easier as the clough progressively flattens out in its lower reaches. Another long section down the valley then has to be completed before your way merges with a less-used path coming down from Shelf Benches. This is near a large stone barn at MR 064944. From this junction a pleasant grassy path leads further down the valley towards

4:2 Devouring the long trail up Doctor's Gate

two ornate stone bridges. Veer R to cross over the smaller of these two bridges and continue walking westwards down the valley. Beyond a swing gate the way leads into the industrialized part of Old Glossop along Shepley Street. Turn L at the end of Shepley Street and cross the lane to enter Manor Park through the gateway almost opposite. Take one of several diagonal routes to reach the SW corner of this attractive recreational area. Leave the park along Corn Street and then turn R down the main A57 road and follow this into the centre of Glossop. The car park is to your L.

Alternative routes

ESCAPES

Once the Glossop Road at MR 035894 has been crossed and you are committed to climbing into the high moorland ahead, opportunities for conveniently curtailing the walk are difficult to select and follow. Therefore, if you need to shorten the route, do so before you reach this area of no return.

There are two sensible possibilities. The first is to spend more time exploring Cown Edge Rocks by walking further S along this escarpment before returning to Glossop northwards along a different path parallel to your outwards route.

The other is further on from the vicinity of Higher Plainstead Farm. At MR 023912 turn L northwards up Monk's Road and a short distance ahead select the path off to the R. From here there is a variety of easy routes back into Glossop over Whiteley Nab.

EXTENSIONS

This is a long, exacting and strenuous route and no extensions are recommended. For those who must, it is feasible, on fine summer days, to continue along the Pennine Way route as far as Hern Stones at MR 092954. From here there is a demanding trek SSW across uncharted peat hags to Higher Shelf Stones. Once this relative sanctuary is reached, follow the natural edge down by way of Lower Shelf Stones, James's Thorn and Shelf Benches to re-connect with the main route at MR 064944.

Route 5: HAYFIELD, SNAKE PATH and KINDER EDGES

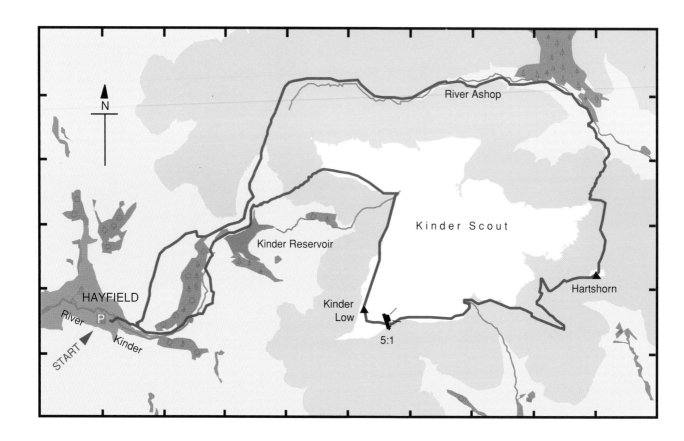

N

River Ashop

Kinder Scout

Kinder Reservoir

HAYFIELD

River

P

Kinder

START

Kinder
Low

Hartshorn

5:1

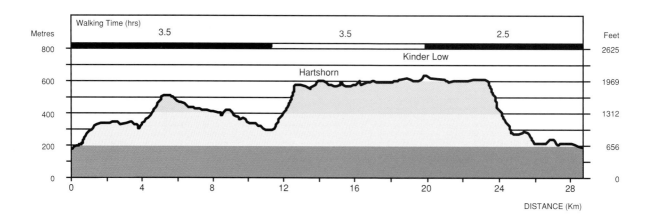

Metres	Walking Time (hrs)				Feet
		3.5	3.5	2.5	

Kinder Low

Hartshorn

DISTANCE (Km)

ROUTE 5

Hayfield, Snake Path and Kinder Edges

●

STARTING LOCATION
Car park at Hayfield.
OLM 1: MR 036869.
Extensive well laid-out car parking facilities.
Toilets, picnic area and Visitor Centre.

ALTERNATIVE STARTING POINT
From Snake Inn.

PUBLIC TRANSPORT
Bus routes 355, 358, 361, 403, 901 and 902.

OVERVIEW/INTEREST
Extremely varied walk with excellent views.
Crossing of Kinder plateau at a relatively narrow point.
Fascinating gritstone and sandstone edges.
Complete solitude the whole day.
Challenging route – one for strong walkers!
Best undertaken in fine weather.

FOOTPATHS
Apart from the crossing of and descent from Kinder, the route is well defined and reasonably straightforward.

Extensive boggy areas encountered around Ashop Head and in other places.
On Kinder, peat hags render the going exacting.
Otherwise, the paths are well-drained and reasonably firm.

GRADING
Difficult/severe.

TIME ALLOWANCE
9½ hours.

STATISTICS

DISTANCE

Excluding Height	28.7 km	(17.9 miles)
TOTAL HEIGHT GAINED	960 m	(3150 ft)
PRINCIPAL HEIGHTS		
Hartshorn	604 m	(1980 ft)
Kinder Low	633 m	(2075 ft)
(Both at edge of Kinder plateau)		

The way to Fair Brook (Woodlands Valley)
Allow 3½ hours

From the car park cross the entrance road and use the underpass opposite to negotiate the main A624 road from Chapel-en-le-Frith to Glossop. Exit from this tunnel along the ramp to the L, then veer R along Walk Mill Road and pass St Matthew's Parish Church. Turn L and cross the River Sett, before turning R up Bank Street passing a branch of NatWest Bank. Follow the road uphill for approximately ½ km (⅓ mile) as it bends to the L. After passing Holly Farm on your R be careful to locate and pass through a narrow opening on your L to engage the footpath informatively signed: 'This footpath to the Snake Inn via William Clough & the Ashop Valley dedicated

for ever – May 29 1897.' Climb the narrow steps, avoiding the nettles! Then bear L along the wide track ahead to pass through a metal K-gate, the first of five such barriers. You are now walking ENE.

Beyond a wooden stile a wide, clearly defined track provides access to more open country further up the hillside. Continue to gain height to the NNE along this path as the other metal K-gates are encountered. On the distant horizon to the SSE the profiles of Mount Famine and South Head come into view. Beyond a stone wall, breached by K-gate number 3, veer L along the narrow path, walking first N and then bearing round to the R (NE). Further height is then gained up an agreeable, shallow gradient as number 4 K-gate is left behind at another stone wall. The peak ahead to your L is The Knott, marking the westerly extremity of Leygatehead Moor.

Open views now appear of quite contrasting countryside. Down below to your L there are tree-covered hillsides. Ahead, barren and dramatically higher moorlands stretch for miles, beckoning you to explore them. Along here there is the first sighting of part of the extensive millstone grit edges of Kinder plateau, now beginning to dominate the horizon to the NE. The fifth and final metal K-gate officially marks the boundary of 'open country' and a sign informs you that you are allowed access to the High Peak Estate along the Snake Path. From here, the obvious way snakes eastwards along a wide, eroded shale path as another path, over from the direction of Glossop, joins yours to the L. The next part of the route is well signed; the signs include 'bog warnings' and bridging set into the path assists you across these.

It is necessary first to veer R, before selecting a L fork that prevents you from descending along a bridleway off to your R. Round the next bend there is a super view of the irregular shape of Kinder Reservoir cradled in the rounded hillsides below Kinder plateau. High above, the distinctive jumble of boulders and rock pitches marking Kinder Downfall can be distinguished in clear weather to the E, almost in a direct line with your continuation path. Your path traverses high above the reservoir along White Brow before it descends to reach the entrance to William Clough stretching away to the N. Bear L here along the higher route following a path not clearly marked on some older editions of the OLM. A fairly level stretch is covered, followed by a short descent, before the long and relentlessly upwards winding groove of William Clough is tackled. A well-established path follows the stream up the narrow enclosed gully as the watercourse cascades merrily over a series of miniature waterfalls. There are alternative ways up the clough and you will be forced to cross the stream several times but this only adds variety to your way up. The exit is to the L up a badly eroded steep slope and across which footholds are relatively difficult to maintain.

The steep slopes peter out into flat, rugged, open moorland and at this juncture a rocky profile

appears on your R marking the northernmost rim of Kinder Scout. Immediately ahead the Pennine Way is crossed at right angles at MR 063902. After this, continue walking NE for some distance across exacting peaty hags, eventually reaching the high ground of Ashop Head. The worst terrain hereabouts can be avoided by keeping to the higher, firmer ground to the L. Securer ground is reached ahead as a clearer, drier sandy path becomes re-established leading E above the infant Ashop Clough on your R. Unfortunately, further 'boggy hags' straddle your direct way forward for some distance and slight detours are inevitable to avoid the ooziest of these. They are finally left behind as more attractive walking terrain is reached along a shallow V-nick in the otherwise featureless moorlands. Shallow downward slopes are then engaged and these follow the course of the now well-established River Ashop leading further eastwards.

Fast progress can now be achieved as the path improves and becomes drier and firmer still. On your R the River Ashop continues to enlarge, swollen by the waters of several merging tributary streams. The Snake Path is then followed for several kilometres eastwards down the clough and eventually this rises significantly above the stream as more interesting wooded slopes come into prominence ahead. These are the extensive Snake Plantations which line the Woodlands Valley in their lower reaches. Then in the vicinity of a dilapidated stone building on your R, at MR 091907, descend along the side footpath also on your R and carefully cross the River Ashop by means of a precariously perched wooden beam. This crossing badly needs some urgent improvement.

On the other side, turn L and walk up the slope ahead along the narrow footpath, continuing to travel E. The way soon climbs to more open ground above the clough and there are fine views down the narrow valley of the densely conifer-forested slopes ahead across the stream. Then the famous Snake Inn comes prominently into view on the opposite side of the valley and in this vicinity be careful to keep along the main path by bearing L at a junction of the ways. Some distance further on, a gentle slope leads back down to the bed of the stream. After this, thread your way through the bracken as the correct route, for a time, becomes less distinct and decidedly wetter underfoot. Then, be careful to locate a distinct, narrow gravel path leading sse up from the flat valley bottom. Along here the next and more demanding section of the route, that up to the top of Kinder Scout far above, becomes progressively revealed. Continue along the obvious path to the r of a recently refurbished stone wall. Just ahead, beyond the Fairbrook High Peak Estate sign, the ways divide. Continue to the l, across the stream (Fair Brook), using the stepping stones provided and then up the opposite slope following the path furthest to the l.

The way to Kinder Low (Kinder Edge)

Allow 3½ hours

Follow the distinct traverse route up the lower hillside along a wide pathway that is invariably dry and firm. Further up, this agreeable path bends to the r to reveal daunting slopes ahead that lead to the stark, boulder-strewn edge of Kinder plateau. The route then veers to the ssw up Gate Side Clough following the course of a dilapidated stone wall. The final pitch to reach the rock formations that line the edge is tough going, so take this at a pace that you find comfortable. The brim in this vicinity is named Seal Edge and the massive boulders are Seal Stones. Once through the configuration of rock pitches, bedding slabs and boulders, continue up the higher grassy slopes, veering l and se to reach the better defined edge path just above. Bear eastwards along this and follow it as it bends round to your r to assume, for some distance, a predominantly southwards direction of progress along the rim of Blackden Moor, now falling away on your l.

When the edge takes a definite turning to the l at MR 117883 and near a tiny watercourse, turn off the main edge route by following a narrower side path up rising ground off to the right, walking due s. A relatively straightforward crossing of the formidable peat hags covering most of Kinder

Scout at one of its narrowest points then follows. Start this by crossing the tiny watercourse ahead, which in the dry periods of summer is often only a parched stone bed, and select a ssw bearing. Keep steadfastly to this bearing, sometimes using indistinct paths through the heather, on other occasions deviating slightly to circumvent peat bogs, but all the time making for the higher ground ahead that marks Hartshorn, located just before reaching the southern edge of the plateau.

Quite soon, in favourable weather conditions, you will be able to make out the distinctive profile of Lose Hill ahead to your l in the se. Then, but a short distance further on, you will reach the edge of Kinder Scout at a point directly above the massive cleft of Grindsbrook Clough snaking down towards Edale. More irregular rock formations are encountered as the green and farmed lower landscape of Edale Valley is revealed. The slopes of Mam Tor and the long ridges leading from this, eastwards to Lose Hill and westwards along Rushup Edge, are clearly visible on a fine day. Now turn r and follow the indented edge westwards along the established rim path. Keeping to the higher ground work your way along the edge, and across more intervening rock formations and watercourses, to reach the top of Grindsbrook. Safely across the stream and the surrounding rock falls, keep walking along the edge by veering l and se using the obvious rocky path. Make for Grindslow Knoll, the high ground directly ahead to the se. Climb this higher hillock along the r hand branch path to reach the precariously balanced cairn positioned there.

After this, start your descent along the faint path to the w. This soon connects with a better defined way as your direction veers r and nw. Your route then re-connects with the main, direct edge path coming in on your r and you bear l along this, walking w once again. After passing a huge cairn, Crowden Brook is crossed by walking over the flat bedding slabs. On the other side of the clough select the narrow, rocky middle path that climbs quite steeply ssw. Continue to climb ssw to reach Crowden Tower, a massive configuration of large, symmetrically rounded rocks. After visiting these, resume your westerly journey along the wide edge path composed alternatively of sand and then peat. Further on, more intersecting rock outcrops are reached, some shapes resembling animals. Amongst these the distinctive profile of Pym Chair can be made out on the skyline ahead as your route threads through the nearer rock formations known as the Wool Packs. Penetrate these, always keeping to the path bordering the edge, and continue to walk w. Views now open up below, exposing the features surrounding Jacob's Ladder, including the arched bridge spanning the stream, at this spot.

5:1 Layered rocks on Kinder Edge

Then the trigonometrical point of Kinder Low comes into view, ahead to the NW. After passing extensive rock buttresses the path crosses an area of high peat moorland along a clear and well-drained route. This leads to the next massive cairn, which marks the location of Noe Stool. At this point turn R away from the edge and proceed along a shallow depression WNW into Kinder plateau, walking in a direct line towards the trig point, the top of which just peeps up above the intervening ground. This is an established route across the corner of the plateau and is not too daunting. Walk directly to the trig point to connect with the Pennine Way once more.

The way back to Hayfield   *Allow 2½ hours*

Now walk northwards along the most westerly edge of Kinder Scout and follow the way that hugs the edge across difficult, peaty slopes. After fording Red Brook you will reach the Downfall at the River Kinder, some 2 km (1.2 miles) further on. Cross this cleft by keeping to the higher ground and the flat rocky slabs away from the precipitous edge. Then follow the rocky, indented edge to the SW as it circles high above Kinder Reservoir. Keep to the higher path that passes round and to the R of the irregular rock configurations of Sandy Heys. Cross over the stiles and continue traversing along the main edge path until you come to a definite spur leading off to the L. This is partly obscured at the top but is situated at MR 070895. Turn L here, off the main path, and walk down the craggy promontory leading SW, directly in line with the reservoir below. On reaching the lower, grassy slopes, a path of sorts is distinguishable but this is not marked on the OLM. Further down still, a steepening section is negotiated by veering R. Continue to descend along the narrow grassy path using the reservoir as your main guiding beacon. The path becomes more distinct and it eventually leads you down towards the indent in the reser-voir at which the stream cascading along William Clough flows into it.

At the bottom, cross the wooden footbridge and then turn sharply L to follow the lower level path round, and to the N of, the reservoir. The path rises and then undulates through a section, buttressed by steps, before it descends along a stony chute to reach the surfaced entrance road to the water treatment plant below. Cross the approach road and use the footpath leading off on the opposite side to cross over the River Kinder. The path then leads down the valley following the course of the stream to reach the lane again some distance on. Bear R along this, using it to re-cross the river, before veering L down Kinder Road and following this into Hayfield. Re-use the tunnel under the main road, to reach the car park.

Alternative routes

ESCAPES
Having reached the Woodlands Valley in the vicinity of the Snake Inn, escape routes are not all that obvious or plentiful. One possibility is to use the path up Fair Brook to reach the edge of Kinder at MR 093891. Thereafter, a crossing of Kinder plateau at another relatively narrow point will bring you direct to Kinder Downfall, just over 1 km (0.6 miles) away to the WSW and where the main route can be conveniently re-joined. Less strong walkers are advised to turn R at the top of William Clough and then to make their way SE along the edge to MR 070895. From this point the spur leading down to the SW and used towards the end of the main route may be followed to short-circuit much of the more demanding part of the main route.

EXTENSIONS
The described route is long and arduous and therefore no additional sections are recommended, not even for strong and fit walkers.

Route 6: THE DERWENT EDGES, DERWENT and LADYBOWER RESERVOIRS

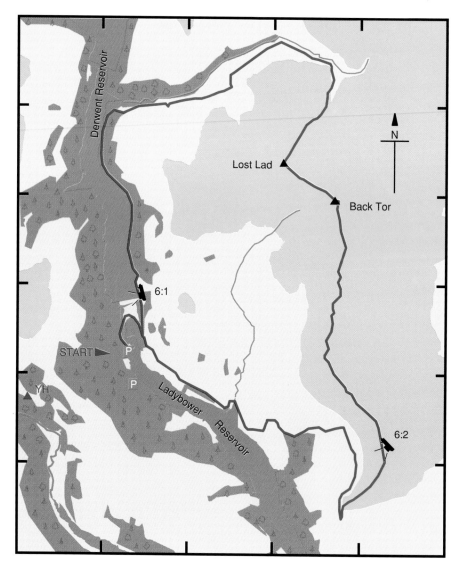

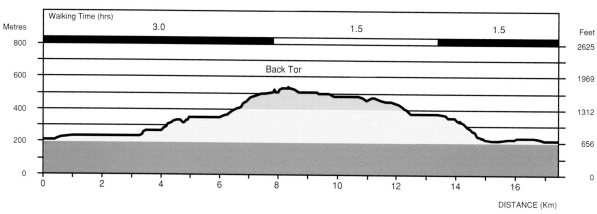

ROUTE 6

The Derwent Edges, Derwent and Ladybower Reservoirs

STARTING LOCATION
Car park at Fairholme Visitor Centre.
OLM 2: MR 173893.
Extensive car parking facilities together with picnic areas, toilets, information centre and in summer months refreshment facilities. Superior starting location!

PUBLIC TRANSPORT
Bus routes 257, 274, 280, 395, 400, 460, 795, 796 and M74.

OVERVIEW/INTEREST
Reservoirs, valleys and moorlands, fascinating edges, rock formations; this walk has it all!
Superb views of never-ending interest.
Part of walk along eastern shores of Derwent and Ladybower Reservoirs.
Scrambling to your heart's content over sandstone and millstone grit outcrops.
A walk to be relished for a long time afterwards.
Choose a dry, clear, windless day for this one.

FOOTPATHS
Always there, even across the highest, exposed moorland.

Much of the way is along very acceptable, well-drained paths.
Along the edges and elsewhere there are areas of boggy peat to contend with but these are part of the challenge.
Much renovation work is underway and the paved sections are a justifiable solution to continuous erosion damage.
Route finding is relatively straightforward and should present few problems.
Signs are quite adequate.

GRADING
Moderate to difficult/severe.

TIME ALLOWANCE
6 hours.

STATISTICS

DISTANCE		
Excluding Height	17.4 km	(10.8 miles)
TOTAL HEIGHT GAINED	400 m	(1310 ft)
PRINCIPAL HEIGHTS		
Back Tor	538 m	(1765 ft)

The way to Lost Lad

Allow 3 hours

The starting location, tucked away within the surrounding forest at the N end of the Ladybower Reservoir, is a real gem. This site developed by Severn Trent Water has deservedly won several awards, including the prestigious Conservation Award from the Institute of Chartered Surveyors and *The Times* together with the Centres of Excellence Award 1993 from the English Forestry Authority.

Leave the centre along the path leading northwards up the valley. Veer R at the macadam road ahead and walk along this to pass the massive twin-turreted dam. The road bends R and at the junction ahead veer L to follow the higher of two paths, which immediately climbs beneath pine trees. Your heading here is NE through magnificent forest scenery. The way leads between rhododendron bushes and emerging from these the route then passes the end of the dam containing Derwent Reservoir. Continue walking NNE and, past a stile, veer L to follow the forest road which winds along the E bank of the reservoir. The views across the reservoir on sunny days, particularly in winter, can be stunning with mirror-like images of the wooded hillsides faithfully reflected on the perfectly still surface of the water. The way leads

6:1 Derwent Reservoir Dam

without fuss towards Howden Dam located less than 3 km (1.9 miles) further N. Along here, ignore (by continuing along the valley) the path off to your R leading to Bradfield and Strines.

Eventually, round a bend to the R, the impressive Howden Dam appears. This fine structure, the uppermost barrier in the reservoir system, is still partly concealed by the abundant foliage, pines and rhododendrons on a tiny island visible in front of the dam. Further on, the route penetrates pines and on nearing the dam bear R along the track signed 'Public footpath to Ewden via Broom-

head for Bradfield and Strines'. (This sign must have been thought out by a former train announcer!) However, about 40 m (45 yd) on, abandon this way as it turns sharply R uphill and instead continue along the broad track ahead. This traverses round the brow of the hillside ahead. These critical manoeuvres are made at Abbey Tip Plantation, MR 171919.

The way then rises more steeply to the E as rhododendron bushes to your R and larches on your L are left behind. For some distance now the route is along an elevated track above Abbey Brook which gurgles away contentedly way below. Beyond gateposts set in a stone wall, more open country comprised of heather-clad slopes is reached. At this point be careful to veer L along the lower of a choice of tracks keeping nearest to a wall and to larches. Height is gradually but progressively gained with seemingly minimum effort and the spirits soar. Past a gate and stile, a tiny stream within a narrow clough is crossed before you tackle the steepening gradient ahead. From along here the best views down into the tree-lined valley of Abbey Brook may be obtained. Far beyond and above this, the flat edge to the NE just hides sightings of the trig point located on Margery Hill. Then Cogman Clough is reached and crossed at the ford. Access from this impressive drainage channel is along the wide track leading up the far steepish bank on a diagonal to your L. Beyond, the path snakes NE above the main valley and the gradient slackens off once more as the route follows the folds of the rounded hillsides.

The way then bends to the R as the contorting cleft of Gravy Clough plummeting down the far side of the main valley is passed to your L. The gradual change of direction brings you to a SE bearing as you enter the more confined and remote higher reaches of the valley. The obvious way continues along an elevated path. Then bedding planes of millstone grit appear as the terrain becomes craggier, but the condition of the superb pathway starts to deteriorate. It then narrows appreciably and sections of rough, waterlogged terrain have to be crossed. To compensate, the land features become more interesting and some distance on an unusual separated spur of rock is passed down to your L which has cleavage faults either side. Opposite this landmark the route veers further R to enter Sheepfold Clough to the S and the serrated edge now directly ahead is that of Howshaw Tor.

Do not be tempted to cross the clough. This is avoided by bearing further R along the narrow but clear path which rises above the clough and which will maintain your southwards direction. You then have to share the route with a descending watercourse up a darkish, peaty way that rises over a gradual gradient. Towards the top of the long incline you are rewarded by the re-appearance of vast, rolling moorlands and as the ground levels off you will find that your direction has imperceptibly changed towards SW. The first sighting of the rocks of Back Tor may now be observed on the skyline to your L, in the SSE, whilst the configuration of Lost Lad, your next immediate objective, may be seen standing out ahead to the S.

Further height is agreeably gained and then, in the clearest of weather, long range panoramic views of the most magnificent moorland scenery appear. In these, the massive outline of Kinder Scout rises to the WSW, with the rolling peak of Bleaklow to the WNW competing for attention. Over to the NNW the impressive and regressive spurs of Howden Edge jut out into the upper environs of the Derwent water catchment system. Altogether the vistas from this full 360-degree viewing platform will be hard to better anywhere in the Peak. The icing on top of the cake is reached a short distance further on, at the isolated stone cairn, as from here the Mam Tor ridge may be observed majestically occupying a postion to the SW.

Additionally Win Hill comes into view to the S signifying the easterly end of a long spur. Veer L from here to reach Lost Lad away to the SSE.

At Lost Lad there is a superb directional compass and view-finder erected by the Sheffield Clarion Ramblers in dedication to the memory of W.H. Baxby. The main land features indicated on this masterpiece are summarized below, moving clockwise round the compass:

- Bleaklow Head
- Holme Moss
- Featherbed Moss
- Abbey Brook
- Howshaw Tor
- Back Tor (your next mission)
- Bamford Edge
- Cakes of Bread (will be visited later)
- Dovestone Tor (will be visited later)
- Win Hill
- Ladybower
- Lose Hill
- Mam Tor
- Lord's Seat
- Seal Stones
- Fairbrook Naze
- Shelf Stones

The way along the Edges   *Allow 1½ hours*

From Lost Lad it is but a short distance ESE to reach the rocky outcrop and trig point on the skyline that signify Back Tor. The route to there is a mixture of sodden, boggy ground and a superb renovated way of huge paving slabs. This way is through wild heathers. The boulders of Back Tor are soon reached and for those with a desire to stand on the very top, there are ways to the trig point which demand some elementary scrambling. This tor stands at 538 m (1765 ft) and is the highest elevation of the entire route. New sightings from these rock formations include Strines Reservoir to the ESE with an outline of some of the buildings of Sheffield forming a faraway back-cloth.

The way continues southwards along the Derwent Edges and down an obvious path. Your next immediate destinations along the edge are soon revealed: in order of approach sequence these are Bradfield Gate Head, Cakes of Bread, Dovestone Tor, Salt Cellar, White Tor and the Wheelstones, but more about these later. The path meanders along the edge and across further boggy sections, the worst of which require occasional short diversions into the better-drained, heather-clad moorland to your L. The ground falls slightly and

6:2 The south westwards panorama observed from Derwent Edge

further on you cross another path, signed 'Abbey Grange to Strines', at right angles. Beyond this intersection the state of your path improves and several long sections of renovated pavements promote swift progress.

A short distance further on, the isolated and aptly named rock configurations of the Cakes of Bread are reached. These are passed some distance away on your L. The next outcrop is Dovestone Tor, which is passed much nearer on your R as the way continues southwards along the edges. The route then drops more appreciably on its approach to the Salt Cellar, a huge boulder appropriately named for its distinctive shape.

After wading through more bog, keep to the R to cross the heather, before making your final approach beside a dilapidated stone wall to reach the Salt Cellar. This routing provides the best views hereabouts. Round the rock configuration, climb back through the heather to your L to rejoin the main edge path.

From here, the ground undulates over gentle slopes and your direction veers to SE before you reach White Tor, the next outcrop. The path then bends to your L and the terrain continues to fall slightly as you approach the Wheel Stones. The local name for this massive coagulation of rocks is the Coach and Horses and once again the nickname is descriptive. Beyond this arresting sight, continue along the edge until you reach the Hurkling Stones. After this, another path is crossed at right angles, this one linking Derwent with Moscar. From here, continue along the wide sandy path making for the brow of the hill ahead and directly in line with the far-off shape of Win Hill. Further on, veer R along the main path near to the edge, ignoring a narrower side path off to your L. Continue to descend along the obvious way. Some distance further on, your line changes directly towards the Mam Tor ridge, viewed end-on. From the next modest group of rocks, Whinstone Lee Tor, there is a superb view down to your R along Ladybower Reservoir and within this scenery your continuation route snaking below and back northwards may be discerned some considerable distance below. At the next junction of paths, a short distance further down, turn R along the bridleway in order to part company with the edges. This is at MR 198874.

The way back to Fairholmes   *Allow 1½ hours*

Following the turn to the R, be careful to continue along the higher of two ways, walking NNW downhill and passing a National Trust sign indicating 'Whinstone Lee Fields' to your L. On no account descend along the steeper, narrower path more to the L and which passes the other side of the National Trust sign. Your path narrows and then deteriorates as it joins company with the stone wall to your L. Keep to the obvious main route along here as it winds round the hillsides, gradually losing height. This means avoiding a way off to your L through stone pillars and, past this, keeping to the lower path to the L as another wide track converges at an acute angle to the R. The way sweeps round the hillside in one long, uninterrupted arc maintaining a fairly constant elevation. Along here, keep to the wide track beside the guiding stone wall to your L. Further on, the outline of White Tor rocks becomes prominent and you should immediately recognize this shape: you were standing on these a short time ago. When you reach a point almost beneath

this outcrop, turn L to follow the bridleway signed to 'Derwent' by passing through a gateway. From this point the route continues W, more steeply downhill.

Lower down, a conifer plantation comprised of Scots pines is reached. Adjacent to this a stile and gate are encountered and beyond these the way continues along a pleasant, grassy band between a fence and a stone wall and more height is surrendered. Lower down, two more gates have to be negotiated to enter the High Peak Estate; further on, another gateway leads to the crossing of a small stream. Then the dilapidated remains of High House Farm are reached past a stile and gate and then another narrow gate, the latter concealed to your L. Exiting from the farmyard, the path bends round to the R tracking NW before turning sharply downhill to the L to level ground at a s-stile positioned just above Ladybower Reservoir.

Turn R along the wide roadway and then avoid the track off to the R towards Ashes Farm. Continue NW for about 2 km (1.2 miles) to reach Derwent Dam again. In achieving this, you will pass the location of Millbrook, the lost village of Derwent, which was flooded during the filling of the reservoirs in 1943–46. On approaching the wall of the dam, veer L downhill and retrace your outwards steps back to the visitor centre.

Alternative routes

ESCAPES
There are several opportunities for conveniently shortening the route by heading westwards along any of the several paths leading down from the edges from Lost Lad onwards.

EXTENSIONS
Sensible extensions are not quite so numerous and the only one advocated is to continue further southwards along the edges before making for the viaduct across Ladybower Reservoir. From here the way is northwards along the road that winds round the E side of the reservoir and this reconnects with the main route at MR 187884.

Route 7: HIGHER POYNTON, LYME PARK and BOW STONES

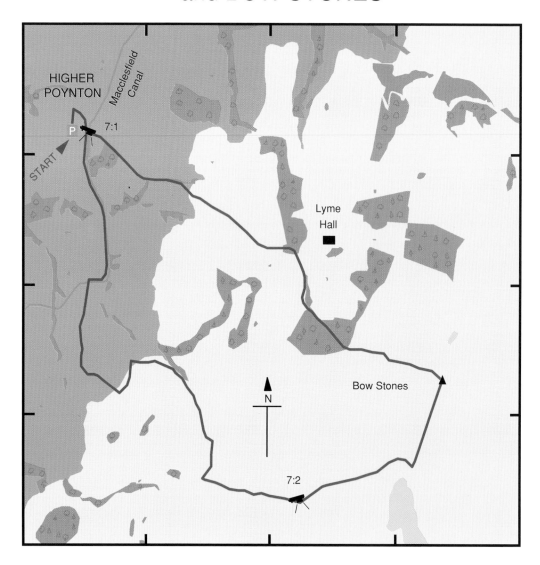

HIGHER POYNTON

Macclesfield Canal

P

7:1

START

Lyme Hall

Bow Stones

N

7:2

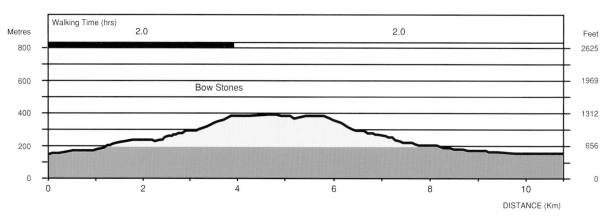

Metres	Walking Time (hrs)			Feet
	2.0	2.0		
800				2625
600				1969
	Bow Stones			
400				1312
200				656
0				0

DISTANCE (Km)

ROUTE 7

Higher Poynton, Lyme Park and Bow Stones

•

STARTING LOCATION
Car lay-by Higher Poynton (along Shrigley Road North).
Pathfinder 741 map: MR 944833.
Space for about 20 cars.
(Additional nearby parking at Nelson's Pit and Poynton Coppice car parks.)

ALTERNATIVE STARTING POINT
Lyme Hall.

PUBLIC TRANSPORT
Bus route 191.

OVERVIEW/INTEREST
Pleasant shorter, lower-level route.
Plenty of interest including Lyme Hall, deer park and boat marina.
Open rolling countryside.
Sections through woodlands and along canal.
No prolonged inclines or steep gradients.
Ideal walk for family groups.
Ancient Bow Stones.

FOOTPATHS
Good and easy to follow for most of way.
Some waterlogged ground beyond Bow Stones.
Excellent canal tow-path.
Route adequately signposted.

GRADING
Easy/straightforward.

TIME ALLOWANCE
4 hours.

STATISTICS

DISTANCE

Excluding Height	10.8 km	(6.7 miles)
TOTAL HEIGHT GAINED	260 m	(855 ft)
PRINCIPAL HEIGHTS		
Bow Stones	390 m	(1280 ft)

The way to Bow Stones
Allow 2 hours

Make your way to the crossroads at the Boar's Head, Higher Poynton, MR 944834. Select the lane, Lyme Road, signed 'Lyme Park – No through road' and, walking E, cross Middlewood Way and the Macclesfield Canal. Macclesfield Canal is crossed at a point full of interest with its nearby extensive boat marina, quacking ducks and patient anglers. Continue along the lane passing in rapid succession Ivy Cottage, the entrance drive to the boat marina and Woodside Cottage, to reach a cattle grid. Immediately after passing through the K-gate at this grid be careful to keep to the R, using the continuation route nearest to the wooded area and rejecting the fork off to your L which leads to Hilltop Farm. Along here, open landscapes ahead reveal the higher, rounded, grassy slopes sweeping up towards Bow Stones. In clear weather the

buildings and telecommunications masts located at Bowstonegate may be observed.

The obvious way continues ahead, passing beneath electricity power lines, and is then obstructed by two further cattle grids before it surrenders height by dipping down to cross a shallow gully just prior to passing through Haresteads Farm. Following this, a short incline leads to the entrance to the extensive parklands which surround Lyme Hall and over which deer freely roam. This is reached at the dwelling now named 'Windgather', presumably after the rocks of that name. It was formerly called 'Four Winds' and is thus described on some editions of the relevant OS maps. The parkland is accessed at this point through a formidable iron railing K-gate.

Continue walking ESE along the wide, gravel way which leads marginally uphill directly in line with Bowstonesgate, silhouetted on the far hori-

7:1 The frozen Macclesfield Canal at Higher Poynton

zon. Some distance along here turn about to observe the fine views to your rear over the village of Poynton and beyond this the vast flatness of the Cheshire Plain extending for miles southwards towards the distant Welsh hills. The pronounced escarpment of Alderley Edge, of both mining and witch ceremony fame, protrudes out into the plain to your L in the wsw. Beyond a combined stile, gate and cattle grid, stretches of deciduous woodlands ahead shelter the more intensively tended grounds of Lyme Hall. Another surfaced lane comes in on your R and a short distance after this, as the merged way bends to the R beneath a canopy of oak and sycamore trees, keep straight on, heading across the intervening grassy slopes before scaling the small tree-covered knoll directly ahead. This hill provides particularly good views overlooking Lyme Hall and its surrounding attractions. These include extensive lawned areas, gardens and its famous Cage.

Turn to your R and descend towards the fringe of the extensive car parking area below. An indistinct path may be followed down to this. Cross the metalled road at right angles and continue along the surfaced branch way directly opposite, walking s. You are now treading along the signed 'Gritstone Trail', which soon breaches the boundary wall ahead at a gate and K-stile. The pathway then rises along the pleasant hillside and you next pass a well-groomed pitch-and-putt course over on your L. (This has a fond memory for the author because on one occasion he achieved the pure fluke of a hole-in-one here, fortunately with reliable witnesses present.) Nearby there is an adventure playground that is bound to delight any youngsters in your party.

Past these attractions, keep to the obvious main path which leads further uphill beside conifer trees, with Scots pines predominating. The way enters Knightslow Wood at a gate and high L-stile ahead. Continue straight on along the main path under the shade of the mature deciduous trees. Some sections along here can be tediously water-logged on occasions, particularly after heavy rain. One compensation for this is that over the retaining wall, below on your L, there are fine views back towards Lyme Hall. The woodlands are left at another high L-stile, where the way to Bow Stones is signed. This is up an obvious, quite badly eroded path that leads over more rugged moor-land slopes which provide further impressive views of the open landscape sweeping upwards to the hilly ridges above. Another L-stile has to be climbed to reach the grassy path leading round the buildings and extensive communications antennae that feature at Bowstonesgate. A final wooden stile provides entrance to the confluence of ways that meet at this lofty, windswept elevation. This is at MR 974813.

On reaching the end of the metalled road at this location spend a little time absorbing the views which abound in all directions from here. In particular, those ahead between E and SE excel. These are down across a wide, shallow valley with lush pastures for countless sheep, and on towards Whaley Bridge, Taxal Edge and Windgather Rocks. To the SW long spurs and rounded grassy hills fan out before the landscape falls to the Cheshire Plain far beyond. These ridges mark your continuation route. The two perpendicular rocks which give their name to this locality are called Bow Stones, for they are purported to have been used in ancient times by bowmen to sharpen their arrowheads.

The way back to Higher Poynton

Allow 2 hours

From your approach direction to Bow Stones turn R, pass through the gate and continue along the walled way, which dips slightly, walking SSW towards the rising ground ahead of Sponds Hill. Beyond another gate and stile, pass by a public footpath on your L leading down to Whaley Bridge and Kettleshulme, and continue, now SW, over the next waymarked stile. After this, abandon the main path which sweeps round more to the L and keep to the R beside the stone wall, passing a sign dedicated to the loving memory of John Lomas and informing you that you are now heading towards Pott Shrigley along a public footpath. This manoeuvre avoids the higher ground of Sponds Hill and changes your direction of travel to W.

The path now becomes less distinct and the next section often becomes waterlogged after rainy spells. Improvised crossings of the worst stretches are in place and with a little care the most treacherous of these can be avoided without significant deviation. The route from here has recently been renovated and this work was still underway at the time this record was taken. Therefore, some of the features now described may since have been further improved. A recently renovated stile is next encountered and this leads to a much better defined, narrow path. This runs downhill for a short distance before the ground rises once again to the rounded hillock ahead. Beyond this knoll the direct footpath to Pott Shrigley is forsaken by veering R along the fork which follows the line of a stone wall to your R but some distance away from it. Keep to the line of the indistinct path parallel to but still maintaining some distance from the previously mentioned stone wall on your R, descending to the SW as you do so. Be careful to cross over a number of obstacles by means of the recently constructed stiles and these very conveniently confirm your correct line of descent. Your final drop to Moor-side Lane is down steeper, rougher, tufted grass slopes beside another stone wall more immedi-ately to your R. A final stile provides entry to this lane at a small group of trees.

Turn R along the lane and pass Keepers Cottage. A short distance further on turn off to your L down the public footpath signed to 'Higher Poyn-ton'. This is achieved by clambering over the stepped stile in the retaining stone wall. The path leads diagonally to your R further downhill and some more swampy ground now has to be crossed. A more agreeable section of the footpath follows and further on a shallow, narrow ravine is crossed down to your L. On the far side of this usually dry watercourse, a more distinct series of

51

parallel paths lead round the brow of a hillock and then down to an enclosed area entered by means of an improvised wooden gate breaching a stone wall. Your approach to this is beside another stone wall on your R. Along this stretch there are other interesting views to your R, this time of the exposed bedding strata in the rock structure of mounds forming the far slopes of Cluse Hay, a small, deepish valley.

Beyond a dip to your L, the way continues down as the path leads beneath hawthorn trees past an enclosure that contains two aging caravans which have been a permanent feature here for some time. After this, there is a further stiled gate for you to negotiate. Then a rapidly widening and improving track guides you down to Green Close Methodist church, Shrigley, at MR 948814. Turn L, and walk uphill along Shrigley Road. After the rise ahead select the next path off on your R, descending slightly to the NW to pass Simpson Lane Cottage. The footpath leads down to Redacre Hall Farm and round to its R, by means of a concessionary path which crosses a stile to the L and which some distance further on will bring you to Mitchell Ford. Your way is signed to this effect. After crossing the stile veer immediately to the L to pass close to the farm buildings at Redacre Hall further over on your L side. After this, follow the line of the hawthorn hedge, once again to your L. You pass by a gateway before reaching a gate and stile in the far lower corner of the field at a muddy approach area.

Continue walking beside the hedge to cross the next meadow and this will take you to another gate and stile which you also cross. From here an enclosed, shaded pathway will lead you down, through two further gateways, to Macclesfield Canal at MR 945821. Cross the canal by means of the bridge and turn R along the towing path to continue E for a short stretch before the canal bends round L to the N. Make use of the tow-path for about 1½ km (0.9 miles) to return to the area of the boat marina at Higher Poynton. This will involve passing beneath an iron latticed footbridge and further on the more substantial road bridge which you crossed on your outwards route.

The correct exit from the delightful waterway is just after passing beneath this road bridge, through a stile and K-gate on your L. Turn down the adjacent lane and from here retrace your steps to where you left your vehicle in the vicinity of the Boar's Head a short distance further on.

Alternative routes

ESCAPES
Many family walking groups will probably wish to spend more time sampling, at their leisure, the many delights of Lyme Hall and its surrounding parkland. The route can be shortened considerably by avoiding the climb and loop which takes in Bow Stones. To do this exit from Lyme Park at West Parkgate, MR 951815. This is reached by descending down the attractive valley containing Hase Bank Wood directly from Lyme Park.

EXTENSIONS
Those walkers contemplating extensions may also wish to see more of Lyme Hall. This can be accommodated by first walking to it, and then using the paths leading E which re-connect with the main route at Bow Stones.

Other alternatives for extending the walk are from the higher ground to the SW of Bow Stones to select a longer descent route, one more to the S of the prescribed main route. There are several of these to choose from, each of varying additional length. However, some of these do become relatively complicated in the locality of Pott Shrigley. One modest extension is to turn L instead of R on reaching Moorside Lane (MR 954805). After making this manoeuvre turn R further on and use the combination of footpaths leading via Birchencliff and Lockgate Farm to reach the canal at Adlington Basin, MR 937816.

7:2 Fantastic snow shapes on Dale Top

Route 8: CHINLEY, SOUTH HEAD and CHESTNUT CENTRE

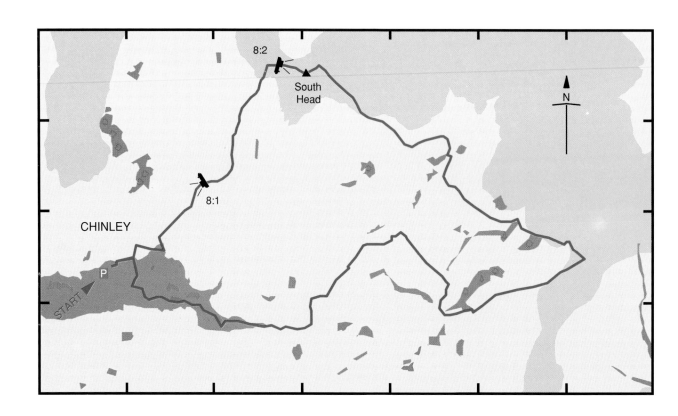

8:2

South Head

8:1

CHINLEY

P

START

N

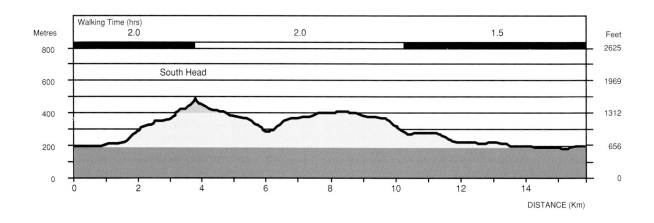

Metres	Walking Time (hrs)			Feet
	2.0	2.0	1.5	
800				2625
	South Head			1969
600				
				1312
400				
				656
200				
0				0

0   2   4   6   8   10   12   14

DISTANCE (Km)

ROUTE 8

Chinley, South Head and Chestnut Centre

STARTING LOCATION
Car park at Chinley.
OLM 1: MR 039824.
Car park near Community Centre holds about 25
  cars.

PUBLIC TRANSPORT
Bus routes 189, 190, 191 and 403.
Train service.

OVERVIEW/INTEREST
Pleasant, enjoyable family walk.
Eminently suitable for sturdy youngsters.
Good open views of surrounding countryside.
Visit to the Chestnut Centre (otters and owls).
Finish through rather industrialized belt.

FOOTPATHS
Good and certain for most of way.

Some muddy areas following heavy rain.
On occasions route finding somewhat complicated
  but no significant difficulties.
No really rough ground.

GRADING
Easy/straightforward to moderate.

TIME ALLOWANCE
5½ hours.

STATISTICS
DISTANCE

Excluding Height	15.8 km	(9.8 miles)
TOTAL HEIGHT GAINED	450 m	(1475 ft)
PRINCIPAL HEIGHTS		
South Head	494 m	(1620 ft)

The way to South Head   *Allow 2 hours*

Return to the B6062 road and turn R by the side of
the butcher's shop. Cross over and walk E through
the village passing a row of shops. Then bear L
following the road which is now signed to Buxton,
walking uphill to pass the Squirrels Hotel. Keep to
the Buxton road by veering back R, passing
between the Methodist and St Mary's churches.
Then walk downhill and immediately after crossing Otter Brook turn L along Alders Lane. The
escarpment rising on your L is Cracken Edge. The
stream is re-crossed before the wide bridleway
passes under a railway line. Keep to this route of
packed earth as it bears round to the R, then
heading NE. The rounded hill appearing immediately ahead is South Head, your first major
objective. After passing a dwelling named the
Alders, bear R round Alders Farm and then veer
further R and pass through the wide gates. At this
point views open up to your L with the higher
ground of Chinley Churn and its abandoned

*8:1 Looking down on Chinley from near the
Hayfield Road*

quarries clearly visible on the skyline. From here, an obvious grassy path leads diagonally uphill passing by a holly tree at a stone stile. Then bear slightly R to follow the course of a stone wall, gaining further height up the hillside. At the top of the brow a wobbly stile provides an entrance to the A624 Hayfield Road.

Cross this busy road with care. Continue walking uphill along the walled lane opposite, passing Wicken Cottage, walking first E but then veering NE as the lane bends round to the L. Keep to this walled lane passing a white farm gate on your R and further on, as more height is gained, an abandoned quarry down to your L. When the lane veers R towards a cattle grid, fork L up the enclosed grassy track, now walking NNE to pass Andrew Farm down below on your R. Then beyond a wooden gate, continue along the edge of a field beside a stone wall on your R. Continue directly across an intersection of ways ahead, still walking NE towards the col linking Mount Famine and South Head, now clearly visible ahead. Ignore a

path off to the L and after this at the next junction, just past a small watercourse, veer L to cross a stone stile adjacent to a wooden gate. A long, steepish, grassy slope now has to be climbed at the top of which you clamber over a P-stile at a stone wall.

On reaching the wide path on the other side, turn immediately R and pass through the wooden gateway ahead. A short distance further on, veer R up the narrow, grassy path to scale the upper, rounded slopes of South Head.

There is a choice of ways to the top. Near to the peak you will find a plaque commemorating Frank Head (1907–1984) who was a leading walker with the Ramblers' Association (RA). This is mentioned because the RA donated funds for the National Trust to purchase South Head Hill for the benefit of future generations of walkers like us. This isolated summit commands a height of 494 m (1620 ft) and the panoramic views from here in clear weather are superb. The associated and not dissimilar peak of Mount Famine rises to the NW, whilst in contrast the endless flat edges of Kinder Scout dominate the horizon to the NE. Several prominent rock features of millstone grit stand out along these irregular edges, such as those at Kinder Low, the Wool Packs and Crowden Tower. The village of Chapel-en-le-Frith lies away to the S sheltered by the edges of Combs Moss that rise high above. Shining Tor and Cats Tor are the rounded hills on the distant horizon to the SW. The view behind to the W includes your ascent route, and the edge beyond is the Chinley Churn escarpment.

The way to the Chestnut Centre

Allow 2 hours

Start your descent to the R of the remains of a dilapidated stone wall heading eastwards down the steep, slippery, grassy slopes to reach the sanctuary of the enclosed bridleway below. You turn R along this. The next section of the route is obvious: just keep walking along the wide bridleway as it descends gently across pleasant, rolling countryside, taking the gates and stiles in your measured stride. There is one quite unusual instruction along here, a sign reading 'On no account disturb the breeding frogs'. The route eventually bends to the L before descending to Roych Clough. Here any youngsters in your party will probably delight in splashing their way through the succession of fords located at the bottom. On the way down, the ventilation shaft serving Gowburn Tunnel may be spotted on the

8:2 Walking towards South Head

horizon to your L. Climb up from the clough passing over further obstacles on the way including a wooden gateway near to the top of the far brow. The continuation way from here can become quite muddy in several places after prolonged rain, particularly so at gateways. The route threads between small copses of deciduous trees, the most extensive of which is Tom Moor Plantation, and crosses further tiny watercourses, including that at Bolehill Clough, before eventually it connects with the A625 road at MR 092825. Turn R along this in the direction down to Chapel-en-le-Frith.

Use the wide verge on the R-hand side of the road to face oncoming traffic, until a short distance further down you select the inviting path off on the L. This is accessed by means of a wooden stile adjacent to a gate. Now veer R beside a stone wall and walk WSW down the wide, grassy way. The next stile marks the entrance to another walled track which continues to descend gradually along Breck Edge through clumps of heather. A stone barn is passed to your L which has an interesting roof, unusually pitched in two directions. After passing a wooden gate and stile, the way leads to a surfaced minor lane, down which you bear R, thereafter walking WNW. A relatively steep slope further on will bring you back to the A625 road at Slackhall Farm and the Chestnut Centre. Cross the road and if you have time a visit to the Chestnut Centre ahead may have some appeal. This conservation park, thoughtfully developed, contains study rooms, a nature trail, an otter haven and an owl sanctuary. On a more practical note, clean toilets and congenial refreshment facilities are also located here.

The way back to Chinley   *Allow 1½ hours*

Afterwards, turn sharp R downhill along the lane running adjacent to the Centre. Ford Hall is situated in the hamlet in the dip ahead where a stream, lower down the valley named as Black Brook, has to be crossed. Keep to the back-lane that winds between the dwellings, ignoring a footpath (Peat Lane) off to your R opposite Ford

House. The route continues uphill along a partly surfaced lane between a stone wall and a wire fence as it leads NW towards the next configuration of buildings around the recently renovated Kinder Farm. These include Roych Barn, built in 1702. After this the lane bends sharp L downhill. Across a tributary stream, be vigilant to turn immediately L to pass through a partly concealed, narrow opening next to an iron gate located only a few metres from the water. After this, keep to the narrow path as it accompanies the meandering watercourse, which becomes progressively enlarged by the waters of several smaller tributaries that feed it. Continue beside the stream, crossing a stile and a driveway in the process. Then the swiftly flowing waters are crossed by a bridge, after which your predominant direction of travel down the valley is resumed by turning R along the opposite bank. There can be boggy areas to contend with from now on.

The path eventually bears L away from the brook, then heads SW directly towards the buildings ahead at Wash. Another pathway is crossed before you reach these. Use the stile on the L by the side of a cottage in your final approach to this habitation. Afterwards, turn R to cross the bridge passing by an old-fashioned red telephone box. Beyond the grouped cottages veer L down the public footpath beside the stream. This path is accessed round a thoughtfully positioned safety barrier. A little further on, the brook is re-crossed, on this occasion by means of some gap-infested woodwork that needs replacing – so watch out until this is done!

Be careful to veer R, off the main path, a short distance ahead to negotiate a wooden stile above. Then walk due S diagonally across the field beyond. In the far corner of the field, at a nasty muddy area, cross a narrow, awkwardly positioned stile. After this, cross the next field following the line of the hedge on your L, walking towards the busy main A6(T) bypass road. The more industrialized scenery you are now approaching contains two impressive, arched Victorian railway viaducts that span the deep-sided valley ahead. Then before reaching the electricity pylon and the more steeply falling ground, turn abruptly through 90 degrees to your ʀ and walk ᴡ towards and through the gap in the hedge ahead.

Following this, bear slightly ʟ to pass through a second gap, this time at a gateway in a low wall. From here, a grassy track leads downhill towards the road. However, before reaching this on a direct line, bear ʟ to pass over a wooden stile and from here turn ʀ and walk to the road. (This is near the premises of Messrs H. & T. Mellor (Engineers) Ltd.) Bear ʀ along the busy A624 road, cross this and then turn immediately ʟ along the public footpath that immediately re-crosses the brook, and a short distance further ahead passes beneath the two railway viaducts, allowing a closer inspection of these imposing structures towering high above.

Further on, climb over the ʟ-stile and continue down the low-lying meadows towards the buildings ahead. More gates and stiles follow before extensive vehicle repair workshops are reached at Bridgeholme Mill. The last one of these ɢ-stiles is a 'rucksacks off' obstruction! Walk between these workshops, keeping to your established direction of travel to reach a gap in a stone retaining wall at the far end. This provides an entrance to the lane beyond. Turn ʟ here and within a few paces turn off ʀ over an unusual, rounded stone bridge that crosses a pipeline, Continue along the overgrown narrow path beside the stream to your ʀ.

Following a ɢ-stile, your obvious path leads uphill to connect with a wider track along which you turn ʀ. You then pass a large bleach works, bellowing steam in all directions. This industrialized establishment does have certain attractions, including the reflections of the buildings in a substantial reservoir containing water for the bleaching processes. Turn ʀ round the far end of the textile mill along a narrow path reached by means of an improvised plank bridge-way across an intervening ditch. The path leads to the mill car park. Turn ʟ at this to exit on to a road along which you turn ʟ before turning back ʀ again to re-cross the stream. Beyond this, the road ahead will lead you uphill back into Chinley, passing Green Hunters Farm (circa 1600) on the way. At the next road junction turn ʟ and then ʟ again by the butcher's shop to return to the car park.

Alternative routes

ESCAPES
The obvious curtailments are: (1) avoid the final, steepish climb to the top of South Head by keeping to the footpath that winds round the hill at a lower elevation, and/or (2) at MR 072838 veer ʀ and use the footpaths and lanes leading southwards to reach the Chestnut Centre on a shorter, more direct route.

EXTENSIONS
One short additional exploration is from the vicinity of the col below South Head to visit the twin peak of Mount Famine. Another interesting possibility is, after reaching the A625 road at MR 092825, to venture along Rushup Edge for as far as you like before retracing your steps back to the departure point from the main route. In fine weather, you will be rewarded with superb views down into Edale valley and along the ridge extending eastwards towards Mam Tor and Lose Hill.

Route 9: HAYFIELD, RUSHUP EDGE, EDALE and JACOB'S LADDER

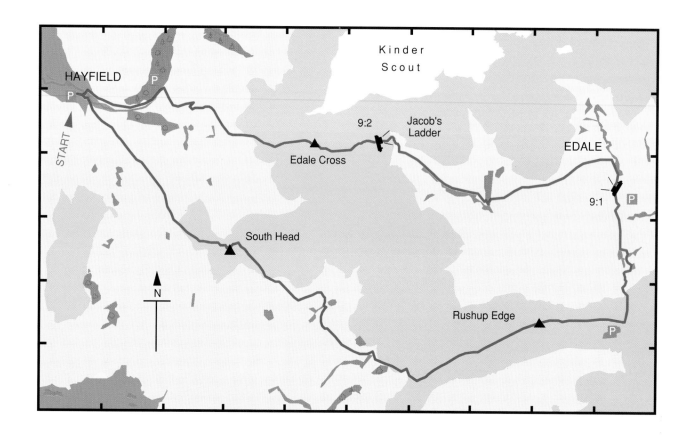

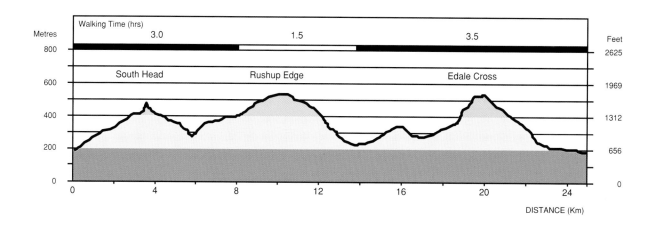

ROUTE 9

Hayfield, Rushup Edge, Edale
and Jacob's Ladder

●

STARTING LOCATION
Car park at Hayfield.
OLM 1: MR 036869.
Extensive well laid-out car park.
Toilets, picnic area and Visitor Centre.

PUBLIC TRANSPORT
Bus routes 355, 358, 361, 403, 901 and 902.

OVERVIEW/INTEREST
Pleasant, undulating circuit.
Fine open views for most of way.
Climbing well spaced out and not too strenuous.
Route passes through Edale, the start of the Pennine
   Way. Initial stretch of Pennine Way covered.

FOOTPATHS
The way is for the most part clear and obvious.
Footpaths good and mostly firm.

Some wet and boggy patches after prolonged rain.
The elevated ridge section affords delightful walking.

GRADING
Moderate to difficult/severe.

TIME ALLOWANCE
8 hours.

STATISTICS

DISTANCE

Excluding Height	24.9 km	(15.5 miles)
TOTAL HEIGHT GAINED	940 m	(3085 ft)
PRINCIPAL HEIGHTS		
South Head	494 m	(1620 ft)
Rushup Edge	540 m	(1770 ft)
Edale Cross	541 m	(1775 ft)

The way to Rushup Edge   *Allow 3 hours*

Cross the road adjacent to the car park and then use the subway opposite to pass beneath the main A624 road to reach the centre of Hayfield village near to the church. Turn R past the George Inn and continue up the road. Further on, select the minor lane, Highgate Road, on your L and walk uphill to the SE passing Rood Nook, Highgate Hall, Windle Croft and Highgate Farm.

At the approach to a stone barn, bear slightly L along the narrow path that leads directly towards Mount Famine. This is accessed through a gate to the L of an adjacent farm track. From here your way becomes enclosed as it continues to snake up the hillside still on a SE bearing. Pass by an inviting footpath off to the L. Beyond this, veer L keeping to the main route as it bends round to the E below Mount Famine. Ignore paths off to the R. After a gate and immediately after passing a dilapidated stone wall with an opening flanked by stone

pillars, bear R along a narrow, grassy path, now climbing ESE. The steep slopes ahead stretch to the top of South Head.

Descend from South Head by the narrow path to the ENE, to join the main path circling the hillside. Turn R along this and follow a more gradual line of descent. Gates and stiles now have to be negotiated and when you reach twin gates be careful to go through the L-hand one. A feature to look out for along this stretch is the ventilation shaft from Gowburn Tunnel away to the ESE. Eventually the path drops appreciably to cross Roych Clough by means of a number of consecutive fords. These are located at MR 077836. Beyond the steep sides of the clough the ground continues to rise steadily for some distance as more gateways bar your way. Then a copse of deciduous trees containing oak and beech is passed on your L and at this point, although it is only obvious from looking at your map, you have passed above Gowburn Tunnel. On reaching

Bolehill Clough, follow the main path round to the R crossing the small watercourse and then pass through another gateway beyond. From here, a clear way threads through more gates and stiles and past a more extensive area of oak trees on the R to reach the A625 road at MR 092825 after crossing another minor watercourse.

The way to Edale
Allow 1½ hours

Just before reaching the road, bear L and follow the now established track uphill, beside the wall dividing this from the road to your R. The direction here is ENE. This leads along rising ground to the public bridleway ahead. Further on, a clear, renovated route directs you towards Rushup Edge where beyond the next gate there is a path down to the L signed to 'Edale via Barber Booth'. Walk past this turning, keeping R along the higher ground along the way signed to 'Castleton and Hope Via Mam Tor and Hollins Cross'.

The path continues its gradual climb as wide, more open landscapes come into view to your R. Beyond the next wooden stile, with your way continuing to rise towards the Tumulus at Lord's Seat located near to the top of the ridge, the magnificent millstone and sandstone edges of the massive Kinder plateau appear to the N. Then the tranquil pastures of Edale Valley come into view down below, also to your L.

The way continues along the apex of the ridge as it falls progressively to reach the road through Mam Nick at a stile. Cross this road and turn L downhill along it. At the end of the immediate lay-by for disabled drivers, turn R and then follow the stony path on the L that descends into the Edale Valley on a northwards bearing. After crossing a P-stile, veer further to the L at the fork ahead. From here, the route curves quite steeply downhill towards the flat valley floor. Before the next gate is reached, views appear to your L of Barber Booth and of upper Edale Valley.

Then an interesting woodlands conservation area planted by Edale School in November 1990 is passed before your path, together with another one coming in on your R from Hollins Cross,

merges into a narrow, surfaced lane. Turn R here, still continuing to descend, and pass round the buildings situated at 'Greenlands', MR 125844. Following this, ignore several narrower side paths and continue down along the lane as it crosses the River Noe and reaches the road along Edale Valley a short distance further on. Turn R along the road and then almost immediately L at the next junction to walk uphill through Edale village. Having passed under the railway bridge the lane leads past the Fieldhead National Park Information and Visitor Centre and the parish church. Towards the top end of the village you reach the official starting point of the Pennine Way at the Old Nag's Head Inn with its 'Hikers Bar'. There is a post office cum shop and a café situated nearby.

The way back to Hayfield
Allow 3½ hours

Use the path opposite the Nag's Head to depart from the village, walking out of it westwards along the Pennine Way. The route is indicated by yellow arrowhead markers, and a series of barriers in the form of K-gates, gateways, P-stiles and S-stiles have to be negotiated as the route climbs up and round the steepening hillsides ahead. There is one important L-hand turn after a P-stile signed 'Pennine Way'. Following this, an obvious paved path leads across fields over rising ground. Many variants of S-stiles over walls follow, as your route continues to gain height.

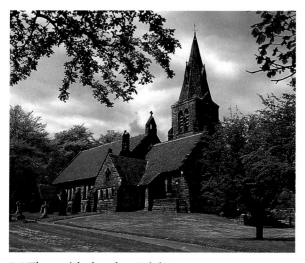

9:1 The parish church at Edale

Eventually fork L along the path signed to 'Jacob's Ladder'. After this a further w-stile marks the start of a prolonged descent. More obstacles follow and through a gateway cross the P-stile to the R. The path leads down to a farm lane, still helpfully signed to 'Jacob's Ladder'. Turn L along this to pass through Upper Booth Farm at MR 103853. At the surfaced lane ahead, reached at a T-junction, turn R, still following the Pennine Way indicators, to cross Crowden Brook. Then continue NW along the obvious way up the valley for about a further 2 km (1.2 miles) to arrive at the foot of Jacob's Ladder, passing through Lee Farm en route. Use the arched stone bridge to cross the stream and climb the formidable slopes ahead up the renovated stepped way round to your R to reach the top of Jacob's Ladder, avoiding all eroded ground to your L. Bear R at the crest of the steepest section and continue to progress w uphill along the path.

Part company with the Pennine Way by continuing ahead westwards, having first passed through another stile beside a gate. Your way w continues to undulate uphill to reach the mediaeval monument of Edale Cross which is passed on your R. Some distance further on select the narrow branch path to your R. This is accessed by means of a stile and is signed 'Public footpath to Hayfield via Tunstead Clough'. The path swings progressively to the R round the hillside to reveal your continuation approach route downwards to Hayfield. Bear L at the fork ahead along the lower path to cross a high stone wall by means of a L-stile. More stiles and gates follow as your way continues down the grassy slopes along a NW diagonal, before you veer L to descend more steeply w towards Tunstead Clough Farm and House. Pass round these to the L, continuing downhill. From here an obvious way winds downhill along the clough to reach a narrow surfaced lane at the bottom. Bear R along this, following it until it joins Kinder Road ahead in the vicinity of an extensive camp site. Turn L down the road and walk by the side of this into Hayfield village, just over 1 km (0.6 miles) away. Use the underpass again to reach the car park passing around the side of the church in doing so.

9:2 Walkers taking a well-earned rest below Jacob's Ladder in Edale

Alternative routes

ESCAPES

Along the approach to Rushup Edge, at MR 099829, select the branch path on the L signed to 'Edale via Barber Booth'. Lower down at MR 010835 you have a choice. (1) Keep L to continue due N directly into Edale Valley to connect with the main valley pathway between Lee Farm and Upper Booth Farm. This will return you to the main route and you may then turn L along it to return to Hayfield via Jacob's Ladder. (2) Veer R and NE to follow the Chapel Gate track down towards Barber Booth. From here there are further choices: either L and westwards along the valley to re-connect with the main route, or select the longer alternative of turning R and walking eastwards towards Edale to connect with the main route and then follow it through the village.

EXTENSIONS

The obvious extension is from Mam Nick to continue NE along the ridge to either Hollins Cross or even further on as far as Lose Hill. There is a convenient and good diagonal path NW from Hollins Cross which may be used to re-connect you with the main route as it passes through Edale.

Route 10: HOPE, JAGGERS CLOUGH, EDALE and LOSE HILL

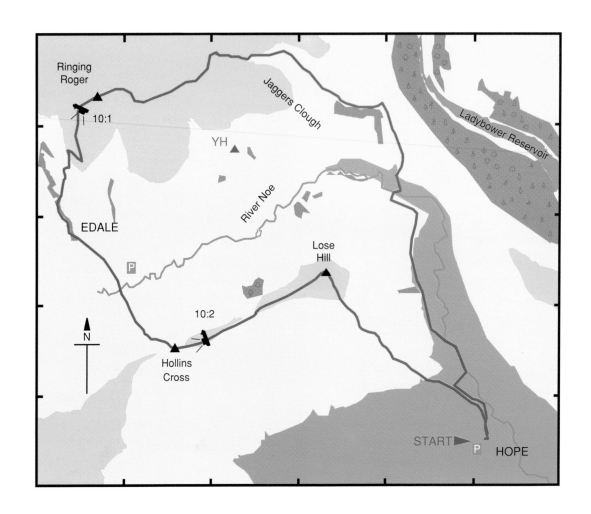

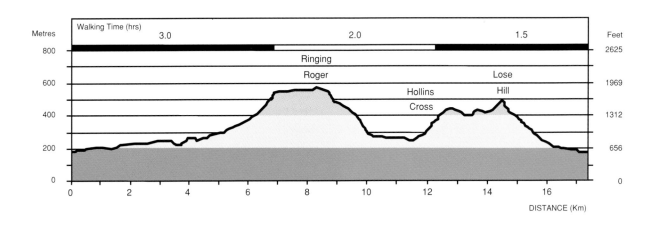

ROUTE 10

Hope, Jaggers Clough, Edale and Lose Hill

●

<table>
<tr><td>

STARTING LOCATION

Car park at Hope.

OLM 1: MR 171835.

Car park space for about 25 cars and 4 coaches.

PUBLIC TRANSPORT

Bus routes 173, 174, 181, 197, 202, 254, 272, 274, 276, 280, 309, 395, 400 and 403.

Train service.

OVERVIEW/INTEREST

Extremely varied route with extensive views.

Open country at start followed by confines of narrowing clough.

Section along Kinder edges and ridge walk to Lose Hill.

Weathered millstone grit rock configurations.

Route passes through charming village of Edale.

Challenging walk with some demanding slopes.

Save this route for a fine day.

</td><td>

FOOTPATHS

Mainly along well-defined paths.

Some interesting variants towards top of Jaggers Clough.

For the most part over firm ground with few boggy patches of any significance.

Some minor scrambling necessary.

GRADING

Moderate to difficult/severe.

TIME ALLOWANCE

6½ hours.

</td></tr>
</table>

STATISTICS

DISTANCE

Excluding Height	17.2 km	(10.7 miles)
TOTAL HEIGHT GAINED	480 m	(1575 ft)
PRINCIPAL HEIGHTS		
Kinder Edge	560 m	(1840 ft)
Lose Hill	476 m	(1560 ft)

The way to Kinder Edge at Crookstone Out Moor

Allow 3 hours

From the car park, cross the main A625 road and turn R passing a garage and a row of old cottages. Beyond these, turn abruptly L through the adjacent gap and walk up the footpath, first signed to 'Losehill Farm' and further on to 'Lose Hill and Mam Tor Ridge'. Go through two K-gates, veer R round Hope Clinic, cross the avenue (Eccles Close) and rejoin the footpath by squeezing through a narrow stone G-stile to the L of Hope County Primary School. From here, a pleasant grass track leads N uphill. Whilst on this gradient the rounded, green slopes of Lose Hill (which marks the eastern extremity of the ridge from Mam Tor) can be seen rising majestically to the NW. To your right the tip of Win Hill just protrudes over the steep intervening slopes rising to the NE. Your way is again signed towards 'Lose Hill'.

Proceed through a swing-gate and a second stile as your path becomes hedged by hawthorn. A disused G-stile is reached before you veer R to avoid private land and negotiate two more stiles, now heading NW. Beyond the next field a railway line is crossed by means of a sagging concrete bridge. After the next G-stile veer L to pass a bungalow, following the direction indicated by the public footpath sign. Continue to the end of the subsequent outbuildings and then turn abruptly R, off the path to Lose Hill, and climb over the stile marked with a yellow arrowhead. Cross the field walking NE adjacent to another hawthorn hedge. A second squeeze is necessary to get through another narrow G-stile, after which climb over a stepped stone stile that provides access to Edale Road, which you turn L along. Walk N, passing Phoebe Croft and Crofthead Farm in doing so. A short distance further on veer L up the minor lane at the location of Underleigh Country House, immediately passing the residence of Ashcroft. (This is just before the valley road reaches Town-head Bridge.)

Ignore a footpath off to the R and continue walking uphill along the surfaced lane, keeping R at the next fork and still heading N. Continue along this lane for about 1 km (0.6 miles) to reach Oaker Farm, having walked past Underleigh and Countrywide Holidays Moor Gate guest houses. The track becomes one of compacted earth and stones and the public footpath is to the L and above the farm buildings. This is accessed by means of a P-stile; the ensuing narrow, enclosed way round the farm can become quite muddy in places. Continue to walk at a fairly constant elevation along the obvious path round the hillside, crossing further stiles. Wilder, more open slopes are quickly reached which support a mix-ture of bracken and brambles before the grassy path swings L following the rounded contours of the hillside. A cart-track is crossed as you continue to walk NW towards the distant south-easterly tip of Kinder plateau. Down below, to the N, Upper Fulwood Farm comes into view to your R with the wooded indent rising towards Jaggers Clough visible beyond. This view reveals the next part of your continuation route.

Following a sharp R-hand bend near a mature sycamore tree and, after another L-stile (once painted white), the path descends quite steeply back to Edale Road, having first passed beneath the adjacent railway line. Turn R along the lane and then immediately L to pass through a gateway on the far side. Veer further R down the steepish slope to reach and cross the River Noe by means of an arched stone bridge to your L. This is Bagshaw Bridge. Walk along the surfaced track to Upper Fulwood Farm, skirting these buildings to the L. This establishment houses the High Peak Estate Office and Warden's Workshop of the National Trust. Just beyond the buildings follow the signed way to Hope Cross and Jaggers Clough by first turning R through a gate round the gable end of the last building and then turning immediately L. There is typical farmyard muck to contend with hereabouts!

The ensuing track initially climbs gradually to

the N between fine specimen trees, including ash and beech, along a pleasant grassy slope. It then veers L to bring you to a stile and wooden gate. Veer L at the fork in the path beyond these features to walk NNW directly towards Jaggers Clough. Sweeping slopes lie ahead that contain a pleasing profusion of trees, bracken, gorse and foxgloves. Your path descends to the stream, after which it follows the course of these waters curving up the clough on their R-hand bank. After reaching a National Trust path sign, the stream is crossed by means of a wooden footbridge and on the far side steps lead up to another stile. A narrower path then leads more steeply uphill through a group of trees. Following the negot-iation of another P-stile, further height is attained under the canopy of foliage. Eventually your secluded path descends to the stream once more to join a more eroded bridleway ahead. This is reached by climbing over a stone wall by means of a S-stile on your L followed by breaching a G-stile. This location marks the boundary of open country at the entrance to Jaggers Clough.

Continue for a short distance along the broad well-used way, walking NW towards the higher slopes ahead. Then abandon this bridle path at the first distinctive bend by crossing the tributary stream and continue to head NW along the narrow path beside the main watercourse, which is crossed a short distance further on. Follow the faint, narrow path along the R-hand side of the stream up the narrowing gully, still heading NW. A long, gradual ascent follows to reach the higher rocky outcrops that mark the final upper reaches of the clough. The climb is relatively undeman-ding but there are some boggy stretches to contend with. The stream is crossed several times in this approach, on one occasion just beyond a rocky bluff which it is necessary to pass beneath.

Following this, the terrain becomes more demanding as the clough simultaneously narrows and steepens appreciably. There are several rock protrusions to get up and you will probably need to use your hands to scramble safely over the more formidable of these. Be particularly cautious to avoid the unstable overhangs of tufted grasses and heathers that cling to the steep slopes

amongst clefts in the rocks and boulders. At times it is convenient to walk up the rocky bed of the stream and when doing so watch out for slippery slabs coated with mosses and lichens. The final pitch is up a downfall of millstone grit where large boulders and shattered rock present a variety of routes to the top of the clough and through which you may individualize your final climb. The path-of-sorts follows the R flank of the downfall almost to its top. Pause for a time during this ascent to look back and admire the fine views to the SE dominated by the proud peak of Win Hill and below this, more to the L, the extensive, forested slopes lining Ladybower Reservoir.

Near to the top, exit from the clough by bearing L along a narrow but distinct peat path and walk southwards along this as it snakes diagonally towards Kinder Edge, still gaining marginal extra height. The way is now certain and obvious as a panorama of the flat outlines of the massive Derwent and other edges are revealed to the ENE. A short distance further on, Win Hill re-appears, this time to the SE, to be quickly followed by sightings, in clear weather, of the length of the undulating ridge from Lose Hill to Mam Tor, leading to Rushup Edge further W. Your path converges with the main edge path; veer L along this to continue walking WSW along part of Kinder Edge.

10:1 Striding along the lengthy descent from Ringing Roger into Edale

The way to Hollins Cross   *Allow 2 hours*

Fast progress is now possible along the established, well-drained edge path and there are continuous fine views down to your L across Edale Valley to spur you on. The skyline directly ahead is filled with protruding spurs, the regressive edges of which are lined with irregular groupings of weathered millstone grit. Bypass the first descent route off to your L and continue walking due W along the R-hand fork in the path. This then climbs marginally to higher ground ahead. Along this edge the highest part of the route is reached and this stands at a height of about 560 m (1840 ft). On reaching some extensively weathered and eroded ground, veer L to approach the configuration of large rocks that mark the outcrop named Ringing Roger (MR 126873). This feature is a series of irregular slabs and boulders of sandstones and grits. Start your descent from here by passing below this spectacular outcrop and then walk along the gritty, sandy path down the SW crest of the ridge. Care is needed here and in particular avoid treading on small loose debris as this unstable surface is liable to slip, transporting you down with it.

67

The exacting steep descent soon leads to a less demanding way down along a wide path which sweeps round to the s across ranging, heather-clad moorland. At a point where the length of Grindsbrook Clough may be observed to the w, your path connects with another route and the consolidated way down is now badly eroded as a result of heavy, continuous usage. From this area, your descent continues southwards into the lowest reaches of Grindsbrook and then into the picturesque village of Edale. On this section, there is one important acute R-hand bend to follow, but this turning is reassuringly signed 'Footpath to Edale'. The final approach to Edale is across Grinds Brook by means of a wooden bridge accessed by flights of steps.

Edale is an ideal spot to stop at for refreshment and the village supports guest houses, inns, a café and a post office cum shop that sells food and drinks. The Old Nag's Head, at the top end of the village, is the official starting point of the Pennine Way. Continue s down the lane from the Nag's Head to the Church of the Holy and Undivided Trinity and opposite the entrance to this turn L over a stile and climb down the steps leading to the stream. (This turning is before reaching the National Park Information Centre, which is well worth visiting.) The route crosses the stream and after the next G-stile turn R down the footpath signed to 'Castleton via Hollins Cross', now walking SE. After squeezing through another narrow G-stile, a barn is passed to your R. A diagonal approach to the valley road follows and this involves crossing beneath the railway line and then veering L, following the way indicated by a footpath sign and a yellow arrowhead. Through the next G-stile, steer R beside the stone wall and walk down to the road. Cross the road and the River Noe, negotiating more stiles along the way, and then continue up the footpath, again signed to 'Hollins Cross and Castleton'. Before reaching Hollins Farm, at a line of hawthorn trees, deviate R to climb more directly uphill, heading SSE. A short distance further on a flight of stone steps will bring you to a gap in an obstructing stone wall, only to be presented with yet another stile. Beyond this, an obvious, eroded path leads diagonally SE to the crest of the ridge ahead at Hollins Cross. The memorial at this spot is dedicated to Tom Hyett of the Ramblers Association and was erected in 1964.

The way back to Hope   *Allow 1½ hours*

At Hollins Cross new vistas appear of the flat lands of Hope Valley and the collapsed road over Mam Tor. The village of Castleton lies down below to the SE, with the buildings of Hope clearly discernible further to the E along the pleasantly wooded valley. Veer L along the undulating ridge to climb the next immediate rounded hillock, now walking due E. The ridge narrows and becomes more spectacular as you approach the crumbling, craggy profile of Back Tor. Use the second of two stiles to cross the wire fence on your L at a point signed to 'Back Tor and Lose Hill'. A cluster of Scots pines soften the otherwise harsh landscape immediately ahead, as you come to grips with the steeper gradient leading up the tor. The best views at the top are near the crumbling NW edge.

From Back Tor, broad, grassy slopes lead first down to the intervening shallow col and then up again to the higher peak of Lose Hill. This commands a height of 476 m (1560 ft), marks the easterly end of the ridge and is alternatively named Ward's Piece. The vast array of impressive major sightings from this elevated viewing platform have previously been identified. However, the correct direction of these, together with many more features, is indicated on the superb illustrated compass seated on the top of an impressive stone circle at this summit. Start your final descent along the obvious path to the SE. This curves gracefully, first R and then L as it follows the contours of the ridge down. Past a wooden stile select the R-hand fork, to pass between a cairn to your L and a stone marker post on the R. After this, cross the remains of a dilapidated stone wall and continue to walk downhill on a SE diagonal. Further down, swerve R to pass close to a copse, walking between attractive clumps of gorse in the process. Continue along the now established SE diagonal, using the path signed to 'Hope' to pass above and to the L of Losehill Farm.

10:2 The Mam Tor ridge in winter

Other stiles and a gap in a stone wall follow and one of these stiles, reached by veering to the R, calls for particular care as there is an unexpectedly large drop on the far side. After clambering over this, continue to surrender height, first walking beside a wall on your R, then crossing a meadow to follow eventually the line of a wall on your L which commences at a disused barn near to which there is a P-stile. At the next signpost another stile to your L has to be crossed on your SE diagonal approach to the village. A further stile follows, under two ash trees. From here, an obvious descent route leads back to Hope. The bungalow you passed on your outwards route is eventually reached. From here turn R and retrace your steps, once again passing over the sagging railway bridge.

Alternative routes

ESCAPES

The exacting climb up Jaggers Clough can be avoided by using the lower footpaths leading westwards along Edale Valley via the Youth Hostel situated at Rowland Cote, Nether Booth, to reach Edale village, where the main route may be rejoined.

EXTENSIONS

The obvious extension in favourable weather conditions, for strong and fit walkers, is to continue westwards along the edges of Kinder for as long as you feel is appropriate before descending into Edale. One suggested descent for doing this is along Grindsbrook Clough.

Route 11: HOPE, WIN HILL and LADYBOWER RESERVOIR

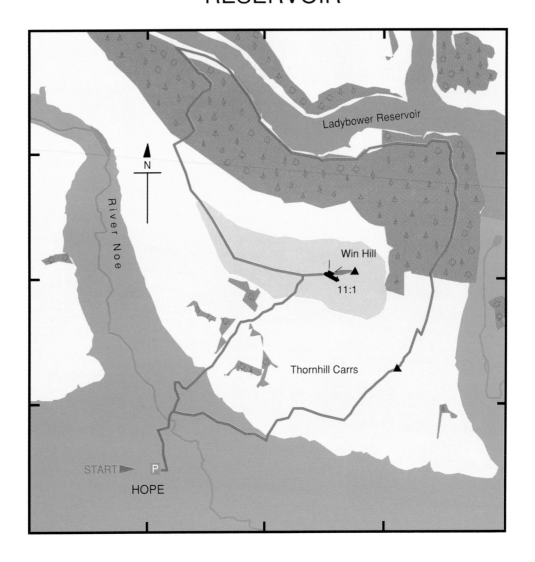

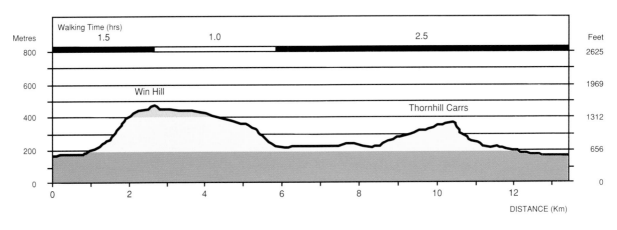

ROUTE 11
Hope, Win Hill and Ladybower Reservoir

●

STARTING LOCATION
Car park at Hope.
OLM1: MR 171835.
Car park space for about 25 cars and 4 coaches.

PUBLIC TRANSPORT
Bus routes 173, 174, 181, 197, 202, 254, 272, 274,
    276, 280, 309, 395, 400 and 403.
Train service.

OVERVIEW/INTEREST
Delightful shorter walk.
Ideal for family groups including older children.
Major climbing completed early on.
Superb panoramic views from summit of Win Hill.
Interesting rock configurations.
Ridge descent across open moorlands.
Section along wooded shores of reservoir.

FOOTPATHS
Overall, very good and easy to follow.
Some steep and at times slippery slopes on way up.
The first woodland paths can become waterlogged.

GRADING
Easy/straightforward to moderate.

TIME ALLOWANCE
5 hours.

STATISTICS

DISTANCE		
Excluding Height	13.4 km	(8.3 miles)
TOTAL HEIGHT GAINED	480 m	(1575 ft)
PRINCIPAL HEIGHTS		
Win Hill	462 m	(1515 ft)
Thornhill Carrs	342 m	(1120 ft)

The way to Win Hill   *Allow 1½ hours*

From the car park cross the main A625 road and turn R, passing a garage and then Woodbine Café. Turn L through the opening between Blacksmith's Cottage and the fruit shop and proceed N along the public footpath. This is signed to 'Lose Hill and Mam Tor Ridge'. Climb the steps and pass through two wrought iron K-gates, veer round the clinic and cross the avenue (Eccles Close) to reach Hope County Primary School. Your first major objective, the pointed peak of Win Hill, is visible from here to the NE above the protruding school buildings. Squeeze through the narrow G-stile to the L of the school and walk up the grassy track beside the wire fence ahead. The summit of Lose Hill appears as you gain height, ahead on your L to the NW. Before you reach the next stile directly ahead, turn R to pass through an unusual flap stile adjacent to an iron gate. From here walk down to and cross the S-stile over a stone wall ahead. A short distance further on, another G-stile provides entrance to Edale Road. Cross this and then veer down the narrower branch lane off to the R, descending slightly whilst walking NNE.

The River Noe is crossed and following this continue along the narrow surfaced lane, ignoring first a footpath off to your R to Brough, followed by another one to Aston. (The second of these is part of your return route.) The lane veers to the L beneath a canopy of overhanging tree branches. An informative Peak and Northern Footpaths Society sign, number 122, is then passed positioned on the R-hand side of the lane. Pass under the railway bridge, turn R and then just one cautionary warning concerning the concise directions presented on the Peak and Northern Footpaths Society sign: the first gate on your L provides access to a field only. Go past this and simply follow the obvious track round to the L through the next large, ungated opening.

A wide gravel farm lane now leads marginally uphill between wire fences. To the L along here there is a small stream flowing down through a shallow, tree-lined depression. Pass through the iron gate in order to avoid stepping over a cattle

71

grid and continue walking uphill to the NE along the compacted earth and gravel track. The route leads directly to Twitchill Farm, located at MR 178847. Just before entering the farmyard turn about to absorb the splendid view below. This contains the village of Hope nestling comfortably in a flattish, wooded valley with the protecting slopes of Bradwell Moor rising serenely beyond. Bear R between the farm buildings and exit through a metal gate. Then veer immediately further R, to climb the steep, grassy hillside, quickly gaining further height to the ENE as you do so. A bridleway is crossed on a tangent at the next gateway. After this, your way (signed 'Footpath only') continues up the established NE diagonal towards the rougher ground ahead. Pass over the L-stile, beyond which an obvious path leads directly to the rocky, pointed pinnacle of Win Hill about 1 km (0.6 miles) further on along a now moderating incline. The final approach slopes are liberally covered with colourful clumps of heather and gorse. The proud, isolated summit of Win Hill commands a height of 462 m (1515 ft) and the extensive area is an assortment of large, fixed bedding slabs of millstone and sandstone grits, with boulders of all shapes and sizes intermingled with loose, shattered rock debris. Vegetation, mostly in the form of heathers, clings tenaciously to life in this harsh regime, seeking out nourishment from tiny areas of soil lodged in minute crevices within the rock formations. Further away, in favourable weather conditions, major landmarks may be observed, including parts of the Ladybower, Derwent and Howden reservoir complex with the lower hillsides leading down to these densely covered with conifer plantations. Walkers with some appreciation of the geology of the Dark Peak will delight in spending time examining the rock structures of the tor. These have been weathered into various shapes, including perfecly symmetrical indentations in the exposed rock faces brought about by the erosion of soluble deposits.

11:1 A snow-capped view of Ladybower Reservoir from Win Hill

The way to Ladybower Reservoir

Allow 1 hour

From the trig point, either scramble down the rocky edge leading w or descend more gracefully to the secure path round and below the rocky outcrop just to the s of it, then walk w, reversing your final approach route. On reaching flatter terrain, keep to the sandy path along the ridge, now shunning your approach route, which falls away on your L. Continue along Thornhill Brink keeping to the way signed to 'Hope Cross' at the next intersection of paths.

Your route more or less keeps to the apex of the descending ridge and this section of the route is exceptionally attractive along a dry path and across ranging moorland. Further on, keep L choosing the wide grassy path down, adjacent to a stone wall to your L.

The ridge bears R and commences to fall more appreciably as your path continues along its crest. The pointed profile of Lose Hill lies ahead to the L on a WNW bearing, whilst away to your R parts of the craggy upper slopes of the ridge from Bridge-end Pasture to Crook Hill appear in the N. Below, Edale Valley snakes away to the NW. The way leads gently and pleasantly down along the well-drained sandy path towards an extensive area of coniferous forest. Beyond this, the slopes of Kinder plateau rear up, marked by several indents, of which Jaggers Clough rising to the NW is prominent. Immediately after passing a dilapidated dry-stone wall and a solitary erect stone pillar, be careful to turn sharp R to enter the forest area by means of a stile to the R of a metal gate. Your direction of travel is now NE and the forest is a plantation of predominantly Scots pines. The ensuing path down through the trees can become extremely muddy and some stretches of this are invariably in this condition. The relatively steep descent path crosses a forestry road at right angles, and following a sharp turn to the L, the final descent to the reservoir is along a prolonged diagonal. Turn acutely R at the bottom on to the wide forestry track leading round and just above the extensive water supply. This is located at MR 172868.

The way back to Hope

Allow 2½ hours

The next part of the walk is along the shoreline of Ladybower Reservoir. This undemanding, sheltered section extends for some 2½ km (1.5 miles) before you head uphill to the forest slopes once again at a point just past the viaduct road bridge visible across the reservoir. The way along the shore is by means of a wide forest road/track that usually provides a sound, dry walking route except when it passes through areas in which tree-harvesting operations have taken place. To start with, the reservoir is narrow but this progressively widens as you walk eastwards. On the far side, above the main A57 Snake Road, rise steep-sided hills covered with forested areas of Scots pines, larches and intermingled broad-leaved trees. Higher up still the twin tors of Crook Hill rear up, their craggy, shattered peaks splendidly revealed.

Further on, more tantalizing vistas open up across the waters including close sightings of the arched concrete roadways over the reservoirs. The track eventually rises to cross a spur of land that juts out into the reservoir, as views of the extensive Derwent edges appear to the NE. Continue along the wide track that follows the contours of the reservoir until you reach a gap on the R across which there is a wooden fence, containing an unusual stile access. Clamber over this and climb up the wide track leading due s over the slope ahead. Your new direction will bring you almost immediately to the forest road which you cross at right angles to continue walking up the hillside. Pass by a pathway down to your L marked by a stile and proceed along the less steep gradient that curves to your R. Along here, the distinctive features of Bamford Edge and Great Tor come into view across the intervening valley, away to the SE.

The next gate and P-stile mark the edge of a plantation of more mature Scots pines and from here these trees keep you company for some distance on your R. Then way down below to your L the massive dam of Ladybower Reservoir comes into sight through gaps between the conifers.

Follow the main path ahead as it veers R marginally uphill. Some distance further on, Parkin Clough is reached and this contains a path crossing yours at right angles. This crossing climbs to Win Hill from near to Yorkshire Bridge in the valley below. Beyond this, your path narrows and becomes less distinct as it skirts the slopes of the hill at a more or less constant height. A fence is crossed by means of a stile and after this the traverse continues along bracken-covered slopes. Continue diagonally up the hillside walking SW towards the brow of the escarpment and following the course of a dilapidated stone wall as you either tread along a slight depression or keep to the faint track above this feature on the L-hand side of it.

Near the top of the escarpment your route converges at Thornhill Carrs, MR 193846, with a wider, better established grassy way just after this superior track commences to descend. Turn acutely to the R, back up this sward for a short distance to reach another branch path veering off above on the L. You need to turn acutely L along this latter branch path after first crossing through a gap in a stone wall. The narrow, grassy path you are now on should be taking you SW, still along a slight incline. It soon parts company with the wall to your L as it escorts you downhill, eventually to the road near to Aston Hall. Before then, Hope Valley re-appears ahead as the path bears round the brow of the spur, and following this your way surrenders appreciable height. Always keep to the main grassy path down as it threads along hollows, maintaining your SW heading. During the descent use the L-stile to cross a formidable stone wall fortified by a wire fence. Be particularly careful in doing this as the ground drops away sharply on the far side. Beyond this, follow the obvious well-used way across the lower enclosed pastures, initially beside a small stream on your L. Across the elongated field, a P-stile in the R-hand bottom corner provides an entrance to an enclosed, wide grassy funnel further down. Along here, there are hawthorn trees to your L and a dry-stone wall on your R. Keep to the L-hand side as this funnel broadens out, walking along a raised grassy bank.

The way narrows and leads to another stile, after which the minor road, Aston Lane, is reached a short distance further on. Turn R along this, immediately passing two adjacent water troughs. Aston Hall is soon left behind, followed in quick succession by Aston Hall Farm. Further on, an inviting footpath to the L should be avoided as this only short-cuts a small loop in the lane at the expense of having to walk along the side of a field that is usually a veritable quagmire! Keep to the lane, avoiding all ways off as further on it loops to the L and commences to lead downhill to the W, passing Crabtree Cottages. Then turn R at the imposing entrance to Farfield Farm, distinctively marked by four stone spheres. Walk down the surfaced road passing the farm on your R. Opposite the farmhouse bear L along the footpath, passing further outbuildings on your R and a water supply point. The descent leads you back to the railway line which you pass under by veering L, having avoided a way off to the R through a gateway. Following this, the path will bring you to the lane used on your outward journey. Turn L here and either retrace your approach route or use Edale Road to return to Hope.

Alternative routes

ESCAPES

During the initial part of the descent from Win Hill the first footpath off to the R will take you down to the forest road skirting Ladybower Reservoir to re-connect you with the main route and this short cut reduces overall distance appreciably.

EXTENSIONS

On reaching Parkin Clough, Win Hill can be climbed for a second time, on this occasion from the E. This might be a particularly attractive proposition if the weather earlier in the day had been overcast and it had subsequently improved and you were after photographs of the area captured in sunshine.

Another feasible alternative is to descend on a wider circle through Thornhill and Brough and then to use the footpath beside the River Noe to return to Hope.

Route 12: MAM TOR, LOSE HILL, CASTLETON and the WINNATS

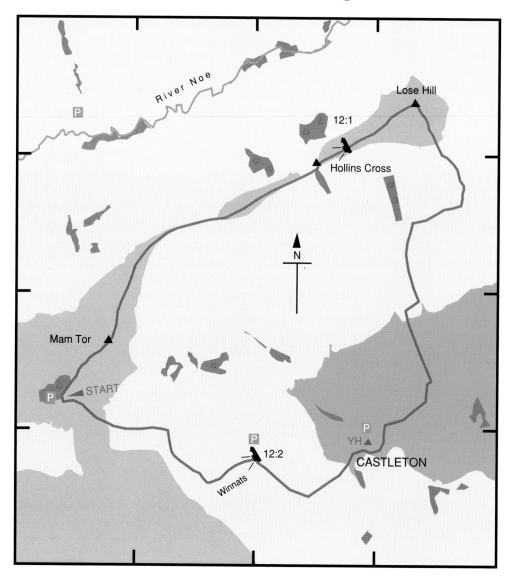

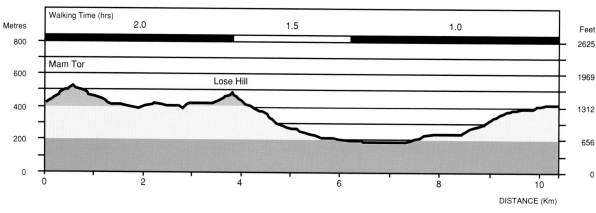

ROUTE 12

Mam Tor, Lose Hill, Castleton and the Winnats

●

STARTING LOCATION
Car park near Mam Nick off A625 road.
OLM 1: MR 124832.
Extensive car parking facilities but these quickly fill up at popular times.

ALTERNATIVE STARTING POINT
Castleton.

PUBLIC TRANSPORT
Bus routes 260 and 403.

OVERVIEW/INTEREST
Superb shorter distance walk.
Ridges, grassy slopes and gorges add to variety.
Excellent panoramic views of Edale and Kinder.
Classic dry limestone ravine at the Winnats.
Opportunity to visit several caverns and a castle en route.
Amenities of attractive village of Castleton.
Perfect hike for older children with plenty to interest them.

FOOTPATHS
Nearly always good and often excellent.
Virtually no waterlogged ground high up, some muddy sections lower down.
Route finding should present few problems.
Part of way across agricultural land clearly signed but somewhat complicated.

GRADING
Easy/straightforward to moderate.

TIME ALLOWANCE
4½ hours.

STATISTICS

DISTANCE

Excluding Height	10.4 km	(6.5 miles)
TOTAL HEIGHT GAINED	460 m	(1510 ft)
PRINCIPAL HEIGHTS		
Mam Tor	517 m	(1695 ft)
Lose Hill	476 m	(1560 ft)

The way to Lose Hill   *Allow 2 hours*

Leave the car park by the far exit from the road. From this, a flight of steps leads conveniently northwards towards Mam Nick. After climbing these, a wide path veering to your R provides an obvious start. As you gain height the indented outline of the spectacular limestone gorge of the Winnats may be observed through the obstructing foliage to your R (you will walk through this ravine on your way back). Further up, the extent of the vast, flat Hope Valley with its villages, farms and industry is revealed. Your path briefly merges with the minor road over Mam Nick before to your R further steps, a great many of them, lead you with minimum effort to the summit of Mam Tor. This area and parts of the path leading eastwards along the ridge from it have been

tastefully renovated by the National Trust. The summit area is now covered with stone cobbles and re-seeding of grassed areas has been incorporated to provide a quite natural appearance. You have now reached the highest point of the entire route standing at 517 m (1695 ft).

The all-round panorama from the top of Mam Tor in fine weather is simply breathtaking. It covers a vast area and is filled with contrasting observations. One of the highlights is the undulating ridge stretching along Rushup Edge to the w and culminating abruptly in the proud, conical peak of Lose Hill to the E. Below, on either side there are views of sheer perfection. To the N lies the secluded valley of Edale with the picturesque village of that name hugging a wooded indent which rises from the serenity of the flat, orderly valley floor to terminate eventually within the mighty, millstone grit rock configurations that line the top of Grindsbrook Clough. Towering above the green valley of Edale are the weathered millstone tors which mark the southern edges of the massive Kinder plateau, the slopes of which rise majestically to over 600 m (2000 ft) at their highest elevations. A more gentle landscape falls away from the ridge to the s. This contains the wide valley of Hope and further away a vast, open countryside of grassy hillocks which stretch for miles in regressive profiles outlined against the skyline.

Leave Mam Tor down the obvious path which leads eastwards along the undulating ridge, initially walking N before the way veers round to the NE. The first part of this splendid ridge walk is along a renovated, sunken flagged way which is being progressively extended eastwards. Fast, enjoyable progress can be made skipping along down this section. This part of the route by way of

Hollins Cross and beyond is obvious: you just follow the path that hugs the crest of the ridge. Therefore, you can relax and concentrate on admiring the many splendid views. Some minor obstacles in the form of P-stiles and gates have to be contended with. From the intersection at Hollins Cross, continue walking E along the ridge, in this vicinity named Barker Bank, towards the distinctive outline of Back Tor with its crumbling N face directly ahead, passing over more stiles in doing so. At the col before Back Tor do not cross the fence on your L until you reach a wooden L-stile and a sign indicating the way to 'Back Tor and Lose Hill'. The correct stile is the second one in this vicinity. The first leans back awkwardly against your approach and should be avoided. Then climb the steeper gradient leading up to the top of the

12:1 Hollins Cross propping up the author between Mam Tor and Lose Hill

tor, where the best views are to be obtained from its craggy NW face; but be vigilant when approaching the crumbling edges.

Beyond Back Tor, undemanding grassy slopes lead down the intervening col and then up again along gradients which are not too severe to the summit of Lose Hill. This easterly culmination of the long ridge commands a height of 476 m (1560 ft) and the fine, rounded hill has the alternative name of Ward's Piece. A quite superb illustrated compass has been positioned at this spot and in good weather you will probably delight in spending some time here positioning the main features indicated in the impressive surrounding landscape. Of the multitude of locations named on this compass, one of the highlights to be viewed from here is the graceful tor of Win Hill rising away to the ESE.

The way to Castleton
Allow 1½ hours

The village of Castleton lies some 3 km (1.9 miles) to the S at the westerly entrance to Hope Valley. To reach it entails one longish descent but because much of the lower intervening ground is farmed the approach is relatively complicated. Additionally, the paths marked on the OS OLM in this locality can be somewhat confusing. However, if you stick confidently to the route directions provided you should not encounter difficulties. The first part of the descent is clear: just surrender height rapidly by following the obvious path down to the SE. The way follows the natural contours of the slopes, bearing first R and then sweeping round to the L. Past a wooden stile, select the R-hand fork to pass between a cairn and a stone marker post. Beyond these bearings, cross the remains of a dilapidated stone wall and continue downhill on a SE diagonal. Further down, swerve R to pass close to a copse of trees bisecting clumps of gorse. Continue using the firmly established SE diagonal to reach a spot just above Losehill Farm (MR 157847) where the path divides. Your continuation route towards Castleton is along the R-hand branch, downhill to the SW across the steep-sided grassy slopes. This path leads to a L-stile at

the corner of a stone wall. Beyond this, continue walking downhill as you head towards the village below to the SSW.

Thereafter, turn R to cross two stiles on either side of a small stream, your direction here once again signed to 'Castleton'. Cross the next field keeping to the well-worn path that threads westwards in this area. This crosses a farm tractor track on an acute diagonal before the way reaches another wooden stile. Exercise care scrambling over this as the ground falls away steeply and rather unexpectedly on the far side. Continue your descent along a farm track (quite often muddy) as it winds down a shallow depression. The outline of Mam Tor with its beds of crumbling shales can be seen looming up directly ahead to the WSW. At the next R-hand bend, and as instructed, be careful to depart from the 'farm-access-only' track by following the continuation of the footpath to Castleton, accessed by a P-stile at this juncture. Your correct way here is signed by means of a yellow arrowhead.

Walk W along the edge of the next field, keeping to the line of the hedge on your R. Across a small stream and another P-stile, turn sharp L to walk further downhill towards Castleton, again following the directional arrowhead and using a farm track which is invariably muddy hereabouts. This leads to another yellow-tipped P-stile where a sign requests you to keep to the side of the next adjacent field further on. A clear path indicates your continuation route down from here beside a tree-lined stream below to your R. A short distance further on, flights of steps lead you across the stream and up out of the dark narrow ravine. Over the next stile, where the field crossing instructions are again politely repeated, turn R and continue downhill along the narrow but well-defined path of packed soil.

Cross over yet another stile, this one bearing a white arrowhead marker, and follow your established diagonal direction of travel southwards with the tree-fringed hollow again on your L. With the appearance of chimneys of buildings close to, through gaps in the intervening foliage, the climbing of a final L-stile will bring you to a narrow surfaced lane. Turn R along this. The lane

79

bends sharply L before straightening out to connect with the main A625 road at MR 155833. Cross this road with care near to the 30 mph restriction sign and proceed into the centre of Castleton by turning R and walking along the pavement. The stream of Peakshole Water is crossed at Spital Bridge and a short distance further on you enter the built-up area of Castleton.

Castleton is a very popular tourist centre for both hikers and more general visitors and it is therefore often uncomfortably busy. If you choose one of the quieter times to reach this cluster of shops, hotels, inns, restaurants, cafés, a castle and caverns, allow time to explore them at leisure. (Bradwell's Homemade Dairy Ices are a particularly delicious investment on hot summer days and a store and tea shop that sells them is positioned right on your approach route.)

The way back to the Mam Nick car park   *Allow 1 hour*

Follow the main road through the village as far as Cross Street. Keep walking straight on here by continuing up Back Street to pass the Nag's Head car park on your L and the parish church of St Edmund on the other side. Although rather dark and austere on the inside, the building is particularly well preserved and is a fine example of a twelfth century church. Follow the road round to the R signed to 'Peveril Castle – Peak Cavern' passing a triangular grassed area to your L which contains several war memorials. Continue along the lane indicated as no through-road for vehicular traffic and again signed to 'Peak Cavern', passing the Peveril Outdoor and Travel Shop. The lane then winds downhill past some particularly pretty old cottages. A stream flowing down from Cave Dale is crossed in the vicinity of the remains of Peveril Castle and Peak Cavern. Both of these make rewarding visits if you can spare the time. Continue up Goosehill and when the lane divides choose the R-hand fork. In passing the private road off to your L here, there are fine views of the perpendicular limestone butts that line Cave Dale. Following this, the lane degenerates as it narrows

into a stony path leading SW uphill.

A gate (difficult to open) provides entry to more open country and following this your way swings round to the R in a graceful curve along fairly level ground. Another gate and an unusual G-stile have to be negotiated before you reach the westerly entrance to the Winnats gorge at Speedwell Caven. Turn L along the road; the cavern and the associated well-stocked gift shop are a short distance further on. A visit to the cavern is a must for all those interested in limestone caves. An adventurous boat trip is involved through a tunnel cut to serve an eighteenth century lead mine. One of the boats used for this watery journey is named 'Titanic' but I think you can safely dismiss any fears of your vessel hitting an iceberg down here! You will travel some 150 m (about 500 ft) below ground. The bottomless pit at the end of your boat journey is millions of years old and contains seven pure stalactites and at popular times in the summer you may have to queue for this popular excursion.

Back in the open again, use the wide green sward on the R-hand side of the road to walk through the spectacular Winnats gorge with its irregular limestone crags. Towards the top, use the wooden boarding across a gap in a dry-stone wall on your R to leave the road. Then walk up the grassy path which first swings to the R before narrowing and sweeping L along a shallow gully. When you reach flatter ground more views appear ahead of Mam Tor, and of the ridge leading E from this hill along which you accelerated down some hours previously. It is then L and R in quick succession to finish up walking W through nettles along a grassy track. Make for the wooden stile ahead, to the L of a gap in the stone wall, and after passing over this continue to walk WNW along the route signed by yellow arrowheads. This will take you round Winnats Head Farm. Further on, cross the B6061 road at MR 128830 through the G-stiles provided and then select the R one of two grassy paths leading over Windy Knoll. The one you want is to the NW. You are now heading on a direct line back to the car park. When you reach the A625 road turn L and the car park is a short distance ahead on the R.

12:2 Awakening at the Winnats Pass

Alternative routes

ESCAPES

There are numerous curtailments possible along this particular route and most of these are fairly obvious from looking at the OLM. If you wish to spend considerable time exploring the many attractions in and around Castleton there is a good, fast, direct descent route SE from Hollins Cross at MR 136845.

EXTENSIONS

Opportunities for extensions are abundant. These include dropping down into Edale from Mam Nick and regaining the ridge at Hollins Cross; venturing further westwards on Rushup Edge for as far as you like before retracing your steps; or from Lose Hill looping in Hope as part of an extended descent route. Only strong and the very fittest of walkers should contemplate a visit to Win Hill and even they should only attempt this during the long daylight hours of mid-summer in favourable weather conditions.

Route 13: SHINING TOR, GOYT VALLEY and WINDGATHER ROCKS

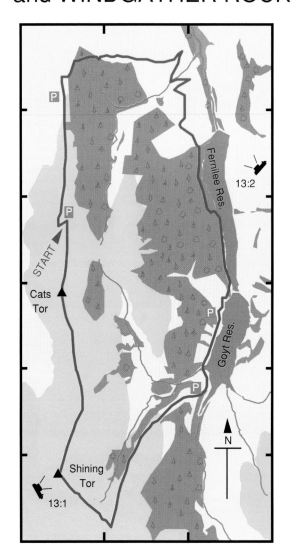

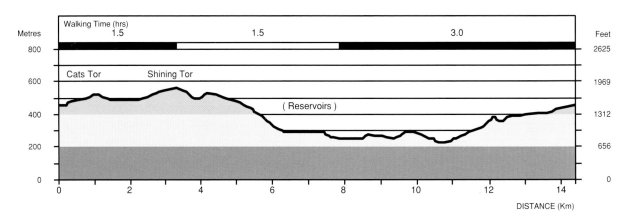

ROUTE 13

Shining Tor, Goyt Valley and Windgather Rocks

●

STARTING LOCATION
Pym Chair car park.
OLM 24: MR 995768.
Car park and nearby lay-bys hold over 30 cars.

ALTERNATIVE STARTING POINT
Goyt Valley (Errwood or Fernilee car parks).

PUBLIC TRANSPORT
None.

OVERVIEW/INTEREST
Enjoyable, pleasant family walk.
Not particularly strenuous with gradients well spaced out.
Plenty of variety from high exposed moorlands to sheltered wooded valleys.
Fine open views of rolling hilly landscapes.
Errwood and Fernilee Reservoirs.
Route passes close to ruins of Errwood Hall.
Jenkin Chapel near starting location.

FOOTPATHS
Well-established and good for much of way.
Substantial waterlogged areas after prolonged rain.
Renovation work to improve paths underway.
Route finding not difficult.
Comparatively few stiles and other obstructions.

GRADING
Easy/straightforward to moderate.

TIME ALLOWANCE
6 hours.

STATISTICS

DISTANCE

Excluding Height	14.4 km	(8.9 miles)
TOTAL HEIGHT GAINED	480 m	(1575 ft)
PRINCIPAL HEIGHTS		
Cats Tor	520 m	(1705 ft)
Shining Tor	559 m	(1835 ft)

The way to Shining Tor
Allow 1½ hours

Pym Chair car park is situated in an elevated position in expansive, rolling countryside. Good open views of the surrounding rounded hills are immediately visible. Walk back to the T-junction of roads just above the car park. Turn L along the road signed to 'Buxton' and locate the narrow path on the R bank of the lane. At the top of the brow veer R over the wooden stile to engage the footpath signed to 'Shining Tor'. Looking back at this point, Windgather Rocks come into view along the continuation of the ridge to the N. The ridge route southwards to Shining Tor, some 3 km (1.9 miles) away, is straightforward and uneventful. Initially the way rises gently to the L of a dilapidated stone wall, sections of which are being rebuilt, to reach the rounded hillock of Cats Tor located at MR 995759. From Cats Tor, the higher and more impressive rock configuration of Shining Tor may be seen to the s. Further away the

dominant, pointed profile of Shutlingsloe rises majestically to the SSE. From this vantage point it is understandable why this fine tor is nicknamed the Matterhorn of Macclesfield.

Beyond Cats Tor a wide, shallow hause leads towards the slopes of Shining Tor, initially up scraggy grasslands and then over higher moorlands which contain increasing proportions of peat supporting clumps of heathers and bilberries. The wall continues to guide your progress southwards, although in places the path deviates some distance away from it. Further on, there are areas where renovations have been carried out to sections of the route, but most walkers will feel much more needs to be done hereabouts. This is particularly relevant higher up where after prolonged rain the going becomes very waterlogged and numerous deviations are necessary to avoid the worst of many gooey black spots.

The ridge sweeps round to the R and a final moderate gradient brings you with minimum

83

effort to the top of Shining Tor. Before reaching the summit you will have passed a branch path off to your R which descends to Lamaload Reservoir, but at this point you continue gaining height ahead along the path then signed to 'Cat and Fiddle Inn'. At the summit use the stout L-stile to cross the wall on the R to gain access to the flat area on which the trig point is positioned. This, at 559 m (1835 ft), is the highest point of the entire walk. The stone column here is often marooned in a pool of water after rainy weather. Walk to the edge of the rocks, just a few paces away, to observe the fine views down below and to the S and W. Take care when peeping over the exposed grit edges, particularly in gusty conditions! Most of the major landmarks have already been noted but one new sighting from this splendid viewing platform is the distinctive, jagged profile of the distant Roaches, visible due S from here in clear weather.

The way to Fernilee Reservoir

Allow 1½ hours

Re-cross the wall by means of the L-stile. Then use the obvious path which bends to the L, and which is waysigned to 'Cat and Fiddle' on a nearby, wooden marker post. The following shallow descent is to the SE along a good surfaced path. The route dips to cross another wide, shallow hause and fast, carefree progress can be achieved along here. At the top of the subsequent rise a gate and S-stile are reached. Over the stile, turn L down the way signed to 'Errwood'. Walk NNE down the grassy slopes by means of a wide track. During the subsequent descent the landscape ahead becomes progressively less barren and remote as groupings of trees appear dispersed amongst more orderly pastures. This becomes intensified with the appearance of the irregular shape of Errwood Reservoir seen beyond a fringe of Scots pines down below to the NE. The slope falls away kindly towards this sighting over grassy slopes interspersed with heathers and bilberry.

Further down, the route passes between disused

13:1 The weathered rock faces of Shining Tor

stone pillars, presumably once connected by a gate, and past these a division of ways is reached. Here veer to the R to continue walking downhill towards the reservoir. The continuation path is signed to 'Errwood car park'. However, before you descend any further, just pop over the wooden L-stile on your L for a view into the deep, tree-covered valley beyond. This is the lower section of Shooter's Clough and it leads down to the ruins of Errwood Hall. Some distance on, a gate and an adjacent L-stile provide entry across a wire fence to more enclosed ground. This contains a grouping of mixed conifer and deciduous trees containing some fine specimens of larch and Scots pine. These are passed to your R. Beyond this feature, the tree-fringed waters of Errwood Reservoir progressively dominate the lower landscape ahead. Above this tranquil setting, high hills to the NNE provide a perfect backcloth. This higher ground in the far distance contains the plateau of Kinder Scout.

At the next division of the paths, keep R following the wider, better used grassy track descending for some distance to the ENE. A path is crossed at right angles. Opposite this intersection pass through another gap between redundant stone pillars, still descending directly towards the reservoir. From here, the way leads down through a further disused gateway to Errwood car park and its well laid-out picnic area. This provides both an attractive setting and utilities for an enjoyable lunch stop. Well fed, bear L to walk across the elongated car park and exit northwards down the approach road running along the W shore of the reservoir. This provides a convenient crossing of the steep indent where the catchment waters of Shooter's Clough enter Errwood Reservoir. Continue along the amenity road towards the dam located at the N end of the reservoir, making all possible use of the grass verges along the roadside. Here, there are fine views across the water, which is often dotted with sailing dinghies.

Near the N tip of the reservoir a second well laid-out car park is passed at Goyt Woodlands. Opposite this, bear R along the lane signed to 'Buxton and Toilets'. Then veer immediately L along a distinct path leading NNE and slightly downhill across a wide grassy slope. On approaching trees

13:2 Part of Fernilee Reservoir from near the Buxton Road

ahead, and with the road just below to your R, veer R down the narrow footpath signed to 'Fernilee'. This direction is still just about discernible on a venerable algae-coated signpost above the path. Keep L ahead, to walk along the higher path which descends marginally into the Goyt Valley, stretching away to the NNE. At the wall ahead, a wooden marker post bearing the number 3 (identifying a forestry trail) is passed. Here there is a fabulous first sighting of Fernilee Reservoir, seen below through the intervening foliage to your R. Now veer L along the better established path which descends more rapidly towards the water. This way then connects with the main pathway round the western bank of Fernilee Reservoir. Veer L along this to pass over a nearby L-stile. Beyond this, clear, unrestricted views open out to your R across the water.

The way back to Pym Chair   *Allow 3 hours*

Continue walking beside Fernilee Reservoir, which stretches for some 2 km (1.2 miles) northwards. The lower path provides the best open views and, apart from the occasional muddy patch, the cobbled way has been well constructed and is satisfactorily maintained. A number of branch paths up to your L may be ignored in order to obtain the best of the unimpeded views across the reservoir from this lower elevation. The way crosses several minor cloughs, but progress is uneventful apart from one brief flurry into the pine forest to get round some more exacting ground. All too soon the pointed towers signifying the dam at the northwards end of the reservoir come into sight and after this you do eventually have to select a path rising to the L up through the forested area. If you go too far, the lower path terminates at a deeper clough and here either backtrack or use the continuation escape route over the remains of a fallen tree to reach the correct way up. The latter manoeuvre is achieved by veering to the L when the tree obstacle is reached, away from the relatively dangerous ground further on and across which there is no sensible route!

The continuation way winds agreeably uphill under trees as part of number 3 forestry trail. This then connects with a broad pathway higher up. Veer to the R along this continuing to walk N. The route then drops gently over sloping ground along a wide forest trail and beneath a pleasant canopy of trees. The path eventually descends to a gate and stile positioned at the edge of the forest area. This is near to a fenced-off zone protecting a 'Wildlife Refuge'. Just after this exit from the trees, veer L along the surfaced farm lane signed to 'Hoo Moor'. Bear R through Oldfield Farm above, located at MR 009778, and leave along the track beyond the far gate. This immediately bends to the L and then traverses at a more or less constant height. The wide, grassy path leads further N, for some distance beside fenced-off woodlands. Further on, height is gradually surrendered as gates have to be negotiated to pass by a large farm outbuilding. Following this, the ground falls more rapidly as your way winds downhill to reach Mill Clough.

The main path veers to the R and you pass through a metal gate at this point to continue to descend to the NNE, with the clough falling and eventually petering out to your L. More fine open views come into sight ahead. The next gate provides entry to a wider farm track ahead, reached at a T-junction. Turn L and descend into Mill Clough, crossing the stream, by following the route round to the R at the bottom. There is a gate and K-gate here. On the other side the main track climbs uphill through a more enclosed channel. A short distance further on, Madscar Farm is passed as the way bends to the L and then passes above this establishment. A short, steeper gradient leads to an acute bend to the L, and further up a bench is passed, presented by 'The Whaley Bridge Amenity Society'. Just past this, Overton Hall Farm is reached and at the far end of the buildings be careful to keep gaining height straight ahead, ignoring a way veering off down to your L. Your direction is now to the W, towards the higher ground above. A cattle grid and a forestry road are then reached and crossed at MR 003786. Straight ahead a signed public footpath leads up steeper, rougher ground towards the skyline. There are further good views from here across the wide Goyt Valley, now down below to your rear.

Over the top of the next brow be vigilant to veer L in order to climb over a L-stile near to the forest boundary. Then veer further L following the route signed by a yellow waymarker. This continues down a conifer-covered dell. At the bottom of this you are confronted with a nasty, muddy water-course, the improvised crossings of which are slippery and far from adequate. On the far side, another waterlogged slope leads uphill towards the ridge footpath and more open ground. Ahead turn L to climb over the L-stile; this one has the top platform missing so quite literally watch your step! Continue walking SSW up the shallow incline between the boundary fence of the forested area and a stone wall.

Quite soon the millstone grit slabs of Windgather Rocks loom up ahead to your R. Beyond another L-stile, grassy slopes cover the final short distance to these outcrops. The rocks and boulders are popular with learner-climbers: their sloping bedding planes afford relatively short, easy routes for these enthusiasts to gain confidence on and to improve their technique under the guidance of more experienced climbers. This vantage point also provides sightings of new vistas to the NW, including the rounded slopes rising to Sponds Hill beyond Kettleshulme. Continue by walking S along the ridge, making use of the concession footpath to avoid having to use the road. A comfortable gradient leads back to the car park situated less than 1½ km (0.9 miles) further on.

Alternative routes

ESCAPES

The route may effectively be cut in two, by descending at MR 005743 into Shooter's Clough and from here making your way by means of Errwood Hall and then NNW along Foxlow Edge (concession path) to reach the road from Jenkin Chapel to Errwood Reservoir. From here, a L turn and a short stretch NW along the road will bring you back to Pym Chair car park.

EXTENSIONS

The most rewarding extensions are to venture into the eastern slopes above Errwood and Fernilee Reservoirs. There are several feasible routes round and above either or both reservoirs and your choice may be easily planned by consulting the relevant OLM of the area.

Route 14: CURBAR, FROGGATT and BASLOW EDGES and RIVER DERWENT

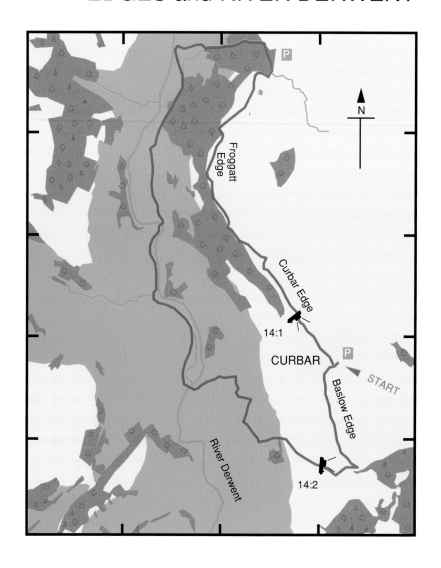

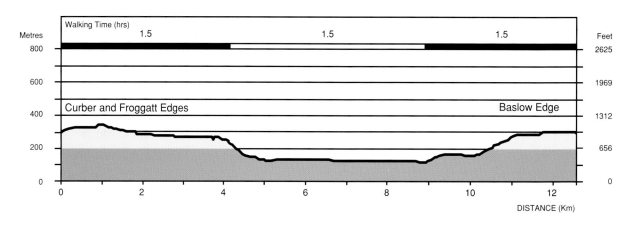

ROUTE 14

Curbar, Froggatt and Baslow Edges and River Derwent

●

STARTING LOCATION
Car park above Curbar.
OLM 24: MR 262747.
Car park up steep gradient, holds up to 40 cars.
Find parking in Calver when roads are icy!

ALTERNATIVE STARTING POINTS
Off B6054 at The Haywood near to the Grouse Inn.
Grindleford.
Calver/Curbar.

PUBLIC TRANSPORT
Bus route (Curbar Village) 277. (Extensive services to nearby Calver.)

OVERVIEW/INTEREST
Superb route along millstone grit edges.
Fantastic rock configurations.
Visit to Wellington's Monument and Eagle Stone.
Excellent wide views.
Sections through deciduous woodlands.
Return along part of River Derwent includes spectacular weir.
Attractive village enclaves.

FOOTPATHS
On the top always impressive and sometimes outstanding; these are invariably well-drained and firm.
The stretches through the woodlands and along the valley become waterlogged after prolonged rain.
Route finding is relatively easy.
Adequate signs and waymarkers.

GRADING
Easy/straightforward to moderate.

TIME ALLOWANCE
4½ hours.

STATISTICS

DISTANCE

Excluding Height	12.6 km	(7.8 miles)
TOTAL HEIGHT GAINED	250 m	(820 ft)
PRINCIPAL HEIGHTS		
Highest point along Edges	340 m	(1115 ft)

The way to the B6054 at MR 255776

Allow 1½ hours

Leave the car park to the N by mounting the steps and walking along the footpath signed to 'Curbar Edge'. Turn L to approach the edge along a narrow fenced path. This bends to the R, and beyond a K-gate adjacent to a brilliant white-painted gate the edge is reached to your L. In progressing northwards from here, take every opportunity to keep as close to the edges as possible. On reaching the first major outcrop of rocks lining the edge at the brow ahead, pause to absorb the views extending for miles down below in a semi-circle from S, through W to N. To the L, below the continuation edges of Baslow and Gardom's, the lush parklands of Chatsworth stretch away to the S and the attractive twin villages of Curbar and Calver lie spread out directly below to the W with sheltering, rounded hills rising beyond. Further away the deep cleft signifying Stoney Middleton is to the WNW, whilst the rounded profile of Sir William Hill, with its telecommunications tower, dominates the far-away view to the NW. Nearer to, the eyes are spoilt for choice as to which particular rock configurations lining the extensive edges to L and R to focus upon. Magnificent!

From here, the route weaves through many fascinating rock features and between huge boulders in its delightful progress northwards. Most of the way is over extremely well-drained terrain, through clumps of heathers, round scatterings of

boulders, along flat bedding planes of rock with innumerable opportunities to peep over the continuously interesting, exciting and on occasions awesome edges. At the more adventurous points a good head for heights is required, and always exercise care and caution when approaching potentially dangerous viewing positions! Be particularly vigilant in icy or windy conditions and also when there are children in your party, who must be kept under constant close observation along here. Further on, Win Hill and the outline of Bleaklow can be seen in clear weather conditions, whilst down below there are more revealing panoramas of the River Derwent meandering placidly along its wide, flattish valley. The route along the edges of Curbar and Froggatt extends for about 3 km (1.9 miles) over fairly flat ground. With so much to take in, the enthralling edge section is over all too soon and the first indications of this are isolated clumps of silver birch trees as the ground begins to fall.

14:1 Looking south east along Curbar Edge

Then there is a small stone circle off to the R, but you will have to look diligently for this. The circle is located at MR 250768 and is reached by means of a grassy side path which loops back to the main route further on. Near here, in the valley below on your L, the sprawling conurbation of Grindleford first comes into view to the NW. A short distance further on the wide, compacted earth path penetrates sparse woodlands just inside of which there is a K-gate. Beyond this, a small stream is crossed as more sheltered terrain encloses the route. The delightful descent continues along an obvious path over more rounded slopes that support an increasing variety of trees and bushes. Some open aspects do prevail and through one of these the far-off village of Hathersage can be made out to the NW. Then in good weather conditions, part of the plateau of Kinder comes into view further to the L of the distinctive pointed tor of Win Hill positioned to the NW. Past an enormous boulder the path descends in a tight curve to the R to reach the B6054 road just below at MR 255776. A K-gate provides access to the roadway. Through this, walk some distance up the road on your side to get away from the dangerous bend before crossing over at a point where you may clearly observe oncoming traffic. Just before reaching the 'Parking 300 yards' road sign, turn L through a swing wicket gate.

The way to Calver and Curbar *Allow 1½ hours*

The gate provides entry into the National Trust Longshaw Estate at the Haywood. Continue by descending the stone steps, after which the path dips down to cross a small stream flowing swiftly over its bed of boulders. The way continues through a gap in a stone wall and northwards up the ensuing brow along a wide cobbled path. Ahead veer L away from the car park area and then further L to walk downhill, passing through a recently constructed wooden gate. Beyond this feature a wide path traverses round the hillside to your R.

Be vigilant to follow a side path bearing off downhill to your L. This way descends through the trees to the NNW. Then the route curves progressively to your L, leading you more steeply down in a westerly direction. After crossing a wider forest track, the way continues downhill oscillating between SW and NW. Eventually, the outline of buildings appear through the trees ahead and a short distance further on a K-gate is reached. Past this, the way connects with a driveway that you turn R along to continue downhill. This track leads to the B6521 road through Grindleford at MR 245778. Contact is established with this road at the Methodist church of St Helen's in the Parish of Eyam.

Turn L along the busy road but almost immediately veer off L through a K-gate positioned before the traffic signals at the bridge spanning the River Derwent. This leads to the public footpath signed to 'Froggatt, Curbar, Calver, Baslow and Chatsworth'. The path veers away from the river to cross the flat meadowland on a SSE diagonal. The way leads to a tiny watercourse near to another K-gate. Bear R after passing through this and then continue beside a stone wall to your R. Then, beyond a G-stile the path clips another small, wooded area.

Ahead, fork R down the lower of two paths. After continuous heavy rain there is an exacting and prolonged oozy section from where a National Trust sign indicates that you are now in Froggatt Wood. Further on, another small stream is passed in the vicinity of erratic boulders. The path then leads to more open ground beyond a gap formed by unusual stone pillars containing several circular holes. Continue southwards from here across the meadowland, keeping to the distinct path of worn-down grass. This leads at a fairly constant height through two gateways and at the second of these pass to the R and below a large stone barn. The route then continues through a wide, open gap between stone retaining walls and another narrow G-stile has to be negotiated. This is positioned to the L of a gate. From here a partially paved track leads between walls, up the next brow. This part of the way is firm underfoot, over bedded paving slabs. Further on, a row of residences signals that you are approaching Froggatt. This is at Spooner Lane which then connects with a major lane named Hollowgate at the Wesleyan Reform Chapel.

Veer R at the junction and continue downhill. A short distance further on the River Derwent is crossed by turning R over Froggatt Bridge at MR 244761. This is a venerable, stone-arched overpass of considerable character and its former use as a packhorse crossing is still evident today in the form of several triangular passing places. Immediately across, veer L to pass through a gap in the quite low retaining wall at this spot. After this, keep to the riverside path to your L. From here, the way continues pleasantly southwards, initially beneath trees. Stiles and crossings of minor tributary watercourses follow as the way continues down the attractive valley.

This delightful section ends all too soon at another road bridge, which is reached at a wildlife refuge. Cross the road directly opposite and to the

91

L of the bridge (which you never quite reach). The continuation path on the far side is signed to 'Calver Bridge' and a short distance further on a wide and spectacular weir is passed. After a gate and s-stile are passed, the path eventually parts company with the river by bearing R towards the buildings ahead. These are dominated by a former chapel which now is minus its bell. A further K-gate leads into parkland in which several caravans appear to be permanently positioned. One of these houses the Derbyshire Village Mission. A macadam drive leads past Calver Mill, away to the L. Beyond this, the village of Calver is entered. Turn L to re-cross the River Derwent by the bridge reserved exclusively for pedestrians and then turn L again by the side of the Parish Church to walk up Curbar Lane out of the village. This is directly opposite the Bridge Inn and is immediately after walking past the entrance to Dukes Drive.

The way back to the car park *Allow 1½ hours*

Use Curbar Lane to walk uphill heading ENE and passing the Old Vicarage on your R. Just beyond the side lane on the L signed 'Pinfold Hill', turn R along Cliff Lane leading to the college of that name. From here there is a superb view of the irregular rock-strewn outline of Curbar Edge rising impressively above to your L. The lane curves to the R. Just beyond the imposing gates of the residence named Curbar Croft, be careful to locate and climb through a stone s-stile on your L. This provides an entrance to a public footpath signed to 'Baslow via Gorse Bank Farm' and the exit from the lane is located at MR 252744. From here, the way continues SE along a narrow path between a beech hedge and a stone wall. A combined gap-and-step stile and the subsequent crossing of a stream lead to an enclosed grassy way, sections of which can become boggy. Turn R along this, for a short distance, walking slightly downhill to the SW.

After passing through a G-stile, veer L over the next s-stile as a preliminary to gaining further height up the grassy slopes to your L. Isolated, erratic boulders litter the rising meadows hereab-

outs. Further on, keep to the wall on your R walking towards the farm buildings silhouetted against the skyline ahead. Then pass through another G-stile, the opening at which is protected by an unusual flap gate. This is adjacent to a gate bearing the notice 'Grislow Field – Keep to footpath'. From here, continue uphill by means of the wide, grassy, diagonal path. The ascent then reaches a wooden gate and on the far side of this veer to the R to negotiate a second gate nearby. Then make a full turn to the L to continue walking uphill to the E beside a stone wall on your L. Your direction now is towards a copse of trees above to your R. After another gate, bear L through the trees to pass over a s-stile in a high stone wall on your L. Turn R to follow the narrow footpath that leads further uphill through extensive bracken into a more open and rugged landscape.

At the next fork veer R to continue SE, then trimming the edge of the clump of trees ahead. Along here, keep to the obvious main path, ignoring narrower side routes off to your L. Some distance on, another wide track is crossed at a tangent and after this continue to climb uphill on your now established SE diagonal. Further up, your way consolidates with another wide path. There are tracks all over the place now and several of these further consolidate along your direction of travel. Then just before another gate is reached, veer L up the higher path and a short distance further up, at the corner of a stone wall, bear L again to climb up a narrow path that gains further height more rapidly up the steepening slope. This latter manoeuvre is made near a distinctive, large flat boulder. This final stretch to the edge above is through dense bracken. The concluding steps to reach Baslow Edge are achieved by veering to the L.

The views from here are quite magnificent and as all the major landmarks have already been positioned, just turn round and admire them again. Then, related to your direction of approach, veer R along the edge walking eastwards to reach the fine edifice of Wellington's Monument at MR 264737. This cross will remind you that the great soldier lived from 1769 to 1832. Your next sightseeing objective, the Eagle Stone, may be observed from the monument. This huge isolated

14:2 The approach to Wellington's Monument

boulder is a short distance to the NW and the walk to it is along a wide, obvious path. The boulder is scaleable with care, but only if you have the right footwear with you and have some skill in climbing techniques.

Beyond this landmark, bear R down the wider path walking northwards across flat, heather-clad moorland. The minor road is soon reached at a point where there are no fewer than three gates. Turn R after these and use the narrow path above the road to reach the car park.

Alternative routes

ESCAPES

The most obvious way to shorten the walk is to walk eastwards from Calver up the minor road skirting Curbar and so back to the car park above. Unfortunately, this variation prevents you from visiting two of the more interesting features along the main route, namely Wellington's Monument and the Eagle Stone.

Another short cut is possible from Froggatt Edge. At MR 249763 there is a steep, narrow path leading down from the rocky edge that will enable you to connect with the path along the E bank of the River Derwent at MR 244760. From here walk southwards along the river to re-connect with the main route at Calver.

EXTENSIONS

The route may be conveniently extended to the N and/or S. To the N keep to the high ground longer before descending westwards along the paths through Longshaw Country Park. To the S, follow the riverside path and minor roads into Baslow before climbing to the NE to rendezvous with the main route at Wellington's Monument.

93

Route 15: MACCLESFIELD FOREST, SHUTLINGSLOE and WILDBOARCLOUGH

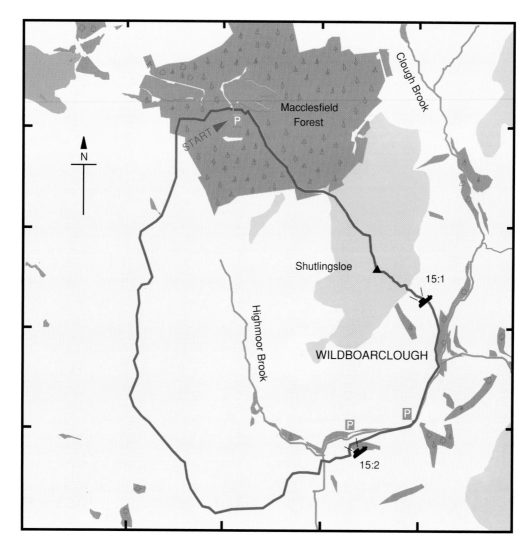

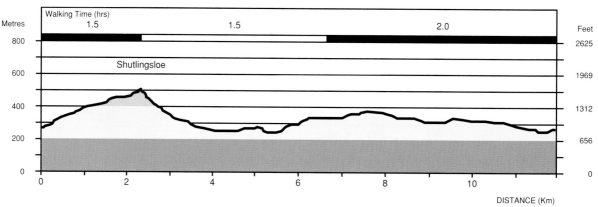

ROUTE 15

Macclesfield Forest, Shutlingsloe
and Wildboarclough

●

STARTING LOCATION
Car park at Macclesfield Forest (near Trentabank
  Reservoir).
OLM 24: MR 961711.
Attractively positioned car park holds about 25 cars.
Information Centre, toilets and picnic area.

ALTERNATIVE STARTING POINTS
Wildboarclough.
Wild Boar Inn (by arrangement).

PUBLIC TRANSPORT
None.

OVERVIEW/INTEREST
Forests, reservoirs, rocky tors, rivers and
  meadowlands.
Pleasant, open landscapes with fine views.
Two hospitable inns directly on the route.
One challenging uphill stretch at start.

FOOTPATHS
The way up to Shutlingsloe is superb!
The rest is mainly good and in most parts well-
  drained.

Several waterlogged stretches in farm meadows
  during return.
Route finding at start very straightforward; the
  homeward journey is more complicated and
  exacting.
Signs are a mixture, more than adequate in places
  but on occasions somewhat lacking.

GRADING
Easy to moderate.

TIME ALLOWANCE
5 hours.

STATISTICS
DISTANCE

Excluding Height	11.9 km	(7.4 miles)
TOTAL HEIGHT GAINED	430 m	(1410 ft)
PRINCIPAL HEIGHTS		
Shutlingsloe	506 m	(1660 ft)

The way to Shutlingsloe   *Allow 1½ hours*

From the car park, head into the forest area along the trail signed 'Forest Walks 1, 2 & 3', walking E with the minor road adjacent on your L before bearing R along the internal forest road. Within 100 paces turn off L down the narrow path and then turn R round the end of a stone wall to reach the well-constructed, direct way leading uphill to Shutlingsloe. Your ascent is now to the SSE. Behind you, good views immediately appear down below over the tree-fringed reservoirs. The path is a delight to walk up with its wide, well-drained surface of compacted gravel constructed in tiered sections supported by retaining timbers.

Further up, the path connects with another internal forestry road. Continue uphill following the route signed to 'Shutlingsloe'. Look back again here to observe the pronounced ridge to your rear in the NW. This landmark contains Tegg's Nose Country Park. The way sweeps round to the L, as further height is gradually and agreeably gained. Veer further L at a sign confirming your correct approach to Shutlingsloe and continue along the obvious wide, dry, stony track as it swings eastwards to enter areas of less densely packed conifers. Ahead, bear R following the signed route towards Shutlingsloe, thus leaving the path leading straight ahead to Standing Stone.

The way continues along a more natural path,

but the going is still pleasantly firm and dry underfoot and the gradient comfortably to scale. Along here, the first views of the rolling, hilly country to your R appear. This terrain houses the telecommunications aerials situated on Croker Hill and these may be observed on the horizon to the SW. The path veers R to reach a stile at the boundary of the forested area. Beyond this, continue climbing along the stepped, paved way snaking up to the SE to attain the higher ground of the ridge ahead. Once more, the care and planning which has gone into the construction of this pathway is evident. The surface of this is likely to last for ever and to become more and more natural-looking as soil and vegetation invade the thoughtfully left spaces between the paving slabs – a grateful 'Well done' to those planning authorities involved with this highly commended project.

More rewarding views appear to your rear. They are over the forested areas now extending below. When the ridge is reached the first sightings of the impressive, conical helmet of the tor of Shutlingsloe appear ahead, jutting out against and dominating the southern skyline. This proud peak of jumbled sandstones and gritstones is still some height above you. A waterlogged section is conveniently crossed by means of a wooden causeway beyond which there is another stile. Climb over this and turn immediately R to walk along the impressive flagged way adjacent to a stone wall on the R. This route leads to a S-stile over the barrier of a formidably high stone wall stretching across your approach. On the far side of this obstacle, stone steps wind to the top of the tor. This section of the way takes full advantage of utilizing natural sandstone outcrops and the final climb is particularly appealing. Just below the summit, erosion control diverts the footpath to the R, before the extensive, flat summit platform is reached.

In fine weather the panoramic views from this lofty, isolated viewing position are superb. An illustrated compass set in a rock face further to the L beyond the trig point will enable you to position all the features in the surrounding vast landscapes to be observed here. To summarize some of the highlights, Black Hill lies far away to the N; Cats and Shining Tors closer to in the NE; further to the

E Axe Edge, Oliver Hill, Ramshaw Rocks and the serrated edges of the Roaches ridges predominate; Tittesworth Reservoir lies down to the SE; Gun Hill is to the S; the SW skyline is occupied by Mow Cop, the long escarpment of Bosley Cloud and Croker Hill; whilst Tegg's Nose rises beyond your previous direction of approach to the NE. There is strong competition for these views from the interesting features underfoot. A particular feature is the crumbling, weathered slopes that plunge along the extensive E face of the tor in a jumble of steep rocky bluffs and intermingled loose boulders.

The way to the Wild Boar Inn *Allow 1½ hours*

Commence your descent along the narrow, rocky path down the precipitously steep E slopes of the tor. This is accessed near the trig point and the start of the way down is helpfully positioned by means of an arrowhead which points along the correct route to the R. The downward scramble zigzags through the rock configurations and there are a couple of interesting sections to test out your technique. There are several alternative routes down each discrete section, so choose a descent route that you are comfortable with. Towards the bottom of the steeper slopes, an obvious grassy track leads down E, before veering SE and to your R, to pass above the isolated hill farm of Shutlingsloe. Keep bearing R along the signed footpath to reach a wall ahead which is crossed by means of a wooden stile. After more obstacles the track down connects with the farm access lane. Veer R along this and then use it to reach the minor road which runs through the narrow valley of Wildboarclough. This is reached at MR 983685. Turn R at the road to pass the nearby Crag Inn.

Carefully continue along the narrow road, with Clough Brook gurgling away to your L, until you reach the Peak National Park vehicle lay-by at Brookside, about ½ km (⅓ mile) further down the valley. Turn L immediately after passing this to cross the stream, using the way leading to the Brookside Restaurant. Then turn sharp R to engage the public footpath that leads further

down the valley hugging the L bank of the river. Ahead, a stile provides entrance to meadowland: veer R over this keeping to the course of a wire fence which follows the meanders of the stream. Further on, keep above a small waterlogged culvert at which another stile is positioned. Safely across this, more open terrain, dominated by the escarpment of Hammerton Knowl rising to the WSW, is once again reached.

Your path then bears L away from the stream and the way continues over rising ground to follow the line of a dry-stone wall positioned to your R. This track leads past two groups of farm buildings, both of which are passed to your R. Just beyond the second of these, be careful to locate and use a stepped stile over the wall on your R, and then follow the way signed to 'Wildboarclough – Owler's Bridge'. The faint path leads downhill directly in line with Hammerton Knowl far above. Cross the meadow below with care for it is often waterlogged. The best course down is beside the wire fence on your R and this line will lead you directly to a stile and wooden bridge over the stream.

15:1 An exhilarating winter's descent into Wildboarclough from the heights of Shutlingsloe

Climb back to the valley road and turn L along it, walking uphill as it bends to the R. Slightly further on, turn off R over the stile from which a footpath leads towards Hammerton Knowl Farm above. A wide grassy track rises pleasantly uphill over gently rounded slopes. This track then swings to the L round the farm buildings. However, the waysigned route is actually through the farmyard and this area is accessed via a metal gate to your R. Leave the farmyard at another such barrier, above and round to the L. From here, an excellent path cum cart-track winds westwards round the lower slopes of the knoll.

A short distance further on, when the remains of a derelict stone building are reached, veer off to the R and climb up the grassy slopes of the hillside on a SSW diagonal. (This is *before* reaching a small copse with a water trough on the R.) As you walk uphill aim for the corner of the stone wall ahead and when you reach this bear L, keeping the wall on your R-hand side. Your continuation way will soon be blocked by another stone wall which you cross at the stile before continuing straight ahead, keeping the stone wall on your L-hand side. At the next field boundary, pass through a gateway, and following this, be careful to aim for a tree directly ahead of you. When you reach it, continue on a straight line, keeping the remains of a dilapidated stone wall just to your L. The next field boundary is crossed by means of a stone s-stile. Beyond this, continue with the stone wall on your L across the next field and then over a L-stile. From this point you should be able to make out the Wild Boar Inn. Trim your final approach to connect with a stile located to the L of the inn.

[Author's note: The previous paragraph, describing this relatively complicated section of the route has been re-written by the National Park Rangers for which I am grateful.]

During your final approach to the Wild Boar, views of the craggy, serrated profiles of the Roaches and Hen Cloud appear in fine weather on your L and to the SE. The inn is a most hospitable place for obtaining sustenance; walkers are made welcome there and by prior arrangement with the proprietors you may, at less busy times, leave your car in their upper car park.

The way back to Trentabank   *Allow 2 hours*

Turn R along the main A54 road to pass or go into the inn. A short distance further on, select the footpath to the R accessed by a stile to the R of a metal gate. This is at MR 958672. Walk uphill along the wide track to pass through the establishment of Longgutter. Leave the farmyard by means of the upper metal gate and continue northwards along the edge of the field above, keeping near to the hawthorn hedge on your R before crossing the stile in the far corner. Following this, continue straight ahead, only deviating round boggy ground, until you reach a grass-covered track that merges into a narrow path of compacted soil. Cross the next fence at the stile beside a metal gate and continue to gain height, walking near a wire fence on your L. Two more stiles have to be

15:2 An abandoned farm above Clough Brook

negotiated before you reach a road. Cross over and walk along Withenshaw Lane, which heads downhill towards Nab End Farm, heading NW. Past the farm and just prior to reaching a small copse of deciduous trees, abandon the lane by veering off up rising ground on your R and then follow a signed footpath leading off beyond a metal gate, also on your R.

Veer L along the ensuing grass track, walking slightly uphill and northwards. Beyond a stone-pillared gateway the track leads down across the rutted, grass hillside towards High Lee Farm. Turn R before reaching the farmyard and pass through a metal gate in a stone wall. This manoeuvre is in order to pass round the farm, with it to your L. From here, veer diagonally L (NNE) down the slope to reach a stile towards the bottom end of a stone wall ahead. After this stile, continue to work your way further downhill beside a wire fence on your L, keeping to a faint grassy track. The farmer here has tried to guide you along the straight and narrow around his farm enclosures and pastures by providing sensible crossing points. However, some strategically positioned directional signs would also greatly assist your (not easy) route finding in this vicinity. I have met and talked to the farmer, whom I found very helpful, and if you should experience problems around here I am sure he will provide the necessary authoritative guidance.

The next part of the way funnels down to the course of a small stream on your R. This is reached via a stone G-stile in the far corner of the enclosure which you are now descending. The beck is crossed just beyond. On the far side, continue walking N, making your way up the opposite slopes of the shallow valley, and then follow the indistinct track further N to pass the entrance drive to Cophurst. This is down to your L. Severely waterlogged areas now have to be crossed and consequently this is a less pleasant section of the walk. Keep above and to the R of a stone wall along here. Having avoided the private way down to Cophurst, cross a wide stile at a rusty iron gate and carefully cross the ground on the far side. In winter this is often oozing with deep, clinging, black mud. There is more of this to come,

particularly at the next watercourse ahead. Past these impediments, continue walking north-wards beside the stone wall on your L. The route then passes through a gap in a stone wall before veering diagonally uphill to your R. Your way connects with a minor road above at a stile on the near side of the road. This point is at MR 953695.

Turn L along this little-used lane and continue down it to pass the Hanging Gate Inn. When the lane bends sharply L more steeply downhill, keep straight ahead by veering off along the side lane coming in from the R. This lane is now used to return to the car park some 2 km (1.2 miles) away to the NE. Ignore all side lanes and farm tracks down to your L and eventually you turn R, following the lane down through the forested area to the T junction below. Turn R up the wider road here, signed to 'Macclesfield Forest'. The car park is a short distance further on to the R.

Alternative routes

ESCAPES

Assuming your primary intention is to climb Shutlingsloe, and this is not unduly demanding, you can then turn about and partly retrace your approach route using the alternative forest trails to descend more or less directly back to the car park below.

Another possibility is in Wildboarclough. From just beyond the Crag Inn, select the footpath off on your R and follow this round the lower slopes of the hillside, through Lower Nabs Farm, to reach the minor road ahead. Then continue down Oaken Clough and use the footpath beyond this to reach Haddon Farm, to re-connect there with the main route.

EXTENSIONS

From the Wild Boar Inn there are a number of interesting circuitous routes extending south-wards towards Wincle and Danebridge. These constitute discrete, additional walking loops and the undertaking of any of them will return you to your departure point from the main route near the inn.

Route 16: THE ROACHES, HANGING STONE and LUD'S CHURCH

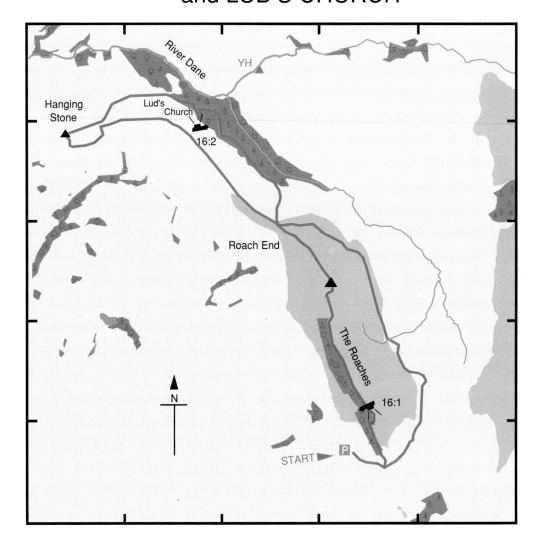

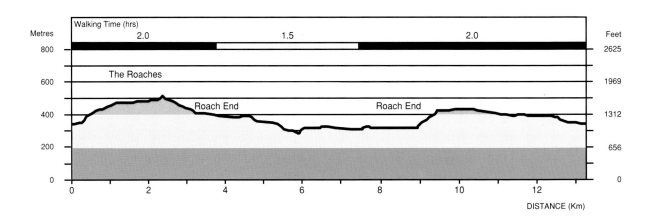

ROUTE 16

The Roaches, Hanging Stone and Lud's Church

●

STARTING LOCATION
Vehicle lay-by immediately below The Roaches.
OLM 24: MR 004622.
Lay-by holds about 25 cars with provision for mini-buses. Turning point 200 m (220 yd) further on.

ALTERNATIVE STARTING POINTS
Roach End.
Danebridge (parking along roadside and short extension necessary).

PUBLIC TRANSPORT
'Park and Ride' service (221) operates at weekends and Bank Holidays from Tittesworth Reservoir car park at Meerbrook: MR 994603.

OVERVIEW/INTEREST
Superb ridge amongst really spectacular scenery.
Fantastic rock formations and rock pitches.
Rub shoulders with climbing fraternity.
Return through woodlands and over moors.
Hanging Stone (rocks) and Lud's Church (cave).
Plenty of animal and bird life including wallabies, grouse, curlews, jackdaws and moorhens.

FOOTPATHS
Outwards route over firm rock with some easy scrambling.
Return, particularly through wooded area, along excellent, well-drained pathways. The odd wet spot across moorlands.
Footpaths fairly obvious along high ridges.
Signs are generally adequate where needed.

GRADING
Moderate.

TIME ALLOWANCE
5½ hours.

STATISTICS

DISTANCE		
Excluding Height	13.3 km	(8.3 miles)
TOTAL HEIGHT GAINED	360 m	(1180 ft)
PRINCIPAL HEIGHTS		
The Roaches	505 m	(1660 ft)

The way to the road at Roach End

Allow 2 hours

The car lay-by is set amongst magnificent scenery, just below the towering, jagged rock faces of The Roaches. Further down the valley the separate tor of Hen Cloud rises in splendid isolation, and far away the shimmering waters of Tittesworth Reservoir catch the eye to the SW. From the lay-by, walk SE downhill heading towards the cheese-wedge shape of Hen Cloud. Turn L at gates and continue uphill along the wide gravel path passing through The Roaches Estate. Ignore three side paths/tracks off to your L and keep bearing eastwards, and to the R, round the brow of the steeper, rocky slopes. The way then winds for a short distance beside a dry-stone wall to your R and passes by a redundant stone pillar. Then veer L up the grassy path which penetrates heather, before rising through the jumble of large sandstone boulders and rocky pitches towering above to your L.

The path narrows and curves further L as further height is quickly gained in threading your way up through this fascinating terrain. There are several alternative routes up individual sections and the higher ground is quickly reached along a route full of interest and one which generously rewards the exertion involved. Further up, the path leads to the R of the exposed edge, as ahead across a shallow intervening col, steeper, almost sheer rock buttresses and slabs rise perpendicularly to another edge teetering above. These pitches are often speckled with the bright garb of climbers edging their precarious way up the challenging rock faces. You pass beneath and round to the L of these formidable barriers. This is

101

16:1 Hen Cloud viewed from The Roaches

achieved by turning R between two stone pillars and following the track along the base of the promontory. However, before making this manoeuvre peer cautiously over the exposed edge on your L to observe the splendid view to the SW of the orderly, rolling landscapes down below.

The obvious well-used path continues NW along a sandy boulder-strewn way but as you gaze at the many rock configurations towering majestically above, be continuously mindful of the severe, dangerous fall-away immediately to your L. Further on, groupings of Scots pines soften the severe barrenness of the surrounding rock formations. Some distance ahead, the path reaches a T intersection. A notice at this spot requests you not to proceed directly forward any further in order that areas dedicated to wildlife should not be entered. Turn sharp R at this juncture to follow the narrower path which then climbs more steeply uphill towards a gap in the rock structures above. Rotted wooden posts mark the route upwards along a stepped path through a nick in the sandstones. Turn full L just prior to reaching the top of the ridge at a point where your way straight ahead is barred by a wooden anti-erosion barrier. On gaining the vantage of the higher ridge there are superb views of the wild high moorlands to the E and of the sombre and distinctively serrated profile of Ramshaw Rocks.

Continue along the elevated path hugging the crest of the escarpment, now walking N towards less dramatic terrain ahead. Further along, keep to the R of the remains of a low dry-stone wall and spurn a gap in this wall with an inviting path leading down beyond. Some less well-drained ground then has to be negotiated. The prominent escarpment now observed far away to the WNW is Bosley Cloud overlooking Congleton. Some distance further on, the distinctive conical peak of Shutlingsloe appears ahead to the NW. The interesting edge continues for the best part of 2 km (1.2 miles) before the descent slopes are reached and the correct route is always along its apex to the NNW, keeping to the main wider path at all divisions. The way passes close by Doxey Pool and a concessionary footpath down to the R should be ignored. The route hereabouts follows part of the Staffordshire Moorlands Walk. A trig point is eventually reached. This is located at MR 001639 and it signifies the maximum elevation of the ridge at 505 m (1660 ft). From here, slopes lead down to the narrow road at Bearstone Rock to the NW. This signifies the termination of the more rocky, upthrust ground. The path down then veers to the L as the falling slopes of the ridge bend towards NW directly in line with the telecommunications tower visible on the distant horizon. The road is eventually reached at MR 996645.

The way to Lud's Church (cave)

Allow 1½ hours

Cross the road and continue NW along the signed public footpath. The path is accessed by passing through a narrow G-stile in a stone wall where a footpath immediately off to your R should be ignored. Across a grassy area, a stile is then mounted as the obvious path leads onwards adjacent to a dilapidated stone wall on the L. The way hereabouts is superb along the flattish crest of a descending spur which affords excellent all-round views. More interesting rocky outcrops and minor tors break up the smooth symmetry of the ridge, curving down gracefully to the L in the far

distance. Further, fast and immensely exhilarating progress may be made along this fine ridge heading towards the area named as Back Forest, although you always remain above the tree-line, down on your R.

Rounded heather-covered slopes abound along here as further on you dismiss a path off to your L which follows the line of a stone wall. Here you will pass a newly erected sign indicating that you are travelling towards Danebridge. Your way continues along the falling crest of the ridge as it curves uniformly to the L through an impressive series of rocky outcrops. Then you cross a concessionary footpath at right angles. The way to the L descends to Clough Head whilst that to your R drops down to Lud's Church; avoid both. Immediately ahead, use the stile to pass through a dry-stone wall. Following this, spurn another way down to the L as you keep to the higher ground along the ridge. The descending spur bears further L, circling far above the farm of High Forest.

After passing over another stile, an undulating slope with an overall gradual descent leads to a combination of a gate and stile. Veer L here over the stile and follow the bridleway signed to 'Swythamley'. This leads southwards, further downhill through a shallow furrow. At the intersection of the ways below, bear R following the concessionary bridleway signed to 'Danebridge' by passing through the nearby gate or squeezing through the narrow G-stile. Continue walking SW downhill veering R along the route, again signed to Danebridge, to pass above a gate and track leading to the property named 'Paddock'. The isolated rock above to your R is called 'Hanging Stone', and your next immediate objective is to stand on (not hang from) the top of this!

Pass through a gateway and then walk across the lanes directly ahead before climbing over a W-stile to the L of a metal gate. Over this, turn sharp R to follow the concession path up the steep grassy slopes to reach the Hanging Stone. Steps provide a final easy way round and to the top of the rocks. After a close inspection, continue up the grassy path beyond the rocks to pass through a gap in the retaining wall which runs along the ridge at right angles to your approach. The panoramic views from this spot in clear weather are fantastic and by now most of the major features to be observed during your 360-degree pivot should be familiar. To recap briefly: Bosley Cloud is the prominent escarpment to the NW, Shutlingsloe rears up to the N, your invigorating descent ridge to reach this spot curls away to the E, The Roaches and Hen Cloud rise to the SE, Tittesworth Reservoir languishes away to the S and Gun Hill appears to the SSW.

16:2 Lud's Church (Cave)

Start your return by walking E, using the grassy path to lead you back towards the rocky ridge. You will find the springy sward underfoot along this section quite delightful. Further on, the crossing of a stone wall is not quite so pleasant! Past a small bog pool appearing in winter, the obvious way leads back, at a configuration of stiles, the first with take-off ramp, to the gully which you have previously walked down. This is at MR 977655. Be particularly careful crossing the stone wall here, for the large coping stone was loose, as were the adjacent ones, when this stile was last used by the author. Turn L up the gully to re-cross the easier wooden stile ahead. On this occasion, select the bridleway signed to 'Gradbach'. The next section is a dream of a walk along a wide path which crosses slopes profusely covered with heathers and bilberries.

Further on, through a more enclosed area, the occasional waterlogged spot may be encountered but these are easily avoided. A gentle descent follows between clumps of heathers and bilberry. (If you pass this way in August, come armed with a container which you can fill with ripe, mouth-watering bilberries.) Then, areas of bracken together with silver birch and Scots pine add great variety to the flora as the route penetrates the aptly named 'Forest Wood'. The way leads to a grouping of exposed, stratified rocks arranged in the shape of twin pinnacles over to your L. These are Castle Cliff Rocks. From here, continue along the higher path which is signed to 'Lud's Church'. The level path continues to lead round the hillside under the shade of the wooded slopes. A short distance further on, the tiny rocky inlet which leads to the narrow but extensive winding chasms named as Lud's Church appears on your R. Walk into, down, along and then up the narrow passageways, spending time to inspect the algae, lichen, liverwort and mosses thriving on the impressive rock faces of this damp and dusky domain. Towards the far end of the cave system, select the R-hand fork and climb out of the narrow cleft up the steps there. Keep further R along here to emerge back into full daylight at the top. Then veer to the L, climbing more steps, and walk round the area protected to combat erosion.

The way back to the car lay-by *Allow 2 hours*

The way continues ESE along more fine paths which meander through further delightful woodlands. A shallow descent follows and this leads to a way descending from the ridge above to your R. Veer L here and then bear R along the path signed to 'Roach End' to continue your journey SE along another well-drained part of the route. After a while you will reach a signpost reading 'Concession path to ridge'. Ignore this and continue down to the T junction, where you turn R following the signed route to 'Roach End'. A small stream is then crossed by means of stepping stones. From here, the path of layered sandstone rises uphill to lead you back to the familiar spot of Roach End. This entails a fair climb up.

Then, be careful to walk past the first gap opening in the wall to your L as the track leading off from here will only take you downhill again, towards Gradbach. Further on, climb over the stile in the corner of the stone wall ahead. Following this, turn immediately L and pass through the gap in the stone wall.

Cross the entrance of the track leading down to Lower Roach End and continue along the narrow lane in an easterly direction uphill. Keep to this remote lane for approximately 2 km (1.2 miles) enjoying the views of the sweeping landscapes stretching away on your L. Eventually, the macadam sweeps round to the L. Just past a cattle grid, turn off the lane to your R and continue along the gravel track signed as a public footpath. This turning at MR 008633 is before the lane reaches the cottage named as Shaw House. The track leads towards Shaw Top but at the entrance gate to this farm the way veers to the L over a wooden stile and then crosses waterlogged ground round and below the buildings. The path leads southwards round the perimeter fence and another stile has to be crossed before a short diagonal to your L takes you to another fenced-off area ahead – you have to veer further L along to get round it, as indicated by the white arrowhead waymarker.

Continue beside the fence and follow this by turning R as it changes direction. You will reach a stile and gate. Turn R again to cross the stile and then walk along the track in the direction of Hen Cloud, the tip of which should, by now, have reappeared ahead to your L. When this track bends L to descend towards Summerhill Farm, peel off to the R over a wooden stile. You will need some deft footwork to avoid the worst of the boggy morass on the far side. After this, bear L along the well-trodden peaty path (which also tends to retain excessive water), initially walking southwards, before the way curves to the R, progressively changing direction towards SW. Further on, a solitary stone pillar is passed. The clearly defined path then descends through more heathers to bisect Hen Cloud and The Roaches ridge through a wide hause.

Further on, avoid several ways leading off to your L which then either climb or lead round Hen Cloud, unless of course you are bent on completing one of the suggested extensions. Instead, keep to the wide grassy path as it leads further SW, veering R round the hillside to connect with ways down from The Roaches before bringing you back to the lane and lay-by.

Alternative routes

ESCAPES
This figure of eight route may be cut in two at Roach End and each loop turned into separate, discrete walks.

A much less severe curtailment is to avoid the end section to the Hanging Stone rocks.

EXTENSIONS
The obvious extension is either to climb or to walk round Hen Cloud and this decision may conveniently be delayed until the end of the day and on the way back.

Another possibility is to venture into Danebridge before circling back along the course of the River Dane to return to the main route at Lud's Church. Due to the many meanders of the river, this is a long and exacting extension which will certainly push the revised walk into the 'severe' category and as such it should only be contemplated by strong and fit walkers.

Route 17: EYAM, HIGHLOW, RIVER DERWENT and STONEY MIDDLETON

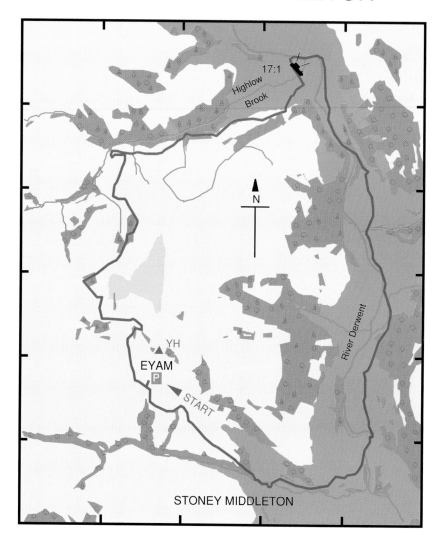

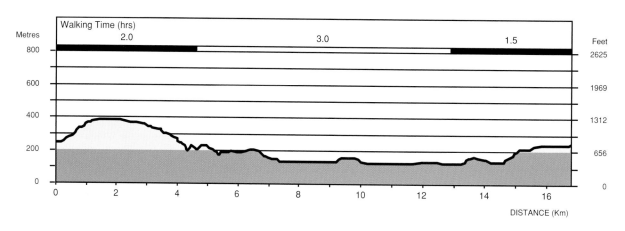

2

THE WHITE PEAK

ROUTE 17

Eyam, Highlow, River Derwent and Stoney Middleton

●

<table>
<tr><td>

STARTING LOCATION
Car park at Eyam.
OLM 24: MR 216767.
Large car and coach park; holds over 30 cars.
Toilets.

ALTERNATIVE STARTING POINTS
Various points along Derwent Valley.
Stoney Middleton.

PUBLIC TRANSPORT
Bus routes 65, 66, 175 and X67.

OVERVIEW/INTEREST
Varied scenery, including open landscapes and
    enclosed riversides.
Pleasant route with ups and downs well spaced out.
Interesting villages and hamlets.
Eyam's historical connection with the plague of
    1666.
Plenty of bird-life.
A route suitable for most family groups, including
    older children.

</td><td>

FOOTPATHS
Paths are a mixture!
Along the tops usually good, firm and certain.
In the valleys, especially in heavy winter conditions,
    stretches become quagmires after prolonged wet
    weather.
Parts of route deserve better signposting.
Watch out for wobbly stiles.

GRADING
Moderate.

TIME ALLOWANCE
6½ hours.

STATISTICS

DISTANCE		
Excluding Height	16.8 km	(10.4 miles)
TOTAL HEIGHT GAINED	410 m	(1345 ft)
PRINCIPAL HEIGHTS		
Above Eyam Edge	381 m	(1250 ft)

</td></tr>
</table>

The way to Highlow Brook – MR 221797

Allow 2 hours

Turn L from the car park and walk downhill along Hawkhill Road. At the T junction below, turn R away from the village centre. Walk past Orchard Bank Victorian shop and continue by the Royal Oak Hotel, ignoring a side lane off on the R. Walk past the birthplace of the poet Richard Furness, author of *The Astrologer* (*Medicus Magus*), and immediately after turn R along the public foot-path, then heading N. At the end of the short, narrow lane the way passes through a farmyard which is often covered in heavy, clinging mud. (A local resident informed me that the farmer here is not too enthusiastic about walkers and that his dogs share this sentiment; so beware! To avoid this stretch see 'Escapes'.)

Beyond the farm, continue N uphill making for the house ahead and walking beside the remains of a dilapidated stone wall on your L. At the corner of this wall at the top of the field, squeeze through the gap on your L and then follow the narrow path adjacent to the private residence, before turning R to cross its approach drive. From here, continue uphill along the now waymarked route. Eyam Edge rises ahead, covered with clumps of deciduous and coniferous trees; the latter are mostly Scots pines. The route then veers L further uphill along a broad, grassy way protected by a stone wall on the R. This is parallel to Jumber Brook, the tree-fringed stream cutting through the shallow valley on your R. Further on, ignore a track on the L and continue climbing along the path by the side of a stone wall, making for the group of Scots pines on the horizon above and veering R along the signed footpath to reach them. The slope steepens as the way passes through clumps of gorse, before winding beneath the Scots pines further up still. Turn round here to absorb the views back down into the valley with the elongated village of Eyam spreadeagled below. A massive limestone quarry scars the otherwise gentle, green, rolling hillsides beyond. Then the path tracks to the R and the steepness of the gradient declines.

The next section is through an attractive wooded area, still uphill but with the direction veering to NE. A stone cairn is passed before the path rounds the brow of the hillside to converge on Jumber Brook. The way bears further R and the stream is crossed before the path winds further uphill to reach a wide, enclosed track above. This track is accessed by means of a G-stile, after which turn L to continue uphill along the track to a surfaced lane opposite Highcliffe Barnes Farm at MR 215774. Turn L along the lane, walking NW to pass by the residence named Trap House. Continue along this lane for a further ½ km (⅓ mile) first W, and then N after the road turns R. At the top of the next brow an open, panoramic landscape is revealed ahead to your L, in the quadrant between W and N. A small car parking area is passed. Beyond this, follow the major lane as it bends to the L, being careful to avoid a minor track off to the R signed 'Unsuitable for motors'. From here, the pointed summit of Win Hill may be

observed in clear weather directly ahead to the NNW beyond the intervening high ground of Shatton Edge. Within a further 100 paces, bear R off the surfaced road down a wide, compacted track. This leads NW towards a small copse, mostly of mature Scots pines. At the intersection of ways immediately past these trees, turn R to climb over a L-style and continue along the wide path leading eastwards.

The next section of the route is along an elevated path through expansive open landscapes of rounded, grassy slopes punctuated first of all by extensive rhododendron bushes and further on by plantations of trees. The way winds gently downhill and the landmark of Stanage House is passed some distance away on the R. Then the impressive, flat and enormously extensive gritstone edges of Stanage and Burbage Rocks appear, far away over to your L in the NE. Much nearer there is a group of Scots pines, silhouetted against the sombre, featureless mass of the Rocks. The way continues down a wide, enclosed grassy area, over a particularly heavy-duty stone s-stile, and through a series of merged plantations. These in approach sequence are named Jubilee, Big Moor and Gotherage. A super, well-drained grassy path leads further downhill; along here ignore the footpath leading off on the L through a gap in the adjacent stone wall. Then avoid penetrating another area of Scots pines through a gap in the wall to the L by veering away to the R and passing round this enclosed area of woodlands. Over another s-stile ahead, veer L and walk downhill past the plantation, first to the NE and then veering L towards NW.

The next section of the way is a sheer delight, down a narrow path which clips clumps of heathers. Lower down the village of Hathersage appears over on your R to the NNE. The descent continues to hug the crest of the hillside and the route bears further L as a branch path from above converges from the R. Further on, another path comes in on the L; this is at an unusually shaped wooden s-stile next to a gate. Continue descending along the elevated path which for a short stretch passes a rocky edge containing interesting outcrops. From here the obvious way leads further downhill to the NNE and lower down another L-stile has to be negotiated. Over this, the descent steepens down rounded, grassy slopes and the well-defined path curves to the R and then bends sharply back L before contorting down towards the narrow, forested valley of Highlow Brook. Lower down, a steep zigzag section culminates with your direction once more being reversed to the R. At this point, just above Stoke Ford (MR 211795), a number of ways converge and here do not be tempted to descend to the bridge below. Instead veer to the R and continue along the path which rises above the valley and Highlow Brook, keeping the stream down below to your L.

From here, a well-defined and much-used path winds uphill eastwards parallel to the stream, now some considerable distance below. The gradient soon slackens off as a more open moorland landscape appears ahead. Further height is then gradually gained up gently rising slopes. The path drops temporarily to ford a tributary stream before regaining its former elevation up the rounded slopes beyond; after which a straightish diagonal leads further uphill, eastwards. Over the next brow, a superb elevated stretch of country is revealed with fine views stretching to the serrated top of Millstone Edge and Bole Hill. Head towards these features as the route forward commences to surrender height. In this vicinity, the slanted, isolated knoll on the far side of the valley on your L is Highlow Hill. The path descends gradually to the valley floor where a double planked bridge provides a crossing, once again out of bounds, of Highlow Brook at MR 221797.

The way to Froggatt   *Allow 3 hours*

Instead of crossing the main stream by the planks, cross the feeder stream ahead to the R and then climb over the wooden stile to continue uphill, walking E further along the valley. Beyond the next gate, the rugged moorland gives way to enclosed lush pastures which are a real joy to walk over. Do this by continuing to walk down the valley, keeping near to a walled forestry area on your L. Round the next bend and further on through the gaps in two stone walls, the most

superb views of Stanage Edge and Burbage Rocks open up ahead to the NE. The obvious way leads above Tor Farm, passing through a wooden gate and then rising slightly uphill. Along here, the large village which appears over to your L is Hathersage. Veer R along the farm entrance lane and over the next brow, where the way continues to descend down the valley. Win Hill is the pronounced peak which re-appears over to your L in the NW and from this viewpoint the summit area reveals its relative flatness whereas from the Hope side the pinnacle appears sharply pointed. Walk past a branch lane leading more steeply downhill at right angles on your L and then bear L along a better established lane. This lane descends further to pass the buildings of Hazelford Hall.

From the Hall, the way leads more steeply downhill to reach the B6001 road at MR 235803. Turn L along this busy road, walking NW along the shaded pavement to reach the conveniently situated Plough Inn, more often than not about lunchtime! The Inn has a sunken garden area. Past the inn, a stone four-arched bridge provides a grand crossing of the River Derwent. Then at the most northerly tip of the entire route, turn S along the public footpath signed to 'Grindleford'. From here, a surfaced drive leads eastwards and then southwards following the course of the river down the broad valley. There follows a delightful stretch of over 5 km (3 miles) along or above the banks of the tree-lined river brimming with wildlife. This part of the route also passes by or through the interesting hamlets of Nether Padley, Grindleford and Froggatt.

Following two cattle grids, the surfaced way terminates at the impressive private residence, Harper Lees. At this point veer R round the buildings along the waymarked path. For some distance now the path keeps to flat meadowlands as you continue southwards down the spacious valley. Stiles and gates come and go as the obvious route leads downstream to the National Trust Longshaw Estate at Coppice Wood. This is entered by means of a wicket gate. The next section of the route can be like a mud-bath after prolonged wet weather as it invariably is in winter. Further on, to provide a change from the more immediate

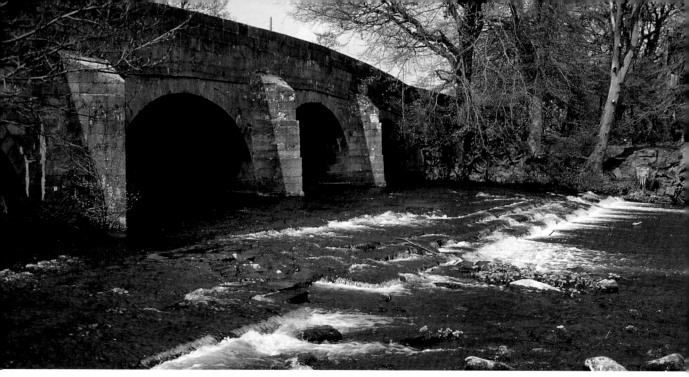

environs of the river, bear L uphill along a path forking off that way and climb to the top of the brow to gain more open and extensive views of the Derwent Valley. Further up, be careful to keep to the signed footpath which veers off abruptly to the L. From here, a narrow, boulder-strewn path leads more steeply uphill to a wicket gate above. Avoid crossing the railway line and instead veer to the R beyond the gate. Proceed across the high meadowland towards two disused stone gate-pillars. Pass between these and descend on a SSW diagonal back down to the river. To do so, walk through convenient gaps in stone walls and cross a farm track at right angles. Towards the bottom, two particularly nasty muddy patches have to be crossed.

Past these minor frustrations, veer L through the K-gate and then use the concrete span to cross the wide side-stream. From here, continue down the valley to re-connect with the series of well-used lower pathways. Along here, the densely forested slopes ahead on your L rise to the serrated top of Froggatt Edge. The next significant landmark reached is the B6521 road, between Nether Padley and Grindleford. This is at MR 246779. Cross over with care and turn R towards the traffic lights at the bridge. However, before reaching this junction turn off L through a K-gate to continue along the public footpath signed to 'Froggatt' (and to several other places).

17:1 The River Derwent near Leadmill

Follow the indicated way across flat meadowlands heading due S and slightly away from the Derwent. Then the path crosses a small brook and through the K-gate on the far side; veer R to resume your now predominant direction of travel, southwards downstream. The route, by means of a narrow G-stile, clips the fringe of Horse Hay Coppice. Further on, more extensive woodlands (Froggatt Wood) are entered. The next section can be extremely demanding with the route continuing through areas of heavy, clinging mud. This is particularly prevalent after prolonged wet weather in winter. Some improvements to the path have been carried out along here but these remain inadequate. Further on, a small stream flowing between large boulders is crossed, and a similar manoeuvre is repeated a short distance further on. Then the way emerges into open country again and the worst of the muddy ground is left behind. The entrance to a more interesting landscape is signalled by a narrow G-stile, the supporting pillars of which contain several large round holes. After this, the route continues across meadowland towards a stone barn on your L ahead. The way circles to the R and below this distinctive feature to reach another G-stile. Beyond this, a paved way leads further S between enclosing walls towards the village of Froggatt, some of the buildings of which are now visible ahead. The tiny hamlet is entered by way of Spooner Lane. This leads to Hollowgate, into which you veer R to continue along the elevated pavement lining the far side of the narrow lane.

The way back to Eyam   *Allow 1½ hours*

Past Derwent Farm, bear R to re-cross the River Derwent at the impressive former packhorse bridge (Froggatt Bridge). Then turn immediately L, to pass over a low s-stile positioned in a stone wall to continue, as directed, along the riverside path. The way then passes beneath a group of trees. After this, a double G-stile has to be negotiated and then, before reaching the sprawling copse of trees and scrubland ahead, bear off R up the grassy slopes following the faint path to pass through a gap in the stone wall above these trees. Veer further R beyond this to climb more steeply uphill. A short distance above, a gateway and G-stile are reached at the top of the field and they provide access to the B6001 road at MR 241756. Cross this road with care and continue W along the lane directly opposite that leads past Knouchley Farm. From here, the way continues to wind uphill passing to the R of the main grouping of farm buildings. At times, there can be a lot more mud about in this locality!

Immediately past the farm, be careful to veer L and to the SW to locate and cross a dilapidated stile in a stone wall adjacent to a metal gate. Be careful making this crossing, for the large stones on top are loose. From here, proceed W round the brow of the hill following the line of a guiding stone wall to your R. Thereafter, a more distinct, narrow path leads downhill, initially through clumps of gorse before it crosses open meadowland to reach Stoney Middleton. Beyond the K-gate, veer L down an internal village lane where you cannot fail to notice passing lamp post 76278! Then, in quick succession, the 'Roman Baths' and the towered parish church of St Martin are passed. Thereafter, follow the lane round to the R, and veer R again to proceed along the lane signed 'The Bank'. This leads to the Wesleyan Reform Church.

Here, keep straight ahead walking along the way signed public footpath to 'Eyam'. Beyond a rocky outcrop over to your L, clamber over the stile to continue up the grassy hillside, keeping to the route signed to 'Eyam 1½'. Your direction is now to the NW up a comfortable gradient. Over the next brow, the buildings of Eyam rise beyond a complicated series of walled meadows.

Through a G-stile, the way proceeds between enclosing, low limestone walling, at the end of which a narrower G-stile provides entry to the final approach back to the village. This entrance is along Lydgate, which bears several poignant testimonials to the dreadful plague of 1666, during which the villagers remained in self-imposed isolation so that this terrible pestilence was confined to Eyam. Cross through the centre of the village past the square (shaped more like a triangle) and continue westwards following the signs to Eyam Hall. This is along Church Street, and the way leads past Eyam Primary School and then the parish church of Saint Lawrence. A short distance past the Rose and Crown Inn, Hawkhill Road (off to the R) will lead you back to the car park.

Alternative routes

ESCAPES

This is a circular route across which there are no obvious satisfactory short-cuts. Therefore set out with the firm intention of completing most, if not all, of the route as described. As previously mentioned, the farmyard near the start can be avoided: turn R uphill from the car park and then use the track off on the L to connect with the main route described at MR 215774.

EXTENSIONS

Satisfactory extensions are not easy to find but one possibility for fit and energetic walkers is from Stoney Middleton: head S into Coombs Dale, then continue past the Sallet Hole Mine and Rough Side before circling back to approach Eyam by means of Eyam Dale, through which the B6521 runs.

Route 18: TIDESWELL, CHEE DALE and MILLER'S DALE

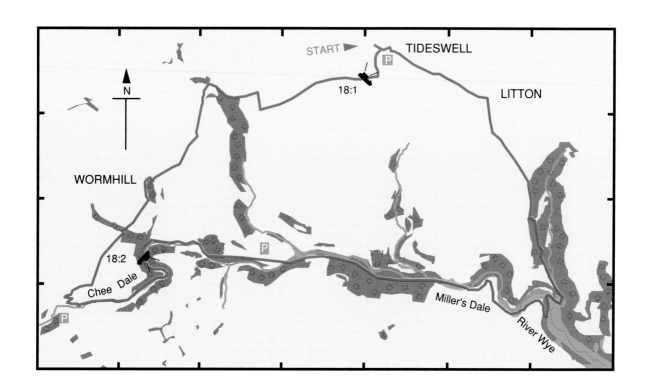

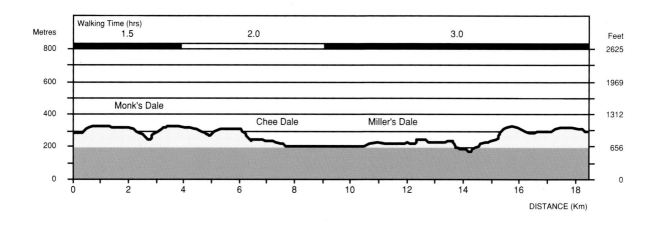

ROUTE 18

Tideswell, Chee Dale and Miller's Dale

●

STARTING LOCATION
Car park at Tideswell (Market Square).
OLM 24: MR 151758.
Spaces for about 15 to 20 cars – get there early!

ALTERNATIVE STARTING POINTS
Chee Dale.
Miller's Dale.

PUBLIC TRANSPORT
Principal town with extensive bus services.

OVERVIEW/INTEREST
Tremendous scenic variety, from open landscapes to deep gorges.
Super walk, one which families including teenagers should enjoy.
Fascinating limestone cliffs, columns and tors.
Lushness of Chee Dale, with interesting stepping stones.
Attractive villages and hamlets.
'The Cathedral of the Peak' at Tideswell.
Stocks and well at Wormhill.
Disused railway and lime kilns.

FOOTPATHS
Very good and dry for most of way.
The route through Chee Dale can be interesting when the River Wye is high!
Route finding is not difficult but patience is needed in some sections.

GRADING
Moderate.

TIME ALLOWANCE
6½ hours.

STATISTICS

DISTANCE

Excluding Height	18.5 km	(11.5 miles)
TOTAL HEIGHT GAINED	420 m	(1380 ft)
PRINCIPAL HEIGHTS		
Highest Point	330 m	(1085 ft)

The way to Wormhill
Allow 1½ hours

Before you depart from Tideswell you might like to visit the parish church of Saint John the Baptist. This quite delightful church is also known as 'The Cathedral of the Peak'. The building is superb and if your visit coincides with a flower festival you are in for a real treat. In 1993 a restoration appeal was launched for the church and this will extend for the subsequent five years.

Leave Tideswell along Parke Road located opposite the NatWest Bank, walking w uphill. The United Reformed Church is then passed on your R. Turn L at the T junction and then immediately R, after which veer L along a bridleway, walking sw still uphill. This route leads straight into open countryside with the village of Tideswell, dominated by its parish church, nestling down below within the folds of the lush, rounded hills. At the

18:1 Looking back over Tideswell

top of the brow select the s-stile on your r, between two gates, and over this the route continues w beside a dry-stone wall. Keep to this direction as a G-stile provides entrance to the next field. Several more of these stiles feature in rapid succession breaching parallel dry-stone walls across your path. Eventually the route bears L along a more distinctive diagonal.

More stiles, mainly of the step and gap variety, follow and at one of these be careful to avoid contact with barbed wire positioned dangerously close. Continue walking westwards; some distance on this will be downhill along a faintly defined path. The countryside hereabouts is a neat patchwork bounded by white limestone walls. Further on, one important stile to locate is at a wooden retaining fence towards the far end of a field and at which again care must be exercised not to tangle with barbed wire. Beyond this, continue beside a stone wall on your L. Then veer slightly r away from the wall to cross another stile. The path eventually reaches a walled bridleway at MR 138751 at which sign 217 belonging to 'The Peak and Northern Footpaths Society' has been re-positioned. Turn r here, walking n towards the road junction near which Monksdale House is situated. This section can be a bit muddy after heavy rain.

At the junction, turn L to walk downhill along the narrow surfaced lane which is part of the signed 'Limestone Way'. The lane leads down to the confluence of Monk's Dale to the se and Peter Dale to the nw. At the bottom of the hill the lane bends sharply to the L before bisecting the two dales. There is an informative 'English Nature' sign here. Turn L to pass through a G-stile and then turn r uphill, following the wide, grassy path ssw. Towards the top of the incline a gateway provides entrance to a fenced-off section as the steepish gradient slackens. Continue through a further G-stile, and then along an alternating stone and grass path between retaining walls. Two metal gates are reached in rapid succession before you bear further r towards the top of the hill, continuing sw along a wide path between stone walls. After passing through another G-stile, veer L along a wide, flat, grassy way between limestone walls.

This narrows further on as more interesting views appear ahead and to your L, featuring the wooded hillsides lining Miller's Dale to the sse. At the end of the walled way veer slightly r across the field ahead to locate a wooden gate and stile beneath a spreading hawthorn tree. The path here is signed and your continuation route is towards Wormhill to the wsw.

The way leads down to a wooden stile and to the r of a large metal farm gate. The stile gives access to an enclosed footpath, the direction of which is signed. Veer r ahead to pass first Holly House and then the entrance to St. Margaret's Church. Continue along the lane to reach Wormhill and the road passing through this delightful conclave opposite Wellhead Farm. This connection is made at MR 123742. The well, of well-dressing fame, is situated in a grassy dell just off to your r. A short distance further on you will come across the village stocks.

The way to the former railway station at Miller's Dale
Allow 2 hours

Retrace your steps to Wellhead Farm and continue s along the road. You will pass an amusing sign on a gate along here that reads 'Never mind the dog beware of the owner'. The road winds downhill and just past the Wormhill name sign be careful to locate a strategic stile on your r which you pass through to reach Hassop Farm, immediately ahead to the sw. Use the farm drive to pass between the buildings and then select the public footpath through the gate signed to 'Flag Dale'. Beyond this, walk diagonally across the adjacent field and then enter the next meadow by another gate. Continue along the established sw diagonal towards Flag Dale. Two stone walls converge at right angles on the next G-stile and through this the steep-sided dale emerges ahead. Part of Chee Dale also comes into view to your L. Descend sw towards Flag Dale and be careful to locate a further G-stile through a stone wall which is somewhat hidden beneath hawthorn trees. From here, a grassy track leads steeply down into the remote dale. No sooner are you at the bottom than an equally steep path leads you out of Flag Dale and you regain the height just previously surrendered. This ascent brings you to another G-stile.

Veer L along the signed footpath ahead, still gaining height to the ssw. Then veer further L to pass through an indistinct G-stile within a dilapidated stone wall next to a retaining post. Cross the field beyond on a ssw diagonal, passing beneath overhead power lines. Breach the next stone wall at the collapsed G-stile and keep on a diagonal which will bring you to the more clearly identifiable stile in the far corner of the next field. This is to the L of a metal gate and when last visited was also in need of repair. Beyond this, a walled track leads ssw beside a plantation towards Mosley Farm situated at MR 730116. The track bears R to pass through an assortment of farm buildings and equipment. Beyond these and at a point where the surfaced farm lane bears sharply R, turn off to the L through a gap in a stone wall to continue downhill along a wide, grassy path. Here, the impressive limestone cliffs of Chee Dale may be observed rising almost vertically ahead to your L. The path veers initially to the R before descending steeply into Chee Dale. The main path then curves to the L and as it does so ignore a side route through a gap in the stone wall on your R.

The path traverses R and then L down into the depths of Chee Dale. Towards the bottom of the valley the official path turns sharply to the R before bending under the disused railway bridge. Emerging from this, another diagonal leads down to the banks of the River Wye. Turn sharply L at the bottom and then cross a stone wall by means of a s-stile. Following this, the path leads pleasantly eastwards beside the fast-flowing, meandering stream through the impressive gorge of Chee Dale. Initially, there are sections of this path which are often boggy; further on there are two series of stepping stones which the river, when in flood, can completely submerge, making progress further downstream relatively precarious.

At the viaduct ahead ignore the bridge across the river and continue by descending the stone steps on the L, keeping to the L bank of the stream along the stony path through overgrown vegetation. The path is somewhat insecure, so watch each step. (Families with younger children may conveniently avoid the worst stretches along this interesting but exacting river bank by utilizing part of the disused railway line above.) Stiles and railway arches come and go before the first set of stepping stones is reached. These lead round a protruding rocky bluff that climbers appear unable to resist. Lower downstream, the river is crossed and then re-crossed at footbridges. When on the far bank, keep to the lower footpath signed to 'Miller's Dale'. Another series of stepping stones is then crossed round a further rocky protrusion and under a rounded overhang where the trick is to avoid the incessantly, dripping water.

Eventually, the way climbs up a rocky staircase and over several tributary watercourses, and a stile in a wall is crossed. After a more open stretch in which water channels abound, veer R at the fork ahead along the lower of a choice of ways. The predominant direction of travel is now almost due E, directly towards Miller's Dale. The manoeuvre up another stepped funnel is repeated as the gorge widens between less steep slopes which become more wooded. Continue beside the river to join the 'Monsal Trail', now along a surfaced path. At the next imposing viaduct, use the steps on your L to depart from the dale, following the direction signed 'Monsal Trail'. Some of the flagged steps here contain crinoid fossils. At the top, veer L along the wide Monsal Trail, which then passes a disused lime kiln. Fast progress can be made to reach the stark and rather sombre remains of the former Miller's Dale Railway Station at MR 138733. There are extensive car parking facilities and toilets here, and also a mobile Peak National Park Information Centre.

The way back to Tideswell   *Allow 3 hours*

From the station continue further E along the Monsal Trail to cross a complicated double bridge system spanning the valley at a great height. Stick tenaciously to the trail, avoiding all side paths as more abandoned kilns are passed. Further on, the route leads beneath an arched stone bridge and beyond this avoid yet another turning off on the L.

18:2 The River Wye flowing through lush vegetation in Chee Dale

This one is signed 'Monsal Trail via Water-cum-Jolly'. This means that you must continue along the elevated way which is somewhat disturbingly signed 'No through way 250 yards ahead'! (The suggested way does in fact lead to a concessionary path.) Walk towards the blocked-off former railway tunnel straight ahead. Before reaching this impenetrable obstacle, escape along a side path signed 'No access – Dangerous'. This is presumably another 'put-off' intended for casual and unprepared strollers, as ahead there is a stile and a dog-gate! Follow the narrower path uphill which crosses another path on an acute diagonal further up. Then be careful to keep to the main, higher path which continues E until, near a distinctive rocky bluff, your path converges with another way coming in on your R.

After reaching a grassy flat area near to a series of disused mine caves, veer L along a clear, narrow path which passes a solitary, sapling ash. Be careful now in crossing some eroded ground but the exposure here is only temporary and then quite minimal. Further on, a lone beech tree is passed. Always keep to the clear path as it follows the meanders of the dale at an elevated height which undulates. After crossing a wooden stile, the going becomes appreciably easier along the now densely wooded dale. Keep to the obvious path along here, passing over another wooden stile. Water-cum-Jolly is then revealed down below. After crossing a small section of loose scree, the path rises in its approach to Cressbrook then drops to pass the extensive former mill buildings situated below. You are now informed (by means of an official Peak National Park sign) that you have been walking along the alternative concession footpath. Just past this belated confirmation of the permissive route, turn acutely back to your L at the intersection ahead, along the Monsal Trail, and then traverse diagonally downhill to the NNE towards the huge, disused mill below.

The bottom stretch is down a steeper gradient by means of stone steps. The River Wye is crossed once more at the bottom, just below an impressive weir. Then bear L across open ground to pass the excavations of the Stancliffe Stone Co. and, following this, the remains of the derelict buildings of Cressbrook Mill. Beyond the entrance to the former mill turn L along the lower of two lanes, which is signed to 'Cresswell and Litton'. The lane climbs uphill by means of a long traverse to the NNW. Further up avoid, by continuing to walk uphill, the surfaced side lane leading off R into Ravensdale and signed 'No through road'. Then at an extremely sharp hair-pin bend to the L, continue straight ahead along the wide, compacted path that leads N beneath trees. Ahead, fork to the L along the narrower, higher path. The way leads up a flight of stone and wooden-buttressed steps. These provide a short, swift and demanding exit from the confines of the valley up steep, wooded slopes.

The way then levels off and leads for some distance beside a stone wall to your L. This leads you into open country once again. The exit from the more confined space is at an elevated wooden stile on your L. Cross the adjacent field on a diagonal to your R, walking towards the village of Litton to the NNW. After passing through a G-stile continue on the established diagonal, now walking directly in line with the village. The pronounced wooded escarpment further away to the NNE is Great Hucklow and Hucklow Edge of gliding fame. Ahead, the distinctive landmarks of Rushup Edge, the Mam Tor ridge leading to Lose Hill and the tor of Win Hill appear to the N, seen through the wide gap in the nearer, lower hills. From here an obvious path leads across fields and through further stiles towards Litton. The final approach

sequence to the village is rather complicated and is achieved by means of a s-stile, crossing a field, a gap, crossing another field, a s-stile, crossing a walled bridleway, another stile, crossing a field containing an electric livestock wire, then crossing another field to reach a s-stile, before a clear path leads uphill over a grassy brow to bring you to a stile that provides access to a walled farm track. (Best of luck with all this!) At this final obstacle there is a signpost seemingly positioned with intent to catch the unwary in the eye!

Turn L and then immediately R to follow the lane into the village of Litton. At the T junction ahead, turn L along the road signed to 'Tideswell and Miller's Dale'. Cross over the road and walk along the adjacent footpath to pass, in quick succession, the primary school, stocks and the tiny Red Lion Inn. The rising, straight road ahead will lead you back towards Tideswell, just over 1 km (0.6 miles) away to the NW. When the road swings to the R on the outskirts of the village, use the footpath off to the L and then branch R to reach the main part of the village below, directly opposite the George Hotel. Turn L and make your way round the parish church back to the car park at Market Square.

Alternative routes

ESCAPES

The most obvious short-cut is to use the footpath through Monk's Dale to avoid the extended loop by way of Wormhill and Chee Dale. The main route can be regained at Miller's Dale, or alternatively, you may continue along the valley to reconnect with it at Cressbrook. Another variant is to use Tideswell Dale on your return, either from the previously mentioned shorter circuit, or from the main route.

EXTENSION

An interesting extension, which can be decided upon late in the day, is to continue further N up Cressbrook Dale and then use Tansley Dale to reach Litton.

Route 19: MILLER'S DALE, CHEE DALE, CHELMORTON and TADDINGTON

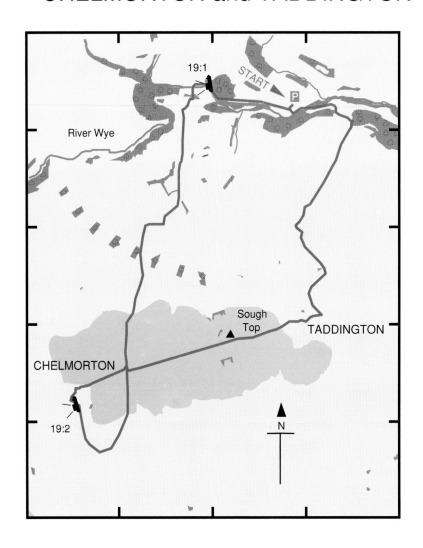

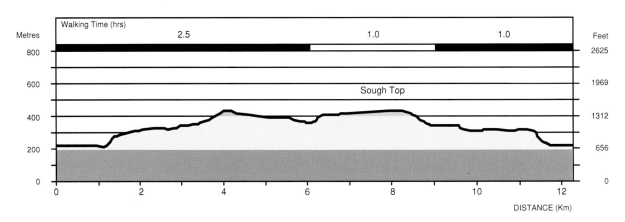

ROUTE 19

Miller's Dale, Chee Dale, Chelmorton and Taddington

---•---

STARTING LOCATION
Car park at Miller's Dale former railway station.
OLM 24: MR 138733.
Extensive parking facilities, toilets and mobile
  information van.

ALTERNATIVE STARTING POINTS
Chelmorton.
Taddington.
(No dedicated parking facilities though.)

PUBLIC TRANSPORT
Bus routes 65, 66, 181, 202, 309 and 795.

OVERVIEW/INTEREST
Exhilarating start along steep-sided Miller's and
  Chee Dales.
Then across pleasant, rolling, open landscapes.
Villages of Chelmorton and Taddington visited.
Opportunity for pub lunch.
Route passes by interesting quarry faces and disused
  lime kilns.
Overall a most pleasant and rewarding walk.

FOOTPATHS
For the greater part paths are good, firm and
  relatively easy to follow.
Route signing is adequate.
Plenty of stiles to squeeze through.

GRADING
Moderate.

TIME ALLOWANCE
4½ hours.

STATISTICS

DISTANCE

Excluding Height	12.3 km	(7.6 miles)
TOTAL HEIGHT GAINED	320 m	(1050 ft)
PRINCIPAL HEIGHTS		
Blackwell Hall	330 m	(1085 ft)
Nr Fivewells Farms	430 m	(1410 ft)
Sough Top	438 m	(1440 ft)

The way to Chelmorton   *Allow 2½ hours*

From the car parking area walk westwards by the side of the former railway platforms, passing by the toilet block on your R. Continue w along the Monsal Trail walking towards an elongated limestone cutting to your R. Towards the end of this cutting and at the termination of the platforms, turn abruptly L down a narrow path signed to 'Miller's Dale'. From here, a clear, compacted path leads steeply down steps into the narrow, winding valley. At the bottom and just before reaching the road, turn R to pass through a stepped G-stile in the adjacent stone wall and then turn back R again in order to continue up the path which meanders w upstream along the R-hand bank of the River Wye. The way leads through an agreeable wooded area and progress along this stretch is absorbing and always full of interest.

Further on, the way passes beneath a massive arched viaduct. Just beyond this ignore a stepped path leading off to your R and signed to 'Monsal Trail'. Instead, continue along the banks of the river up the path of firm, compacted soil and stones. A short distance beyond, the slopes on the near side of the dale begin to assume greater interest in the form of impressive limestone outcrops which rise to your R. The way then leads to an elevated footbridge over the river, which you cross. This is at MR 128734. The continuation way is uphill to the s and is signed to 'Blackwell'. This tiny settlement lies across the rolling hillsides just over 1 km (0.6 miles) away, but first you have to climb out of Chee Dale. To do this select the less

119

19:1 The crossing of the River Wye in Chee Dale

distinct path which veers slightly to the R up the grassy slope ahead, being careful to ignore a more pronounced path on the L. The correct ascent veers further R and the path becomes better defined higher up. Following this, the remains of a dilapidated limestone wall are breached at a gap as the way climbs the grassy slopes.

Higher still, the path runs for some distance beside a wire fence which encloses a copse of deciduous trees. Be careful along one narrow passage here for you come perilously close to some barbed wire! When you reach the remains of another dilapidated stone wall leading off southwards at right angles to your direction of approach, turn L beside it and continue up the more gentle final slopes of the hillside, initially keeping the remains of the wall to your R. Your direction along here is SSW. Further up, pass through one of several gaps in the stone wall. Just ahead lies a surprise for first-time visitors, for over

the brow of the slope is a really stupendous view down along the deeply-cut, contorting, narrow valley of Chee Dale.

When you have seen enough, veer L along the grassy ledge being circumspect about the deep fall-away immediately to your R, and continue SE with the remains of the stone wall to your L. Further on, the way passes above a series of almost vertical limestone cliffs and from here there are further magnificent views down into the looping dale. When your guiding wall bends away at right angles to the L, simply follow it. A short distance further on, your circuitous route connects with the main, signed public footpath, which does not provide comparable viewing positions to those you have just visited. Turn R along this path to continue due S along a wide, grassy sward. Ahead, you reach a S-stile which provides a crossing of a stone wall. Be careful here because the smooth limestone blocks can be quite slippery! Walk round part of the perimeter of the next large field, hugging the boundary wall along the R-hand edge. This typifies what follows, as the next part of the route crosses a flat, rural landscape which contains orderly meadows punctuated by isolated clumps of trees. Veer R at the end of the field to pass over another S-stile and, after this, proceed along the obvious enclosed way round to the L to maintain your southerly direction of travel.

A gate then provides access to a farm track which you follow to reach the extensive buildings at Blackwell Hall, but not before another tight squeeze through a particularly narrow gap to the L of a wooden gate. The Hall is situated at MR 126723. Pass through the extensive farmyard area and exit via the access lane on the far side. From here, the continuation route dips pleasantly downhill along a minor surfaced lane. Rolling green hills beckon you ahead. When you reach the entrance gates to the Hall, veer R along the lane walking W towards Cottage Farm Caravan Park. Neat cottages and farmsteads are next passed over to your R and further on a huge barn appears before you reach the caravan enclosure. Then the lane bends sharply to the L and some distance further on the main A6(T) road has to be crossed. Do this with care. Then continue southwards along the lane directly opposite, walking slightly uphill towards the green slopes occupying the horizon ahead. The lane bends sharply to the R and a short distance beyond this, just before reaching the double gates marking the entrance to a quarry in-fill area, veer L to pass through a metal gateway. From here, a grassy bridleway leads further uphill between stone walling.

The route then passes through another metal gate near the brow of the hill. Just beyond this, ignore a way off to your L signed 'Concession path to Five Wells Cairn only'. Instead, continue straight ahead, walking due S to pass over the brow. As you start your modest descent you are rewarded with revelations of another massive landscape of rolling countryside, this one partly spoilt by savage quarrying operations. The excellent way progresses further S down gentle slopes

and before long you will be standing at the intersection of the lane leading to Fivewells Farms. In this vicinity two footpaths, one leading off to the L and the other to the R, are spurned – but mark them well for you will make use of these later on. Instead, keep walking steadfastly down the dead straight lane ahead (now macadam) as it provides a quick crossing of elevated terrain. Further on, the lane connects with the back road linking the villages of Taddington and Chelmorton. Bear slightly to the R along this, heading towards Chelmorton. Then veer further R when you reach the major road ahead at MR 119696.

A short distance further on, turn R again along the side lane which leads NW above the main part of the village which can now be seen down below on your L. Pass by a path leading down towards the lower part of the village and retain your height by continuing along the lane leading directly towards the spired church. This is located at the dead-end, topmost part of the sprawling conurbation. Follow the road, in the form of Church Lane, round to the R and a short distance uphill you will come to St John the Baptist Church. Opposite the church is the Church Inn, where walkers are made welcome.

The way to Taddington   *Allow 1 hour*

The village of Taddington lies less than 3 km (1.9 miles) away to the ENE. To reach it is relatively straightforward but it does involve having to pass through a multitude of narrow G-stiles. Start by walking uphill away from the village and then veer R at the fork ahead. From here, the route continues up a wide, grassy enclosed way. A short distance further on, you must ignore a stile and narrow path leading off on your L. The path widens as it leads above the church and, following this, the way straightens out along a diagonal pointing E up a gradual incline. Further on, the loop is completed when you arrive back by means of a G-stile at a point you have previously visited. This is located at MR 121706. Turn R, but only retrace your previous steps for a few paces before, on this second visit, turning off to the L over the S-stile. This is along the path signed 'Taddington 1½'.

The next part of the route is along a bee-line ENE to reach the elevated Sough Top Service Reservoir positioned at MR 134709. To get there cross the first field on this exact bearing to reach the first of several step stiles which cross limestone retaining walls running at right angles to your direction of approach. The way then leads beside limestone walling immediately on your L. Before reaching a trig point towards the edge of the high ground you are walking across, you will have to pass over or through no fewer than 10 more stiles. One of these contains a boarding which has uncovered barbed wire stapled to it, so watch out for this!

The trig point is eventually passed to your L and just beyond this the elevated reservoir is reached. At this point the path veers R to pass below the tiny water catchment. Cross the adjacent field on a diagonal, walking down the slope to the R to reach another S-stile at which there is a sign confirming that you are using a public footpath! At this point and in clear weather, the shape of Monsal Dale can be made out far away to the ENE. Now bear further R and continue down the broad, grassy band which leads towards the village of Taddington nestling below. The route continues along a well-used path and further down the hillside a stone wall has to be breached at a point where the way is again signed to 'Taddington'. Then the steeper part of the descent terminates at a narrow S-stile followed by a G-stile positioned at a minor

lane. Cross this lane to continue your diagonal approach downhill towards the buildings below where another G-stile soon has to be negotiated. At the bottom of the final field, a stone S-stile provides an entrance to a narrow ginnel which in turn leads into the village at Humphrey Gate. Cross over the road and pass through the wrought iron gateway before walking along a narrow, walled pathway which leads to the paths across the church grounds. The fine spired church is St Michael and All Angels parish church of Taddington.

The way back to Miller's Dale   *Allow 1 hour*

Exit from the church lands by means of the G-stile in the top far L-hand corner. Continue N beside a stone wall to your R to reach and cross once again the main A6(T) road. The road is reached at a combined gap-and-step stile. Having crossed at a dual carriageway section, turn R and within 50 paces you will come to a similar exit stile positioned on your L. Over this, turn R to follow the broad path leading NE. You will then come to an enclosed wide, grassy track and at this point be vigilant to locate and pass through a G-stile in the wall on your L. From here, walk NNW towards a small group of trees where another G-stile is located. This enables you to cross a stone wall barring your line of approach. Beyond this, continue downhill along a much clearer path, walking

19:2 The view westwards beyond Chelmorton

NW and passing an English Nature sign which may be of some marginal assistance to you. Keep to the indicated public footpath which then winds further downhill to your L. Lower down, two miniature G-stiles are used and a short distance past these the first buildings of Priestcliffe are reached. Two more G-stiles line the crossing of a muddy farm track and more churned-up ground has to be crossed before cleaner, grassy slopes are scaled. The correct route here is indicated by yellow daubings.

At the top of the slope you will reach a high s-stile which is quite awkward to get over due to the way it slants. Then turn R along the narrow lane and then bear further R at the wider lane immediately above. This almost instantly leads you out of the village and you next veer to the L to pass round Lydgate Farm. This is along the way indicated by the sign reading 'Miller's Dale'. Continue for a short distance down the wide track with a grassed-over middle section before turning off to your R to pass over a stile before walking along the path on the far side, again signed to 'Miller's Dale'. From here, proceed downhill following a diagonal to your L to then pass through a gap in a stone wall, also on your L. Thereafter, maintain this established direction of travel to the NE as it leads up hill and down dale across undulating terrain. The route along this section is easy to follow through a succession of stiles of varying shapes and sizes. There are seven of these in all.

Then quite suddenly there are stupendous sightings down into narrow limestone gorges, this time along part of the lengths of Miller's and Monk's Dales. Additionally, across the flat plains on the far sides of these rifts, the tips of the buildings of Tideswell can be observed to the NNE. From your vantage point follow the path by turning first sharp R and then veer L along it to commence your adventurous descent back into Miller's Dale. The way is down a narrow path of compacted earth which can become slippery when wet. Extensive former quarry workings scar the steeply falling slopes to your L. Be extremely careful along here and make good use of the protective iron barrier rail to help control your rapid rate of descent! The route then swings to the L and at the bottom of the slope, when a natural flattish ridge is reached, veer further L to follow the concessionary path which then enters a nature reserve established in 1974.

From here, the correct route is helpfully indicated by a series of white-topped posts. The way then undulates and you should have little difficulty locating each successive marker post, although the occasional one is quite cunningly concealed. Some distance further on, the massive twin viaduct spanning Miller's Dale and the remains of the station come into view. This respresents your cue for descending into the dale and this you do a short distance further on by following the path as it bends back acutely to the R and then traverses down towards the valley floor along a straight diagonal. Part way down you will come to a battery of four disused lime kilns, well worth a cursory inspection. Below this feature, a concrete, stepped path descends steeply to the Monsal Trail. Turn L, cross the impressive viaduct, and the former railway station is on the R.

Alternative routes

ESCAPE

The obvious short-cut is when you first come to MR 121705: turn L and head straight towards Taddington, thus cutting out the loop which takes in Chelmorton.

EXTENSIONS

It is feasible for strong walkers to continue further W along delightful Chee Dale before selecting one of a number of alternative longer routes which lead southwards across open country to connect with the main route at Chelmorton. If you decide to do this, beware of the following two constraints. Firstly, Chee Dale contorts all over the place and a seemingly short direct map distance almost invariably takes longer to complete than you might plan. Secondly, there are two series of stepping stones in the dale which become submerged beneath fast-flowing water when the river is in spate.

Route 20: ASHFORD in the WATER, LONGSTONE VILLAGES and MONSAL DALE

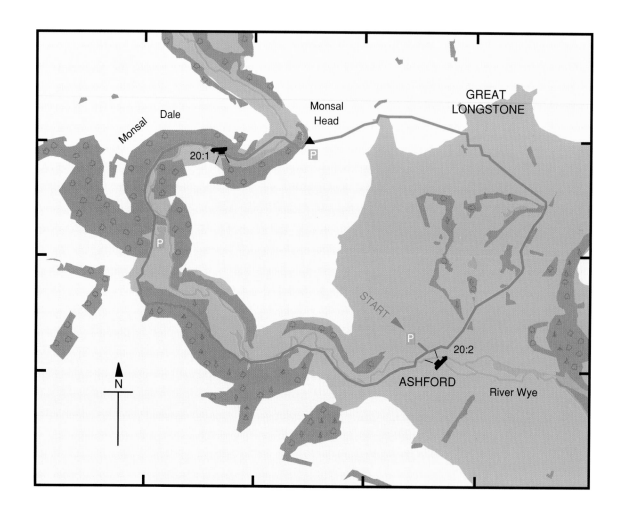

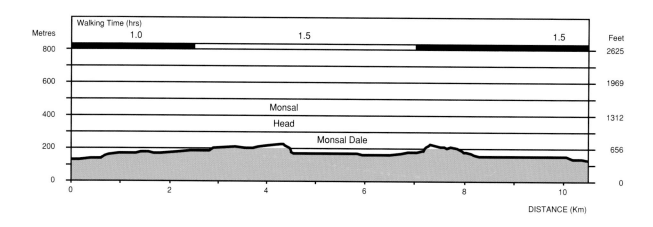

ROUTE 20

Ashford in the Water, Longstone Villages and Monsal Dale

•

STARTING LOCATION
Car park at Ashford.
OLM 24: MR 195698.
Tiny car park with toilet facilities; holds between 10 and 15 cars depending upon neatness of parking!
Additional parking within village.

ALTERNATIVE STARTING POINTS
Great Longstone.
Monsal Head.
White Lodge at Lees Bottom.

PUBLIC TRANSPORT
Bus services 58, 68, 153, 173, 202, R1 and X23.

OVERVIEW/INTEREST
Great family walk full of interest.
Good scenery throughout with some really exciting views.
Fine halls and other stately buildings.
Varied countryside ranging from rural landscapes to spectacular limestone gorges.
The fairytale setting of Ashford.

Plenty of animals, both farmyard species and wildlife.
Save this one for a warm, sunny day!

FOOTPATHS
Excellent throughout.
Muddy patches rare.
The route is well signposted for most of the way and route finding presents few challenges.

GRADING
Easy/straightforward.

TIME ALLOWANCE
4 hours.

STATISTICS

DISTANCE		
Excluding Height	10.5 km	(6.5 miles)
TOTAL HEIGHT GAINED	200 m	(655 ft)
PRINCIPAL HEIGHTS		
Monsal Head	235 m	(770 ft)

The way to Great Longstone   *Allow 1 hour*

Turn sharp R on leaving the car park to squeeze through a narrow G-stile which provides the entrance to a children's play area. Walk NE along the macadam path running adjacent to and above this recreational area. Exit through a wider gap and continue along the subsequent enclosed pathway. Turn R at the T junction ahead and walk down towards the centre of the village. Cross over the B6465 and continue along this road until you reach a junction opposite the Ashford Hotel. Turn L along Church Street and take the next turn to the L to reach the main A6020 road to Baslow. Walk NE along this, using the pavement.

Just before reaching a progressively sharpening bend in the road to the L, cross the busy thorough-fare with care and select a public footpath leading off on your R. This is entered by means of a G-stile. The way crosses a tiny brook, then beyond a latched gate proceed up the opposite slope, passing through a small plantation of sapling trees. Clamber over the stile at the top of the brow. From here, a diagonal route to the L across the adjacent rising field will bring you to another stile, this a ladder one. The approach direction is to the ENE. From here, there are fine views back down into the valley towards Ashford. In competition Long-stone Edge rises to the N.

Keep to your established NE diagonal to reach another L-stile, in a limestone wall. The path veers to the L beyond this, round the grounds of stately Church Dale Hall. Thereafter, the way for a stretch is across flat but interesting meadowlands which are pleasantly sprinkled with trees. An obvious way leads to yet another stile and following this bear L along the macadam in the direction indicated by the public footpath sign. Follow the lane round to the right and away from the hall, walking towards Churchdale Farm, which is passed on the L. Continue down the lane until you reach the somewhat complicated intersection of busier roads below. This is at MR 206709. In your approach to this intersection the village of Great Longstone first comes into view ahead on the L nestling beneath the long escarpment.

Carefully cross over the roadway immediately in front of you and then continue up the road signed to 'Gt Longstone and Rowland'. Pass beneath the Monsal Trail before taking the next footpath off on your L signed to 'Great Longstone ½'. Your path then threads NW for a short distance below the main Monsal Trail through scrubland, with open views to your R. Then abruptly select a continuation path off to the R which is accessed by means of scrambling over a stone S-stile. Past this obstacle, veer L to strike a NW diagonal across the adjacent meadowlands making directly towards Great Longstone, which is over the brow of the hill ahead.

Further on, pass through a G-stile before the way continues NW and passes between two more G-stiles, after the second of which the route turns sharply to the L to lead along an enclosed path beside dwellings. This brings you to the cul-de-sac ending of one of the avenues of a housing estate. A kind lady resident then suggested the following route through this built-up area: 'Cross over and continue down Grisedale Road East. Pass by Croft Road leading off on the R and proceed to the far end of Grisedale Road East. Then use the continuation pavement on the L-hand side, bearing L and then R to enter Grisedale Road. Walk to the end of this road passing by The Close and at the T junction ahead turn R to pass round the immaculately maintained gardens of Windy Acre and continue along the road. Cross over and, a short distance further on, veer L down the public footpath starting from MR 199716.' The final path mentioned is accessed through a gap in limestone walling.

The way to White Lodge car park

Allow 1½ hours

Another G-stile provides entry to open country again. The next section of the route is westwards through an attractive rural landscape, the rich pastures of which support sheep and the raising of spring lambs. The way is directly towards the twin village of Little Longstone situated less than 1 km (0.6 miles) away. Further on, as the ground ahead dips, the distinctive outline of a deep limestone dale stands out ahead to the L – this is part of Monsal Dale, your next major objective. The obvious well-trodden way leads further westwards across numerous meadows and a series of minor obstructions: two G-stiles, the crossing of a farm track, two more G-stiles and a final S-stile. This succession leads down to the road which connects the two villages and is reached at an unusually complicated arrangement of gates and stone S-stiles which accommodate another path converging at this spot.

Over whichever stile you choose, turn L along the road and pass through the village, using the pavement provided. The route leads conveniently right past the Pack Horse Inn. After this, ignore a footpath off to the R signed to 'Wardlow' and instead continue WSW along the road out of the village, heading directly towards Monsal Dale. In doing this you will pass the tiny Congregational Church of Little Longstone. The B6465 road is reached at Monsal Head, directly opposite the hotel of that name. Cross the road with care, as this intersection can be frighteningly busy at times, and continue along the side road which is signed to 'Upperdale and Cressbrook'. Walk to the edge of the short-term car park on the R, to observe the superb views from here down into Monsal Dale. Directly opposite this car park, select the footpath leading down into the dale and waysigned 'Monsal Dale Viaduct and Trail'. This path is accessed by means of a G-stile in the limestone parapet.

Through the stile, veer R and walk down the stepped way. Turn L part-way down, to follow the path waysigned to 'Viaduct and Monsal Trail'. From here, the route leads more steeply down to reach the Monsal Trail. Turn ʀ, away from the blocked-off tunnel and use the impressively high viaduct to cross the River Wye. It is interesting to ponder in passing over that this viaduct, now listed as being of historical and architectural interest, was once the subject of fierce controversy as the invasion of the upper Wye Valley by the railway aroused heated opposition from numerous quarters at the time.

The views from the viaduct, in either direction, are a sheer delight in fine weather and the spaciousness of the high-level crossing is almost overpowering. Immediately the far side of the valley is reached, pass through the swing gate to your ʟ and descend down the steep, narrow path,

off on your ʟ again, to the valley floor below. The route then continues along the wide valley path away from the viaduct, downstream. To your ʟ the River Wye is almost motionless, its waters momentarily trapped on a flattish stretch, prior to entering the (by comparison) white-water rapids a short distance further down the valley. Above, steep-sided and densely wooded slopes complete a picture of charm and tranquillity, the quietness of which is usually only punctuated by the squawking of waterfowl splashing about in the calm waters.

20:1 Cosy family picnic beside the River Wye in Monsal Dale

Further on, the dale develops more gorge-like characteristics as massive, craggy bluffs of exposed limestone invade and punctuate, with their sharper and more irregular features, the otherwise rounded, steep grassy slopes lining the valley. Then a weir is reached and this particular one has a surprisingly large drop. Continue past this down the dale, keeping to the R-hand bank of the river by avoiding a footbridge spanning the stream. Further on, you will come across a fallen tree which straddles the path and which is still causing an obstruction despite someone's valiant efforts to cut through. When you arrive at a choice of ways ahead, keep to the path nearest to the river in order to maintain the better, more open views along the near bank of the meandering waters. From here, continue downstream along the spacious dale to connect eventually with the main A6(T) road at MR 171706. Just before reaching this major highway, a side stream has to be crossed by means of stepping stones in a locality which can quite often be muddy, and following this, at the top of the far brow, stone steps lead to a G-stile which provides an entrance to the road. Cross this busy road to reach the vicinity of the White Lodge car park located at Lees Bottom.

The way back to Ashford   *Allow 1½ hours*

Make towards the first parking area but, before reaching this, peel off to the R and walk up the slopes leading to a S-stile above. At this stile, the route beyond is waysigned 2 and 3. (These numbers refer to local walks.) Ahead, continue along the lower path waysigned 3 and this indicative number will remain with you as you return to Ashford. The way then leads towards limestone cliffs rearing up almost vertically ahead on your R. The path bears R in line with these pinnacles and your immediate surrounds become more enclosed for a time as the way threads through a narrow, rocky gully.

When the limestone crags branch quite spectacularly ahead, keep to the L-hand fork by clambering over the S-stile to your L as indicated by walking route 3. From here, a rocky path winds up the steeper slopes between impressive limestone faces. The next section of the route is steeper still and the going is relatively demanding for a short spell. Along here, further progress is made to the S before the route swings westwards and then along a continuation footpath signed to 'Ashford and Sheldon'. Again route 3 is indicated. Further height is then quickly gained along a steep, straight traverse. Higher up still, be vigilant to fork L and to the E, back towards the River Wye, now far below. This is achieved by crossing over a wooden bridging of a gap in the stone wall to your L. The correct way is again denoted number 3.

From here, a narrow, exposed path curves to the R round the steep contours of the hillside and in negotiating this stretch be particularly vigilant of the steep fall-away on your L. Should there be younger children in your party, take the precaution of grasping these in a vice-like hand grip until the potential danger is passed. Fortunately this occurs very quickly indeed. Height is then gradually but progressively surrendered as the path winds down eastwards through extensive woodlands. These fine, mature trees are located in Great Shacklow Wood. Further on, ignore a footpath off to the L almost indistinguishably signed to the 'A6 road'. The correct way straight ahead is signed to 'Ashford and Bakewell'. Immediately after this, another way has to be avoided, on this occasion one that leads uphill to the R by way of wooden steps.

Connection is once more made with the River Wye in the vicinity of several attractive pools situated to the L in a shaded area. A wide path continues from here further E down the valley, for a spell tenaciously following the meanderings of the river. Along this stretch, a most unusual derelict building is passed. This is Shacklow Mill, which once required water power: there are two large, rusting water-wheels on either side of the dilapidated structure. Just beyond this interesting feature, bypass the arched bridge spanning the river, keeping steadfastly to the R-hand bank of the stream. Then another stile has to be climbed, again in company with walkers following route 3, and at the following stile and wide gap (which presumably represents a former gateway) veer L,

20:2 Sheepwash Bridge spanning the River Wye at Ashford

keeping to the valley pathway. From here, the route leads back towards the village of Ashford. Then a final L-stile provides the opening to a lane that you veer L down. This in turn winds down to the A6(T) road which you again have to cross with care, on this occasion crossing opposite the venerable, medieval packhorse bridge which is now called Sheepwash Bridge. Across this, veer to the L along Fennel Street and the car park is reached following a final R-hand turn.

Alternative routes

ESCAPES

The most obvious short-cut is from MR 206710 to use part of the Monsal Trail to reach the viaduct below Monsal Head. There are also direct paths leading NNW from Ashford to Little Longstone which avoid the necessity of visiting the larger, more intensively populated twin village of Great Longstone.

EXTENSIONS

An interesting addition is from just beyond Lees Bottom at MR 169702: instead of turning to the L, turn R, and from here circle through Deep Dale and the village of Sheldon before tracking N again to re-connect with the main route in Great Shacklow Wood at MR 176698.

129

Route 21: BASLOW, CHATSWORTH PARK and EDENSOR

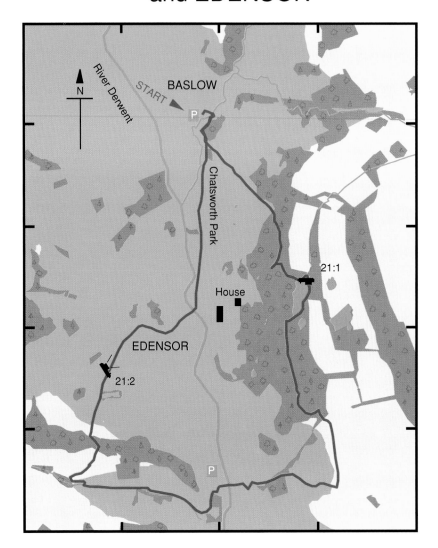

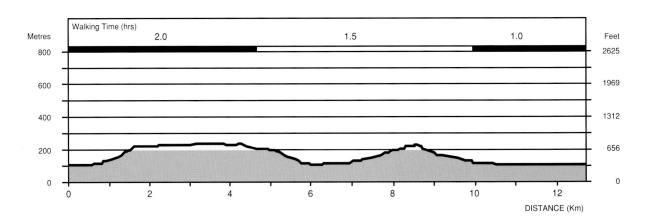

ROUTE 21

Baslow, Chatsworth Park and Edensor

●

STARTING LOCATION
Car park at Baslow.
OLM 24: MR 258721.
Large car park with toilets.

ALTERNATIVE STARTING POINTS
Chatsworth Park.
Edensor.

PUBLIC TRANSPORT
Principal town with extensive bus services.

OVERVIEW/INTEREST
Fine, enjoyable family outing.
Interesting views all the way.
Chatsworth Parklands, Gardens and House.
Deer Park.
Attractive villages and churches.
Pleasant, sheltered landscapes.

FOOTPATHS
Good, and usually dry and firm.
Notable absence of waterlogged ground or difficult
   terrain.
No appreciable steep gradients.
Route finding straightforward.
Way well signed.

GRADING
Easy/straightforward.

TIME ALLOWANCE
4½ hours.

STATISTICS

DISTANCE

Excluding Height	12.7 km	(7.9 miles)
TOTAL HEIGHT GAINED	260 m	(855 ft)
PRINCIPAL HEIGHTS		
Edge above Chatsworth	240 m	(785 ft)

The way to Beeley Hilltop (MR 268685)

Allow 2 hours

Turn R out of the car park to pass Lana's sweets (old-fashioned varieties) shop on your R. Cross the stream, Bar Brook, by the hump-backed bridge and then turn immediately R along the public footpath signed to 'Chatsworth' to pass a group of thatched cottages by walking S. The way leads to an entrance into Chatsworth Park accessed by means of a high wrought iron K-gate but before reaching this, avoid passing through another K-gate on your R. There are several recognized routes across the flat, cultivated parklands and the one advocated is the concession footpath signed to 'Stand Tower 1 ml and Beeley 3½ mls'. This is followed by walking SE, initially keeping to a faint cart-track which leads across the lush meadowland. There follows a delightful section across open parkland passing beneath a scattering of mature deciduous trees including horse chestnuts, oaks, sycamore, ash and decorative cherries. The route crosses the main surfaced drive to the Hall and further on the wooded slopes of Gardom's Edge may be observed rising on your L to the NNE. Beyond these slopes, the distinctive profile of Wellington's Monument may just be discerned by those with good vision. Ahead on the R, the top of Stand Tower (former hunting lodge) appears above the dense, intervening woodlands away to the SSW.

Make for the gap between two clumps of trees ahead, crossing a wide gravel track in the process. Past this, veer to the higher ground on your L, still maintaining your SE bearing, and crossing several sheep tracks. Higher up the hillside, extensive views to your rear are of gentle wooded landscapes with an artificial lake occupying the lower

131

ground down below. The continuation way threads between more large trees, just clipping a group of beech and sycamore. Beyond these, another track is crossed before the way leads up a more pronounced grassy bank to reach a s-stile positioned in the stone wall ahead. Climb over this to enter the thick woodlands that cover the steeper slopes protecting Chatsworth Park.

A good path of compacted earth leads up through the wooded area, initially maintaining your SE diagonal but then veering more s beneath a cooling canopy of foliage. In May, when these slopes are covered with masses of bluebells, the next sheltered section of the walk is a sheer delight. Your upwards diagonal leads to the forest road which runs N to S close to the edge of the escarpment. Bear R along this, walking s in the direction signed 'Concession Footpath – Stand Tower – Beeley 2½ Mls'.

Stand Tower is soon reached. Bear R at this point to get a good look at this tower but please respect the fact that it is now a private residence. The structure, with its four observation turrets enclosed in stone and glass frameworks, is very well maintained. Walk to the edge for a most rewarding view of Chatsworth House, down below to the SW. This fine building is set within extensive ornamental gardens maintained to the highest standards. Beyond this ornate masterpiece the unpretentious small village of Edensor may be observed occupying a wooded dell, part way up the hillsides that rise from the parklands below. The central feature of the village is its fine spired church.

Retrace your final approach steps to the Tower, before bearing R along the forest track directing you towards 'Hob Hurst's House and Beeley', now walking SSE. Bear L at the fork ahead to follow the way indicated by an unusual purple arrow painted on a large stone. The way then leads round the narrow, indented, northern tip of Emperor Lake, a large oasis in a woodland setting. Then be vigilant to locate and turn down a narrow path to your R which winds round the eastern fringe of the lake, still heading S. A delightful section follows through almost tropically luxuriant undergrowth which allows tantalizing glimpses to your R of the lake and the extensive bird-life it supports.

All too soon, you will arrive at the southern tip of the lake but in achieving this be careful always to keep to the narrow paths nearest to the water's edge and studiously avoid any branch paths leading off on your L. Along the way there is one challenging jump across a feeder brook which might cause some temporary excitement. Bear R round the tip of the lake, ignoring several paths off to your L. The way leads towards a small jetty that contains a sluice gate but before reaching this feature, turn L along the obvious forest road as the path round the lake terminates. Turn L again at the T junction ahead to resume your southwards direction of travel along the continuation of the forest way. Just ahead there is a view of sheer perfection through the trees on your R where a short branch path will lead you to an observation point at the tiny holding pool above the water cascades falling dramatically through the land-scaped garden surrounding Chatsworth House. Keep a tight grip on younger children in this vicinity because there are some dangerous drops here.

Afterwards, resume your progress s by turning R to follow the way along the edge. A straight section through more delightful woodlands follows before the way descends gently to reach a major service road. Veer L here, in the opposite direction to that indicated by another purple arrow, and a short distance further on, bear R along a wide, grassy path to resume heading s. This sward connects with another gravel forest track, at which you turn R. The path leads to a gate and P-stile breaching a relatively high stone retaining wall. Over the stile, the openness of Beeley Moor stretches ahead on your L. After walking in this direction along the gravel path for no more than 100 paces, bear off R, downhill, along a narrow waymarked path.

A pleasant downwards traverse follows across bracken covered slopes to the more sheltered, farmed pastures below. The way leads to an elaborate configuration of stiles in a high stone wall near a wooden gate. Over these, cross the adjacent field on a direct, downwards diagonal to your L, making for the farm buildings below to the wsw. Another s-stile provides access to a farm lane which you turn R down. From here, the way leads round the extensive cluster of buildings located at Beeley Hilltop, including the farm and the unusual assemblies of toadstool-shaped stones.

The way to Edensor   *Allow 1½ hours*

A steeper descent along the back-lane leads to Beeley Lodge. Beyond the lodge, turn R along the B6012 road to pass over the arched stone bridge across the River Derwent. Another entrance to Chatsworth Park lies just ahead and near this veer L to cross a wide gravel path reserved for fishermen, before selecting a narrower path leading uphill on the far side of the open space. This will lead you sw round a wooded area. Ahead, keep veering to the R up the steeper slopes to reach the fringe of one of the extensive car parking facilities serving Chatsworth House and Park. Turn L here

through a gate and continue along the surfaced lane signed to 'Forest Office and Sawmill'. These are located about 200 m (220 yd) further on, down on your L. Beyond a private drive another gate is reached.

Your gravel way leads NW and height is progressively gained along a comfortable gradient. Further up, a wooded ravine through which a small stream meanders becomes established down on your L. Pheasants and other bird-life abound in this friendly environment. The gradient then steepens up a long, relentless incline. Eventually, the footpath swings acutely to the R at a group of farm buildings and cottages. This is at Calton Houses, located at MR 245685. Further extensive views are revealed from this vicinity, particularly to your R of part of the route you have already

21:1 By the side of Emperor Lake in Chatsworth Parkland

completed. Past a gate, at which there is a waysign, the path continues to gain further height, narrowing as it climbs. Fork R after the next gate, and then veer further R to walk along a wider, grassy path leading up a further modest slope, beside a stone wall. Your new direction is for a short distance ENE before it bends L at the top of the brow to adopt a more northwards bearing. The way then passes beneath power lines and ahead use the narrower path to cross a level meadow, bisecting another path in this process. Continue along the way signed to 'Edensor and Chatsworth'. More gates and stiles are used in quickly passing through a narrow belt of woodland on a diagonal to your L.

On emerging from the wooded area, a revealing view of Chatsworth House and its surrounding parkland appears down below to your R. A pleasant descent to the NNE over gentle, grassy slopes follows and this direction will lead you towards clumps of trees further down the hillside. The way is well signed and slight deviations are necessary to avoid fenced-off areas. During the descent the fine spire of the church at Edensor appears above the trees directly ahead and it progressively dominates this particular view. Lower down, bear to the L to assume a line of approach above and to the L of the church spire. The way leads to and down an interesting flight of steps, accessed by means of an iron stile. These will lead you into the attractive village of Edensor. Turn R at the bottom of the steps and follow the road towards St Peter's Church, to admire its impressive spire at close quarters. The small enclave also boasts a village shop, post office and café, all of which are welcome sights to hungry, thirsty travellers.

The way back to Baslow   *Allow 1 hour*

Leave the village to the NE passing through an elaborate gateway near a cattle grid, cross the road ahead and then veer R up the pathway, initially walking eastwards into the parkland. An elevated path then bends to the L, leading towards Chatsworth House, and from this location impressive views may be obtained of the general layout of the main buildings and of the ornamental water cascades plunging towards them. The path connects with an internal drive through the parkland and an ornate stone bridge spanning the River Derwent is crossed. On the far side of the river, turn L down a path which is reached by passing through a gate. Before this, the House and Gardens may be visited if so desired.

The continuation way leads due N through flat parkland following the course of the river upstream. There is much to catch your attention along here including Queen Mary's moated Bower. Further on, the path becomes upgraded into a surfaced lane and this leads back to the wrought iron entrance K-gate that you passed through several hours previously. From here, retrace your outwards steps into Baslow.

Alternative routes

ESCAPES

The suggested route may be conveniently curtailed at several points by simply descending from the higher ground into Chatsworth Parkland along one of the recognized public or concession paths. The ultimate short-cut is to stay in the parkland sampling the many attractions which this stately home offers to discerning visitors.

EXTENSIONS

Beyond the confines of Chatsworth Park continue S along the higher ground before dropping down to the village of Beeley, where liquid refreshments may be obtained. From Beeley there are various return routes possible that venture further W and that make use of the elaborate system of paths through the extensive woodlands snaking away up the slopes to the NW. Several loops of varying additional distances are possible and the route most suitable for you may easily be planned by consulting the OLM of the area.

21:2 Chatsworth House observed across the rich meadowlands near Edensor

Route 22: LONGNOR, EARL STERNDALE, CHROME HILL and HOLLINSCLOUGH

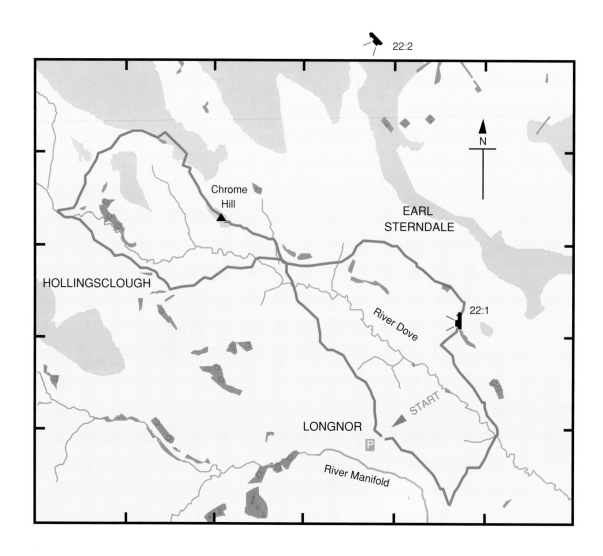

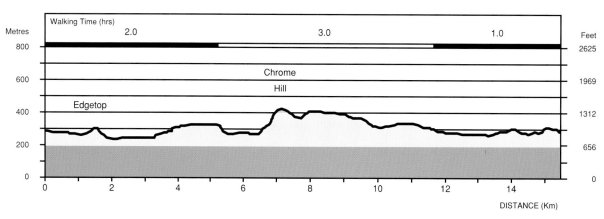

ROUTE 22

Longnor, Earl Sterndale, Chrome Hill and Hollinsclough

●

<table>
<tr><td>

STARTING LOCATION
Car park at Longnor (village square).
OLM 24: MR 089649.
Parking for up to 20 cars, with further space along verges of some access roads.

ALTERNATIVE STARTING POINTS
No obvious ones with dedicated parking facilities.

PUBLIC TRANSPORT
Bus routes 442, 445, 446, 456, 460 and 464.

OVERVIEW/INTEREST
Superb ridge section along Chrome Hill.
Good, open views and varied landscapes.
Interesting villages of Longnor and Earl Sterndale.

FOOTPATHS
Footpaths mainly good with very few waterlogged areas.

</td><td>

Waysigning somewhat mixed, leading to occasional doubts concerning route.
The exposed edges of Chrome Hill demand care.

GRADING
Moderate to difficult/severe.

TIME ALLOWANCE
6 hours.

STATISTICS

</td></tr>
</table>

DISTANCE

Excluding Height	15.4 km	(9.6 miles)
TOTAL HEIGHT GAINED	460 m	(1510 ft)
PRINCIPAL HEIGHTS		
Edgetop	305 m	(1000 ft)
Earl Sterndale	340 m	(1115 ft)
Chrome Hill	430 m	(1410 ft)

The way to Earl Sterndale   *Allow 2 hours*

The car parking area at Longnor is surrounded by inns and hotels, including the Crewe and Harpur Arms Hotel, the Grapes Inn and the Horseshoe Inn, the latter sporting an enterprising notice: 'Walkers welcome'! To escape from these temptations, depart along the road signed to 'Crowdecote ¾, Sheen 3¼ and Bakewell 9', walking SE to pass the post office followed by the Cheshire Cheese Inn. Ignore the footpath opposite the inn but select the next signed public footpath off to your R which initially leads down a wide, surfaced lane past Manifold House. Then veer L through the farmyard and exit via a S-stile in a stone wall. Following this, bear R round a barn and walk downhill across a field to locate a further S-stile. From this stile follow the path signed to 'Brund via Crofts and Over Boothlow'.

The way continues ESE across a series of narrow, walled pastures and over limestone walling. A gate and several G-stiles bar the way as it leads agreeably downhill on a diagonal towards the River Manifold and to Crofts Farm. Turn R at the farm as indicated by the huge white arrow daubed on the stone wall. Then bear L and walk further downhill and follow the signs to pass through a red-painted gate. From this position, veer slightly to the R and continue down the slopes to cross a field before passing to the R of the lower edge of a white-painted stone wall. Another helpful footpath sign has been placed on the tree trunk above this spot. Continue beside a hawthorn hedge, now walking S. At the end of this hedging and at the start of a continuation stone wall, be careful to pass through a narrow G-stile to your L and from here walk further downhill beside the stone wall, now on your R. The direction is still to the S and the route leads to a wooden stile to the R of a metal gate. The approach to this can be extremely muddy.

Now walk uphill towards a dilapidated barn but before reaching this turn L. Then be careful to locate and use a narrow stile at the end of the stone wall to your L. From here, the continuation way is clearly signed 'Footpath to Crowdecote'. This path leads to another G-stile at Boothlow Hayes. Exit across the water channel and up the waysigned public footpath that leads uphill across open fields towards the buildings situated at Edgetop. The direction is to the NNE. At the top R-hand corner of the field, keep to the established route which passes to the L of the buildings and which entails using the original G-stile to leave the meadow. From here, the route leads to a narrow lane which is reached at MR 099646. Super views are revealed here, down across the valley below towards the tiny farming community of Crowdecote. The fine escarpment rising above this is High Wheeldon. Catching the eye on the far L are the 'Twin Peaks' of Parkhouse Hill and Chrome Hill to the NNW.

Cross the lane on a diagonal to your R and exit through a G-stile in the wall ahead. After this, the continuation footpath veers to the R, initially along the grassy rim before it plunges down the steep slope along a diagonal to the L, where it then passes between clumps of hawthorn bushes. Lower down, the descent becomes better established to the E. The route then crosses a small gully, covered with a mixture of gorse, bramble and more hawthorn, before a stone wall is reached. This is crossed by a wooden stile that may require some care in locating. Continue downhill over meadowland, keeping near to a tree-lined watercourse to your L and heading towards Bridge End Farm below. Make directly for the farm buildings and then cross the infant River Dove at a footbridge where three paths converge. This is at MR 102649.

Turn L along the lane ahead and follow this into the tiny hamlet of Crowdecote. At the road junction ahead, veer R to walk uphill past the Pack Horse Inn. After this, branch L along the side lane. Just past the row of cottages on your R, turn L

22:1 Climbers on disused quarry face at Aldery Cliff (site owned by the British Mountaineering Club)

down the public footpath signed to 'Glutton Bridge'. The broad gravel path immediately swings to the R to pass Meadow Farm with the buildings to your L. Some distance beyond these, a S-stile next to a metal gate provides entry to more open country. From here, the continuation route is along the valley to the NW, for a short distance beside a limestone wall before it veers away to the L of this feature. The way then passes through a metal gate before it bears R towards a strategic S-stile, positioned in a stone wall. This stile provides the entrance to the approach lane to Underhill Farm, ahead to the L. Veer R here, away from the farm and use a short section of the farm lane to reach the road ahead at MR 097661.

Bear L along the narrow road and follow this through the dry limestone ravine into Earl Sterndale about 1½ km (0.9 miles) further on. The chasm you walk through separates Aldery Cliff from High Wheeldon. The route passes by a disused quarry gouged from the face of Aldery Cliff and this area is now owned and maintained by the British Mountaineering Club. Beyond this feature, the road leads into the rather stark village of Earl Sterndale which is on an exposed, wind-swept hillside. The way leads directly to the village green which is situated between St Michael's and All Angels Church and the inn named 'The Quiet Woman'. The latter, built in 1891, has an unmistakable sign depicting a headless lady, hence the name!

The way to Hollinsclough
Allow 3 hours

Depart from Earl Sterndale along the road to the NW and opposite Dale View pass over the partially concealed stile to the L of a metal gate on the L-hand side of the road. From here, veer L up the grassy slope away from the track to your R. The way is to the W and it passes just above the abrupt end of a limestone wall, before leading over the brow of the slope ahead to another S-stile. From this position there are magnificent views towards the pointed peaks of Parkhouse Hill and Chrome Hill to the W. The continuation route leads downhill through another stile breaching the limestone walling ahead. This is daubed with yellow paint and these directional daubings are a feature for some distance on. An obvious steep,

grassy diagonal completes the descent round the lower slopes of Hitter Hill, passing through further obstacles before the road below is reached at a wooden stile (MR 085668).

Cross the road and exit over a similar stile. Then walk across the field, on occasions ploughed over, making for the stile positioned at a metal gate on the far side. From here, continue round the lower slopes of Parkhouse Hill, walking due W over the brow directly ahead and to the L of the craggy summit area way above to your R. The way then leads through another stile, after which it traverses the hillside at a fairly constant height. A short distance further on, you will pass by an isolated, round limestone tower, named the Sugar Loaf. Your route then converges on a surfaced lane which you turn R along. This is at MR 078668. The lane provides access into remote and tranquil Dowel Dale lying to the N.

The lane crosses a small stream and between this and the cattle grid ahead, turn L to pass over a wooden stile. This provides the entrance to the path waysigned to 'High Edge via Chrome Hill'. Bear L to tackle the steep, grassy slopes leading up

22:2 Distant view at twilight of Parkhouse and Chrome Hills

to your R. These lead to the narrow ridge which rises in a series of pitches to the summit area of Chrome Hill. The climb is really exhilarating, there is exposure without danger, and the views back of the spectacular, serrated limestone edge of Park-house Hill terminating abruptly in the Sugar Loaf are exceptional. Do exercise great care when treading across the exposed limestone rock, for this has become smooth in many places due to pounding by countless footsteps and these rocks do become extremely slippery when wet. Further up, the symmetry of the climb is temporarily broken by crossing a stone wall by means of an inevitable s-stile near a mature sycamore tree. From here, the final section of the climb is quite demanding, up steep, grassy slopes, but the fantastic views below more than compensate for the effort. At the top, in fine weather, the all-round panoramic views are really breathtaking, as they reveal part of England's 'green and pleasant land' for many miles in all directions.

Start your descent to the NW and be careful to keep to the recognized paths. These broadly follow the several separate hillocks along the falling spur. Again, exercise care making this descent as there are both steep fall-aways and crumbling edges to contend with. There are also some relatively difficult rock pitches which may be avoided by planning your route down and following the paths which lead round these places. Eventually, you will arrive at a wide gap in the craggy spur and at this point your route bends round to the L to descend westwards along a grassy cleft towards the valley below. Lower down, the way passes over a s-stile in the wall on your R and the directional sign here points you towards another, but much less severe, climb up more grassy slopes extending to the N. This is along a narrow but obviously well-used, signposted path barred by yet another s-stile.

Thereafter, the route veers R up a steeper slope and the correct heading is towards the marker post on the skyline directly above. Towards the top, bear L and then follow the line of a stone wall to your R along the way indicated. A gentle descent follows across green pastures and two further wooden s-stiles have to be negotiated in

this section. Keep to the higher ground until you reach the next signpost and then follow the diagonal path down to your L. This is signed to 'Booth Farm'. The change of direction is above Stoop Farm and is to the W, where further on another marker post is reached. After traversing round the hillside for some distance beyond this, the path descends to the wide, compacted track below, reached at an iron gate. Bear R along this track. Past a stile and cattle grid, veer L along the superior surfaced lane. This leads gently downhill before swinging round to the L.

Ignore both a footpath leading off to the R and then a branch track across a cattle grid to your L, by keeping to the lane which bends R to enter Booth Farm by means of a metal gate. Directly opposite the farm, veer L downhill along the next track. From here, an elevated way winds along the hillside at a more or less constant height affording views into the deep, wooded valley cut by Swallow Brook, snaking away down below on your L. The farm of Leycote is reached a short distance further on and you will find the farmer there very affable and kindly disposed to walkers. At the farm, venture through the gate directly ahead and then exit from the adjacent fenced enclosure by means of the older iron gate on the far side. Continue downhill from here keeping to the R-hand side of a stone wall, as you descend to the SW. Along here a muddy stream has to be crossed and this may test your ingenuity! Keep walking down the slope and further along be vigilant to locate and pass through a G-stile where the descending walling gives way to a hedge. Beyond this, a better defined path traverses to the R and to the WSW down into the upper reaches of a narrow, enclosed valley.

The way leads to Washgate Bridge, the natural meeting point of several former packhorse trading routes. Having passed through a G-stile, the arched stone bridge is used to cross the gushing stream. Turn sharp L on the far side and proceed along the track which follows the main stream, having to cross a tributary watercourse to do so. Then continue along the lower of two public footpaths, selecting the one accessed by means of a wooden s-stile. The route continues adjacent to the main stream, initially leading SE where it immediately crosses another feeder brook. A narrow waterlogged area has to be crossed before a clearer path climbs uphill to reach an elevated terraced way. This is waysigned. Further on, after crossing a boggy stream-bed, the path leads past a derelict stone building, before undulating higher uphill, still maintaining a SE bearing. Some distance on, a wooded area is reached, then another tiny watercourse and a S-stile at a stone wall. The route continues SSE and then gradually descends back to the valley floor, after which it veers R to climb a more enclosed section before reaching a surfaced lane at MR 064666. Veer L here and use the back-lane to descend the short distance into the hamlet of Hollinsclough.

The way back to Longnor   *Allow 1 hour*

In Hollinsclough bear L to pass the Methodist chapel, the residential centre and the schoolhouse. Keep to the lane, ignoring footpaths off to both R and then L. Then select the next escape path off on your L which is accessed by means of a stepped G-stile in the corner of a stone wall. Continue towards Parkhouse Hill following the course of the meandering stream on your R and passing through a narrow G-stile on the way. Further on, ignore the tractor crossing of the brook but continue down to the metal-railed footbridge which you cross. Continue towards Parkhouse Hill, crossing a cattle grid and stream before your track converges on the lane ahead at a point which you walked past earlier in the day. This is at MR 078668.

Almost immediately, depart from the lane over the W-stile on your R and prepare yourself for an awkward climb down. Then head SSE to cross the adjacent field on a diagonal, rounding the corner of a limestone wall ahead. After this, veer R to cross the stream ahead at the footbridge lower down the slope. A moderate traverse follows to pass above the buildings situated higher up the hillside. The way levels off there and two more G-stiles have to be negotiated before you arrive at a narrow lane which you bear R along. This, in turn,

leads to the B5053 road into Longnor. Veer R along this, walking uphill. After passing the buildings ahead, select the next farm lane off to the L leading to Yew Tree Grange. Then ignore a grassy footpath leading off to the R, after which veer R to follow the track which passes above the farm.

Across a cattle grid, pass to the R of the next buildings to locate and follow a waysign directing you further to the R over a stile. Veer L uphill on the far side so that you can then veer L along a track to pass above Underhill Farm. Above the farm entrance, veer L along the lower part of a path, which loops at this point, to walk SE further along the valley. A short distance beyond the next gateway, veer R up the signed public footpath, but register that this particular sign is a little prematurely positioned and therefore walk past it for a few paces before making your turn in order to avoid the unnecessary crossing of waterlogged ground. The ensuing short, sharp climb leads to another stile and over this veer L to follow the line of a stone wall heading towards the village of Longnor, with its towered church now visible. A final series of obvious stiles and steps leads down to a narrow lane which you turn L along. Continue downhill using a ginnel to arrive back at the village square.

Alternative routes

ESCAPES
The route forms a figure of eight and therefore the most natural curtailment is to use each loop as a separate walk. This is achieved from the intersection of the loops at MR 078668.

EXTENSIONS
The obvious extension is to climb to the summit of High Wheeldon which commands a height of 422 m (1385 ft). For those who are not keen on walking along exposed ridges, the longer route by way of Dowel Dale will avoid the necessity to climb Chrome Hill and the main route may be rejoined to the NE of Stoop Farm. However, you will miss a lot in selecting this alternative!

Route 23: LATHKILL DALE, BRADFORD DALE and CALES DALE

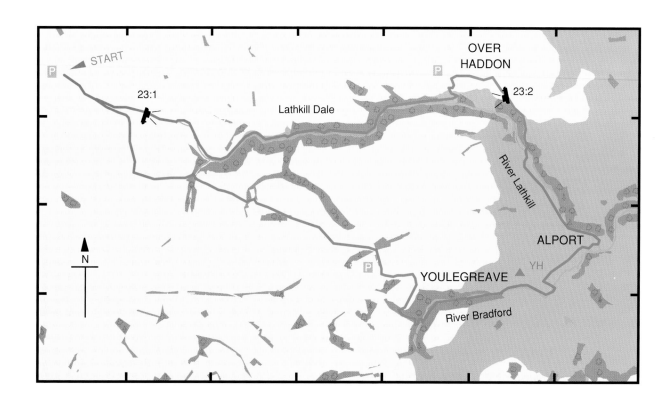

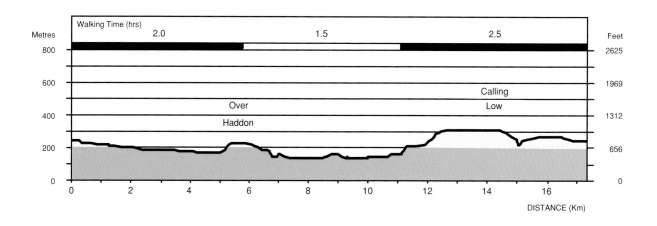

ROUTE 23

Lathkill Dale, Bradford Dale and Cales Dale

●

STARTING LOCATION
Car parking lay-by near Monyash.
OLM 24: MR 158665.
Parking for between 15 and 20 cars.

ALTERNATIVE STARTING POINTS
Over Haddon.
Alport.
Youlgreave.

PUBLIC TRANSPORT
Bus services to Monyash 57, 177, 192 and 446.

OVERVIEW/INTEREST
A route packed with continuous interest.
Three superb dales are visited.
Impressive limestone rock formations.
Tranquil riverside scenery.
Extensive wildlife and flora.
Caves and weirs.
Attractive villages.
Disused lead and calcite workings.

FOOTPATHS
The paths are extremely good with very few
    waterlogged or boggy sections.
The route is clearly signed and sections are along
    waymarked local trails.
Route finding is therefore straightforward.

GRADING
Easy/straightforward to moderate.

TIME ALLOWANCE
6 hours.

STATISTICS
DISTANCE
Excluding Height	17.3 km	(10.8 miles)
TOTAL HEIGHT GAINED	320 m	(1050 ft)
PRINCIPAL HEIGHTS		
Over Haddon	230 m	(755 ft)
Calling Low	310 m	(1015 ft)

The way to Over Haddon   *Allow 2 hours*

Opposite the main lay-by, select the footpath waysigned 'Local Walk 2' and walk SE along a broad, grassy path. This leads slightly downhill through a shallow valley towards Lathkill Dale further to the E. The path is accessed via a stone stile next to an iron gate. The path is obvious and although minor obstacles, mainly in the form of stiles of the gap variety, are encountered, the route is easy to follow as its meanders eastwards into Lathkill Dale. Always keep to the main route leading down into the valley, ignoring several inviting tracks off uphill, both to your R and L. For some distance your way continues to follow the clearly waysigned walk number 2. Lathkill Dale is a national nature reserve managed by English Nature and you will shortly pass one of their colourful information signs headed 'From Monasteries to Mines'.

The scenery becomes more rugged and interesting as you descend further into the valley and as the sides of the dale steepen and exposed limestone cliffs and butts appear, exposing their horizontal banding. Each of these bands represents several million years of crinoid and other primitive sea-creature deposits. Then rockfalls are reached and at the second of these, which intrudes on to the path, follow the way round to the R. Several notices should be observed, including one which indicates dangerous mine shafts. The route continues SE along a narrowing, rocky path and further stiles have to be either climbed over or squeezed through. Then the dry dale is enhanced by the sudden emergence of a watercourse. This appears from a small cavern in the limestone bedding planes, some 100 m (330 ft) or so below the tree-lined fringe of the top of the cliff towering above. The waters are sparkling clear and the path veers to the L of these thus avoiding any necessity

23:1 The western entrance to Lathkill Dale near Monyash

to cross the infant stream at this location. In summer this spring is often dried up.

At the footbridge ahead you part company with walk 2 which continues across the stream. Your way is still SE down the valley with the river to your R and you therefore also ignore the way up steps to your L at this point. Further on, a mighty limestone cliff is approached, its profile falling along a perfectly proportioned 45° slope into the dale ahead. To compete for your attention, miniature but impressively wide weirs and waterfalls begin to arrest the smooth drop of the river and these break up the flow of water into a series of tranquil catchment pools divided by stretches of white-water. The stream is now wide and powerful and, together with its bordering flora, it supports increasing fish and bird populations, the latter including moorhens and mallards. Another steep path up to the R needs to be avoided as you continue over a stile at a gate ahead. Further on, the way widens into an elevated track. At one point keep to the path nearest to the stream in order to avoid waterlogged ground in a shallow depression to the L.

Then the remnants of some dilapidated stone columns are reached, after which two cairns signify that other pathways are intersected. After this you pass an interesting notice directed at walkers coming in the opposite direction. This reads: 'This privilege footpath is closed for shooting on several occasions from October to January.' You might well wonder how a footpath might be used for such purposes! Lathkill Lodge is reached at MR 203662 and at this point you temporarily part company with the river. The departure is primarily to enable you to visit Over Haddon, an attractive small village where refreshments may be obtained, and also to provide a change from walking along an enclosed dale. In order to climb out of the confines of the valley, bear L to pass round the two wooden gates just above the lodge and continue up the winding, narrow lane into the village. On the way up, tiny St Anne's Church is reached. This is superbly well maintained; its interior is refreshingly simple and it has links with St Silas. When you reach the grass triangle ahead, bear R round Yew Tree Tea Room and Country Store. From here, proceed due E through the village to pass another café. At the fork ahead, veer R in order to continue obtaining uninter-

23:2 The cascading weirs of the River Lathkill near Haddon

rupted views of the fine landscapes down to your R. Follow the lane round to the L and up the brow to reach The Lathkill Hotel.

The way to Bradford Dale   *Allow 1½ hours*

Just beyond the hotel the lane bends sharp L and at this point exit via the narrow G-stile ahead and then veer immediately R to walk downhill back towards Lathkill Dale along the wide grassy way, heading SE. The obvious, diagonal route down leads through more stiles and some of these are grouped in twos to provide convenient crossings of narrow enclosures which bar your way at right angles. Along here there are tremendous views of the steep-sided dale to your R and of the many weirs spanning the River Lathkill. Lower down, the descent steepens and eventually you have to squeeze through a narrow G-stile in a low wall to your R. Another G-stile below provides access to a minor road. Turn R along this road and use it to cross the River Lathkill at Conksbury Bridge, located at MR 212656. Keep to the road as it winds uphill and then select a footpath off to your

L. This is reached by passing through an old gateway in the retaining stone wall. From the road, a well-bedded stone and gravel path leads first S and then SE further downstream above Lathkill Dale. The next section of the route, towards Alport, is straightforward along a clearly waysigned path. Numerous stiles need to be negotiated but these are sighted in obvious positions, usually adjacent to gates.

Further along, closer contact is once again established with the River Lathkill. After this, gentle slopes lead down to the small conurbation of Alport. The road linking Alport and Youlgreave is reached by means of another G-stile directly opposite a red telephone kiosk. This is at MR 221645. Turn R along the road, walking to the w slightly uphill to pass other popular car parking places situated on both sides of the roadway. Past these, cross over and turn off through a narrow G-stile in the retaining wall on the L-hand side of the road. From here, a path leads SW above the approaches to Bradford Dale. A short distance further on there is a terrific view, through gaps in the trees, of a vertical limestone cliff. The waymarked path bears R and ahead, where there

145

is a somewhat confusing series of divisions, keep to the L-hand forks nearest to the dale below. The twin villages of Bradford and Youlgreave, which together extend for quite a distance, are passed to the SE and on your R. To do this, pass through another G-stile on your L and then ignore several side paths to your R leading into the village centres. The way does, however, lead down to the sprawling outskirts of the quite extensive populated area. This is reached at a lane by means of passing through yet another G-stile. This is opposite an attractive, terraced cottage named Meadows Reach.

Veer immediately L to walk down Braemar Lane, not allowing the sign to 'Alport' to shake your confidence! The narrow lane leads directly down to the River Bradford, which you cross by means of the arched stone bridge. On the far side turn R in the opposite direction to Alport and immediately pass a wooden seat sheltered beneath a protruding limestone bluff. The waters in the stream hereabouts are so clear that one lady walker who knows the area well informed me that crayfish inhabit this stretch of the river. The path follows the stream round to the R and the water is re-crossed before the path leads you back to the road. Cross this and then pass through a G-stile to the L of wooden gates. At this point, avoid the temptation to cross the stream again at a low stone footbridge.

The way continues WNW along delightful Bradford Dale and you have to bypass two further tracks leading up the slope on your R into Youlgreave, now above you. The route is then upstream past a succession of low weirs along an excellent path which leads below the wooded slopes of the dale. Further along, the stream is crossed at a stone footbridge. Continue up the dale on the opposite side of the river, passing more attractive weirs along the way. The still waters trapped behind these support prolific growth of a variety of plants which could grace any aquarium. Trout swim contentedly in these clear waters. Higher up, the dale becomes progressively more enclosed as the wooded slopes on either side steepen appreciably and you are informed that you are treading along the Limestone Way. You

eventually reach two gates separated by a large stone pillar. There is a waymarker sign here which alerts you that you are now back on route 2. Then cross the stream by means of the wide stone bridge and you are ready to exit from the dale. This is at MR 199636.

The way back to the car lay-by

Climb the well-used path which first veers to the R before tracking back uphill on a diagonal to the L. Two less clear paths off to the R, one back alongside the river and the other up into the side dale, need to be avoided. Then the remains of a dilapidated stone building are passed on your R and from here an obvious path zigzags up the steep slope which, as height is gained, affords superb views back along Bradford Dale. The incline leads to a minor road at a hairpin bend. Turn R where, a short distance further on, the route passes by Lomberdale Hall. Following this, when the road bends sharp R, veer off along the continuation footpath to the L. This is accessed at a G-stile next to a wooden gate. The correct way is again numbered 2.

Bear R to climb to the brow of the slope ahead, walking northwards to reach another minor road at a stile, once again positioned at a bend. Cross over on a diagonal to your L, spurning the path directly opposite which is signed to 'Over Haddon'. As the road straightens out, select the next footpath off to the R. This is again waysigned as route 2 and is accessed by means of a stone s-stile. From here, a clear path leads further uphill along a diagonal to your L towards the W. Further on, beyond a s-stile over a stone wall, the way curves slightly but progressively to the R and eventually leads you northwards. More stiles are reached before the way brings you to a narrow lane. This in turn leads to a minor road where the popular Moor Lane car park and picnic area are located at MR 194644. Turn L at the road and walk W to converge, at an acute angle, onto a busier roadway a short distance further on. Cross this second road on another diagonal and then leave it through a low, stone s-stile, where there is a sign indicating 'Monyash 2'. Strike off across the meadow on a diagonal to your L, walking WNW to go round and then follow for a short distance an intermittent limestone wall, keeping to the R of this. Maintain your now established diagonal to arrive at a formidable stone wall to your R and cross this by means of another s-stile. Continue along the well-trodden NW diagonal to cross a large open meadow along a wide path which does become soft and muddy in wet weather.

The way leads to, and clips, sparse deciduous woodlands before another s-stile is reached at the corner of a stone wall. From here, the route leads across more flat fields to reach the substantial farm buildings at Calling Low. A diverted footpath provides a way round these to the N and this is accessed by means of a R turn through a K-gate. After crossing an area that can be muddy, several more gates have to be negotiated before a path through a strip of woodland indicates that the diversion is nearing completion. Beyond the trees a wide landscape of rolling green hills, interspersed with clumps of trees, stretches for miles in all directions.

The route continues downhill and it then veers R to pass through another K-gate. After this, a diagonal to the R leads further down the slope more directly towards Lathkill Dale, the narrow scar of which may now be clearly seen to your R. Through another K-gate, the way continues to lose height as it passes through rural scenery. More gates are encountered together with a colourful sign depicting 'Lathkill Dale'. Then the steep sides of Cales Dale loom up immediately ahead. Your visit to this dale is a quick down and up. The descent is by means of steps, many of them! Be careful during this climb down for the exposed, polished limestone rock and compressed soil in between can become very slippery and there is a frightening drop.

At the bottom there is some choice of ways. Select the middle path which zigzags up the equally steep W slopes of the dale. The route is still signposted as route 2, 'Limestone Way'. Near this sign veer L into the small limestone gorge ahead. The way traverses up the R-hand side of this along a narrow, rocky path, and towards the top a small rockfall has to be crossed. Then a somewhat complicated twin stile is negotiated before open terrain is crossed in your approach to One Ash Grange Farm. This establishment is skirted to the R, but the way does pass between some of the farm outbuildings. These are reached up steps which lead to a G-stile. Continue westward beyond the farm by veering R and then slightly R again. The route then leads marginally uphill passing the last farm building, a huge barn to your L. When an iron gate is reached, continue along the cart-track signed 2A. This leads N over the shallow brow of the hillside directly towards Lathkill Dale. (Route 2 continues at right angles, westwards, into Monyash.) Past a metal gate near a water trough, veer L down the hillside towards the cliffs of Lathkill Dale ahead. The way bends further L to follow the line of a stone wall down into the dale. Through a gate at the bottom, veer L and retrace your outwards steps back to the car lay-by about ½ km (⅓ mile) further on.

Alternative routes

ESCAPES

For those who do not enjoy climbing, one modest short-cut is not to venture up to Over Haddon. This loop is avoided by keeping to the footpaths bordering the River Lathkill down in the valley to rejoin the main route at Conksbury Bridge.

Another possibility is to use the series of footpaths leading S from Over Haddon through Meadow Place Grange, and then to walk SW along the minor road to re-engage with the main route at MR 193645.

EXTENSIONS

Interesting extensions which avoid excessive use of roads are not all that obvious. However, one suggestion is to visit Haddon Hall and Park from Over Haddon. This is achieved by using a somewhat complicated series of footpaths which link with the main route at Alport. This will entail a long, hard day and is only suitable for the fittest of walkers.

Route 24: ELTON, BIRCHOVER, STANTON MOOR and WINSTER

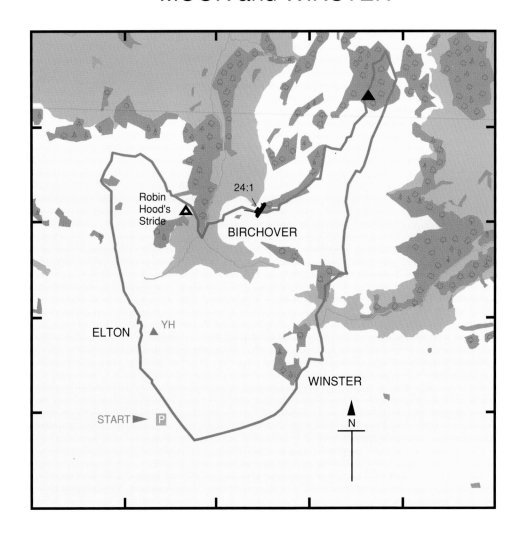

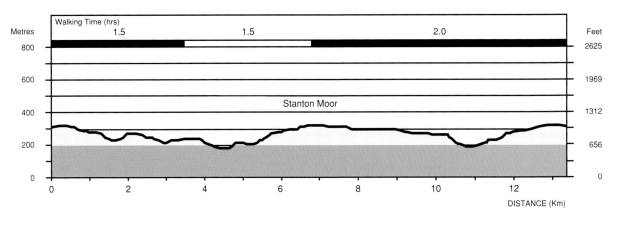

ROUTE 24

Elton, Birchover, Stanton Moor and Winster

•

STARTING LOCATION
Isolated car park between Elton and Winster.
OLM 24: MR 226599.
Extensive car parking in field with picnic area; field closed off in winter with space then for only about 5 cars outside fenced-off area.

ALTERNATIVE STARTING POINTS
Villages of Elton, Birchover and Winster but no dedicated car parking facilities.

PUBLIC TRANSPORT
Bus routes to Elton 170, and Winster 57B, 170 and 172.

OVERVIEW/INTEREST
Route of many contrasts from gentle rural scenery to rugged high moorland.
Continuous variety and constantly changing landscapes.
Several interesting villages.
Rock formations and outcrops, including Robin Hood's Stride.
Route suitable for family ramble in dry weather.

FOOTPATHS
A real mixture; good, certain and firm over the high ground, less obvious and inclined to be waterlogged and muddy in wet, wintery conditions across the lower farmed terrain.
Some walking along minor roads is involved.
Signs are intermittent.
Bridging of the worst muddy areas along public footpaths is badly needed.

GRADING
Easy/straightforward to moderate, depending upon ground conditions.

TIME ALLOWANCE
5 hours.

STATISTICS

DISTANCE

Excluding Height	13.4 km	(8.3 miles)
TOTAL HEIGHT GAINED	350 m	(1150 ft)
PRINCIPAL HEIGHTS		
Robin Hood's Stride	270 m	(885 ft)
Stanton Moor	323 m	(1060 ft)

The way to Robin Hood's Stride

Allow 1½ hours

Turn R from the car parking area and walk NW up the narrow lane leading to the village of Elton situated about 1 km (0.6 miles) away. Soon revealing views open up, ahead and to your R, of the expansive, rolling landscapes towards which you are heading. Further on, bear R along the major lane signed to 'Elton ½'. After this, the route leads pleasantly downhill into the hamlet of Elton, with its buildings huddled around the towered church of All Saints. The final approach into the village is along Moor Lane. Pass through the hamlet, cross the main road signed to 'Winster 1, Youlgreave 5' on a diagonal to your L and proceed down Well Street on the L-hand side of the church perimeter.

Then fork L along the surfaced way signed 'Public Footpath to Youlgreave' and at the metal gate ahead, turn L to pass through a narrow gap adjacent to the gate. This will bring you onto two waysigned footpaths. Turn immediately R and follow the path leading off at right angles downhill over grassy slopes which can often become muddy. At the bottom of the hill you will locate a redundant G-stile and from this position there is a good view of the interesting escarpment of Anthony Hill with its almost vertical westerly face. Also from here you will be able to make out the well-used continuation route to the N snaking up

149

the far hillside. Before reaching the minor road at MR 219617 the way passes through five more G-stiles in stone walling, the last one of which provides entry to the surfaced lane. At the second of these be mindful of the overgrown hawthorn!

Cross over the lane and continue along the footpath directly opposite by passing through another narrow G-stile. The path is signed to 'Youlgreave 2'. Another stile follows as you continue walking uphill. After this, the way bears R, to maintain your direction of travel northwards and another G-stile, reinforced by angle iron, has to be negotiated. From here, the obvious way leads to the crest of the hillside. Cross the barbed-wire fence, stretching across your direction of approach, at the wooden boarding and continue walking across lush meadowlands. Your way then crosses a farm track where a s-stile in the retaining wall demands some awkward stretching. The track is to Cliff Farm.

Continue walking northwards along your established diagonal to pass over another s-stile where the far side is often muddy. The route than skirts below and to the L of two small wooded areas containing Scots pines and larches with a sprinkling of oak. The second of these is named Tomlinson Wood. At the next narrow G-stile you are requested to keep to the path and several more of these notices follow as the public right of way passes through farmland. Then the way curves round to the R and after passing through a gateway the footpath, now signed to Robin Hood's Stride, leads downhill. It then bears NE following the line of overhead electricity cables.

Through another G-stile, veer R to pass through a wide opening before walking uphill along the way again signed to the Stride. This area is often very boggy, with the ground churned up by farm tractors. The continuation way leads E to pass by Harthill Moor Farm with its extensive barns and outbuildings. The route bends to the L round the farmhouse and from here the first sightings of the fascinating jumble of rocks and boulders named Robin Hood's Stride can be made out ahead on your R and to the SE. To get there, follow the track as it bends sharply R and then leads you to a narrow minor road. Cross this, pass through the G-

stile on the far side and then follow the continuation footpath by veering R and walking SSE across meadowland to reach the jumbled rock formations. The last part of this approach section is along the Limestone Way and more stiles have to be negotiated, the step down from one of which is tricky. At the approach to the rocks, there is a route round to the R which commences as a straightforward path and ends up as an easy scramble along a fault line amongst the boulders to reach the top of the rock configuration. Do not be tempted to use any of the routes on the L as these demand some exacting scrambling and are relatively difficult and dangerous. The quite magnificent panorama from the top of the rock slabs, together with the close-up views of the massive boulders, more than compensates for the marginal extra effort of the climb.

The way to Stanton Moor (trig point)

Allow 1½ hours

Descend from the rocks by retracing your approach route exactly. At the bottom, bear round the rocks to re-engage the Limestone Way. This leads downhill along a clear path passing below a group of larches to your L. Beyond another G-stile, a second band of exposed rocks appear over to your L. This one is a near vertical cliff with a dwelling nestling below its protective bulk. Use the farm track leading downhill to connect with the B5056 road at MR 228618. Turn L along the road and cross over well away from the bends. Within about 100 paces, abandon the road by passing over the stile which provides entry to the public footpath veering off uphill and signed to 'Birchover'. There is more mud hereabouts!

Climb up the steepish slopes to your R making for the tree-fringed hillock dominating the skyline directly above. As height is quickly gained, turn around for a revealing view to the rear of your approach route, including the two prominent rock features. Further up, another path converges from the R and the merged ways traverse round the hillock at a fairly constant height, passing by a dilapidated stone building. From this elevated

24:1 Looking north west towards Youlgreave from above Birchover

position there are fine views down to your L of neat farmsteads and enclosed pastures. Beyond the flatness of this rural scene, a long edge rises to the NNW; this marks the boundary of high ground leading to Harthill Moor.

Past the next stile, a most delightful grassy track leads downhill further E, before it curves to the R to merge into a better established track which leads down into the valley, passing by a small pool with its own cascading feeder stream. From here, the way leads E, marginally uphill, to pass in rapid succession The Old Vicarage, the tiny bell-towered church of St Michael and All Angels and then 'The Old School' building. At the road junction ahead, the Druid's Inn at Birchover is reached. Cross the road on a L diagonal and then locate the footpath leading uphill through trees over a surface of compacted earth. The start of this is directly opposite the inn.

Soon you are walking above the roof tops of the elongated village of Birchover. Further up, divert to the L through heathers to obtain a stupendous view over the flatter lands below and towards the large village of Youlgreave, far away to the NW.

Back on the main path, the route meanders through a wooded area, still gaining height. This section of the way terminates abruptly at a road which is reached opposite a factory, Ann Twyford Dimensional Stone Works, at MR 241625. Cross over and turn L to walk uphill along the road. Keep to the road for about ½ km (⅓ mile), passing extensive, disused quarry workings, and then locate a distinctive path leading off to the R which immediately passes round two sets of boulders. Over a s-stile, continue up a slight incline along a sandy and stone-slabbed path, walking ESE.

The way soon leads to a really interesting area where there is a large boulder, the 'Cork Stone', complete with steps and iron hand grips. These aids allow a relatively easy and safe way up. In this immediate vicinity, if you are fortunate, you could spot a goshawk. Veer L round the massive boulder to pass above a shallow, disused stone quarry, now walking NE along a quite superb grassy way. When this path divides, choose the R-hand fork and this will lead you directly to the trig point on Stanton Moor. This is positioned at a height of 323 m (1060 ft), and is the highest elevation of the entire route. Further extensive views stretch away in all directions from this feature.

The way back to the car park   *Allow 2 hours*

From the trig point, continue NE choosing the obvious main route from several that thread their ways through a most unusual landscape of purple heather interspersed with isolated clumps of rhododendrons. A communications pylon sticking up ahead on your L completes the picture. The route then descends gently along the crest of the wide spur and further down a wooded area of mostly silver birch is penetrated. Through this, the way leads to a wider path, approached on an acute diagonal. The place where these paths connect marks the northern extremity of your route; therefore, turn back sharp R here to commence walking s along the wide and obvious pathway leading that way. This new direction is maintained for the next 3½ km (2 miles) to reach the village

of Winster. In the first part of this section, there are wide-ranging views down to your L and these contain Darley Dale to the E and the town of Matlock to the ESE. The buildings discernible on the far horizon are Ryber Castle, which now houses a zoo.

The compacted, wide sandy path is a sheer delight to walk along and fast progress can now be achieved. A shallow descent follows and along here your path crosses another one at right angles. Continue SSW over falling ground to reach a minor lane, accessed by means of a wooden stile, at MR 246625. Veer R along this lane, but within 50 paces select the continuation footpath leading off to the L. This leads into a much mellower landscape. The route then leads down to and round Barn Farm where the extensive farmyard is entered through a G-stile to the L of a metal gate. From here, walk round and below the farm to pass through another G-stile towards the far end of the buildings.

Now continue further s along the signed footpath, ignoring another path leading off at right angles to your L. Green meadowlands stretch ahead; be careful to keep to the R-hand edge of the first one of these, and then squeeze through a narrow G-stile in the wall at the far end. From here, continue downhill veering R. Then avoid a side path on your R leading off through another G-stile. Past an often waterlogged area, the way leads to the equally muddy approach track to Uppertown Farm, which your route bisects. There is a brand new sign here helpfully informing you that Winster lies ahead. Leave this track through the R of two gateways and walk slightly uphill along a track obviously also used by tractors. Your direction is still towards s. Further on, abandon the continuation of these tractor tracks as they veer away to your R and instead continue straight ahead, keeping to the hawthorn hedge on your L. Repeat this course further on when the unwanted track veers off through an iron gate to the L.

Before descending along the narrow path into the valley ahead, spare a few moments to move over to the higher ground on your R in order to obtain a really splendid view across the wide, shallow valley to the village of Winster sprawling along the top of the far hillside. Beyond the next G-stile, the path bends sharply R and, following this, further height is surrendered along a straightish downwards diagonal. At the end of this, veer L to walk more directly downhill, passing through another narrow gap in a stone wall ahead. Then some exacting, waterlogged ground has to be crossed and this includes the fording of a small brook flowing across your direction of approach. Care is needed here to avoid slipping and inevitably getting your behind wet, as I did on one quite unforgettable occasion!

Pleasant grassy slopes are soon reached and these lead more steeply downhill to where the valley floor is crossed. An obvious way leads from here directly uphill through several more stiles, and across further boggy ground which assumes quagmire characteristics following prolonged wet weather, into the village of Winster. Your path up to this village eventually connects with a surfaced track which in turn leads to a lane. Continue straight ahead up this narrow lane to pass a row of cottages, one of which is prominently signed 'Wildflower Cottage'. This passage is Woodhouse Lane and it connects with the main street of the village.

Turn R to walk through the village, where there are opportunities to purchase refreshments of several kinds. At the far end of the main street, turn L along West Bank but then ignore the public footpath to the R leading through the grounds of St John the Baptist Church. Your continuation way leads quite steeply uphill through the upper, tiered part of the village to connect with the B5056 road at the top of the hill, near the Miners Standard Inn. Bear L here to reach the major road, cross it with care, and then almost immediately veer off it to your R along the side road signed to 'Elton 1½, Newhaven 4½, White Peak scenic route'. Just over 1 km (0.6 miles) further on, turn R towards the village of Elton and the car park is located a short distance down this lane on your R.

Alternative routes

ESCAPES
There are several opportunities for shortening the route described and these possibilities are obvious from examining the OLM. Two suggested shortcuts are to avoid the loop to the N which passes by Harthill Moor Farm and/or to bypass the section over the high ground of Stanton Moor.

EXTENSIONS
The most attractive countryside is situated in the northernmost part of the route; therefore, the most rewarding extensions are to venture further N, perhaps taking in the area surrounding Stanton-in-the-Peak and Stanton Hall. Another appealing possibility is to spend more time exploring the edges and rock formations lining Stanton Moor.

153

Route 25: MANIFOLD WAY, WETTONMILL and GRINDON

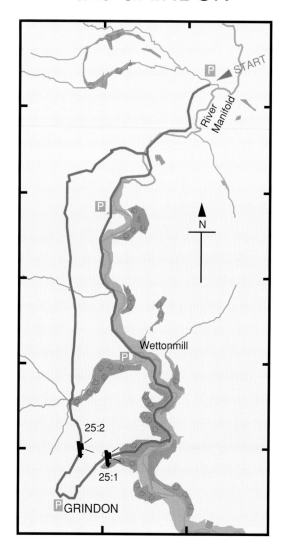

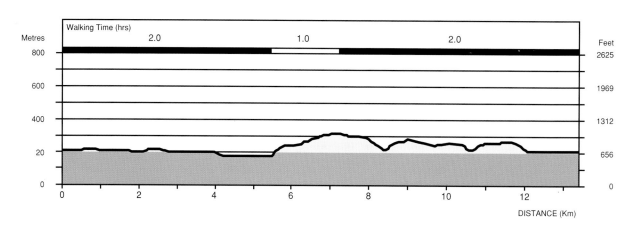

ROUTE 25

Manifold Way, Wettonmill and Grindon

●

STARTING LOCATION
Car park at Hulme End.
OLM 24: MR 103593.
Extensive, well laid-out car parking facilities.

ALTERNATIVE STARTING POINTS
Wettonmill.
Grindon.

PUBLIC TRANSPORT
Bus routes 202, 441, 442, 445, 446, 456 and 464.

OVERVIEW/INTEREST
Spectacular limestone gorge of River Manifold.
Wettonmill area and Thor's Cave.
Absorbing views with plenty of variety.
Dales, woodlands and farmlands are visited.

FOOTPATHS
The Manifold Way is excellent but watch out for
  cyclists!

Other paths are mostly also very good but there is
  the odd waterlogged patch, and in one area on the
  return, route finding is obscure.
However, generally the route is well waysigned.

GRADING
Moderate.

TIME ALLOWANCE
5 hours.

STATISTICS

DISTANCE

Excluding Height	13.4 km	(8.3 miles)
TOTAL HEIGHT GAINED	300 m	(985 ft)
PRINCIPAL HEIGHTS		
Grindon	320 m	(1050 ft)

The way to below Thor's Cave   *Allow 2 hours*

Depart from the narrow sw end of the car park, walking on to the Manifold Way at its northern extremity. The broad, elevated macadam way immediately winds through an attractive landscape of rolling hills covered with copses. The dominant feature is the rounded, grassy slopes of Ecton Hill over on your L to the s. A fast start can be achieved along the absolutely flat (in walker's terms) and exceptionally well-drained course of the former railway line (Leek and Manifold Light Railway route). Footpaths lead off to both L and R but these, together with others ahead, may be ignored. Further on, the way curves to the R to enter the upper Manifold Valley, passing between slopes of exposed rock bedding planes to your L and symmetrically rounded, grassed-over slopes to your R. Both are liberally covered with a mixture of deciduous trees, including hawthorn,

beech and sycamore. Then the meandering River Manifold is crossed by means of a sturdy wooden bridge. The way continues down the narrowing dale with the broad, shallow river gurgling merrily away over its pebbly bed to your R.

Further on, a side lane is crossed at gates and from here your continuation route is signed towards 'Swainsley ¾'. Ahead, the valley system widens appreciably as the higher and more barren, curving slopes of Ecton Hill increasingly dominate the forward landscape. Then Radcliffe's Folly comes into view, the conglomeration of buildings containing an obtrusive pale green spire. The river is then re-crossed and beyond this there is a clearer view of the folly, to your rear. From here, the way continues along a narrow, elevated shelf above the river and from this position there are further compelling views ahead along the dale. The sheltered, tree-enclosed way leads past a small parking area (which might provide an alternative starting point) and beyond this the way develops into a narrow lane.

Next, the tributary stream of Warslow Brook is crossed and immediately over the bridge a single-track road is reached. Then walk through the long, illuminated tunnel, being constantly on guard against the possibility of having to share this gloomy passage with vehicular traffic. Side spaces are provided to get out of their way if need be. (I once went through this tunnel intermingled with a car rally of about 300 MG enthusiasts but hopefully you will not have to contend with such formidable competition!) Emerging into daylight once more, the narrow road leads further down the dale to cross another tributary stream about

½ km (⅓ mile) away. Beyond this, the appealing surrounds of Wettonmill are reached. There are further parking opportunities here and refreshments are also available, both on your side of the River Manifold from 'The Mobile Kabin' or across the waters at Wettonmill, which also boasts toilet facilities and a play area beside the stream. The coffee served at the mill shop is excellent.

Leave the mill area by continuing down the Manifold Way along the lane signed to 'Wetton 1¼ and Alstonefield 3'. The route then passes another tributary stream, this one descending over a number of shallow weirs. Then, more impressive limestone cliffs loom ahead as the route passes a camping area in a perfectly flat field.

25:1 Walking towards Grindon from the direction of the Manifold Way

25:2 A tranquil view taking in the heights above Thor's Cave

The river is crossed once more, this time by the less attractive of two parallel bridges. The other arched one is beautifully proportioned and of pleasing red sandstone. The route leads to further parking areas and here the Manifold Way resumes its former discrete identity, separating itself from the roadway by means of another bridging of the river. Continue southwards down the dale and spare a moment to turn round for a good view of the pinnacle of Wetton Hill away to the NE. Then look ahead to the L for your first sighting of Thor's Cave, way up in the far limestone crag. (The cave is visited and commented on in some detail in Route 26.) Along this stretch you may be surprised at the reduced water level in the River Manifold: the explanation of this is that by now most of its former contents have disappeared underground at watersinks. Further on and just below the cave, ignore the footbridge across what remains of the river but prepare to depart from the attractive dale.

The way to Grindon   *Allow 1 hour*

Just past the footbridge, select the footpath leading uphill to your R to climb out of the steep-sided dale. This is at MR 098551. The path is accessed over a wooden stile, complete with doggy access. The ensuing climb is up the slopes of Ladyside, a hill owned by the National Trust. This is the first climb of the day and is a stiff one along a much-used way that gains height very rapidly. Keep always to the main route, making use of a series of steps buttressed with tree trunks. When more open ground is attained higher up, the views back across the dale towards Thor's Cave are superb. The way continues uphill but fortunately the steep gradient slackens off as the way leads to another composite stile and you will need to turn L to cross over it. From this point, a narrow but well-drained path traverses the hillside at a more or less constant height. The way here is across the densely wooded westerly slopes of Ladyside.

157

The wide variety of vegetation along this stretch includes hawthorn, ash, Scots pine, brambles and many species of woodland flowering plants including primroses. The route curves round to the w, high above the deep, wooded side valley; and a stile (of some rarity in these parts) is reached. Some distance further on, the way rises above the extensive wooded area where it leads to a wall which is crossed by means of steps, thus avoiding a footpath leading uphill off to your R. On the other side of the wall, follow the footpath leading off to the L which is faintly signed to 'Grindon'. For some distance the path is quite indistinct and through this section keep the wooded area immediately on your L as you cross the grassy slopes above the treeline. Your continuation route is then to the sw as the top of the church spire at Grindon comes into view, providing a helpful landmark.

Thereafter, a much more clearly defined footpath leads towards this spire. The way reaches and then follows the course of a tiny stream, appearing on your L. Then the route climbs up a grassy brow to pass over and through a combined gap-and-ladder stile. Following this, and as directed, bisect the stream at the second obvious crossing point. Continue walking southwards up the brow on the far side of the watercourse, initially following a direction to the L of the church. Higher up, another signpost is reached and from here the way leads straight ahead beneath a natural archway formed by the spreading branches of a huge sycamore tree. Further on, a stile-and-gate combination signal the entrance into the village of Grindon. Turn R along the lane and from here the way leads slightly uphill to and then round the Gothic church of All Saint's. Continue beside the perimeter walls of the church grounds, turning R to pass the picnic area and car parking facilities across the road.

The way back to Hulme End   *Allow 2 hours*

Leave Grindon along the narrow lane, walking downhill to the NE to pass a cattle grid by means of a stile on the L. A footpath leading off to the L is

therefore ignored. Further downhill, a succession of indistinct paths on the L are likewise avoided. Then select the combined footpath and bridleway on your L which is located opposite a path leading in the other direction and signed to 'Thor's Cave'. This departure is at a stile and gate. Walk due N, diagonally to your R, away from the boundary of the adjacent field. Pleasant, rolling countryside beckons ahead with the village of Butterton now in view spanning the hillside on your L. The way then descends across rounded grassy slopes. Past one of several stile-and-gate combinations, the descent steepens as the route veers to the L away from Ossoms Hill Farm above to the R.

The next part of the route passes through a series of bridleway gates and associated s-stiles for more agile foot-sloggers. The steep valley of Hoo Brook is then crossed, and the stream at the bottom by means of a concrete bridge. At this crossing follow the combined way signed 'Bridleway to Wettonmill, Footpath to Butterton'. Part company with the footpath leading to Butterton at the next stile, where you climb uphill to your L away from the stream, keeping to the line of the hedge on your L and walking N. The valley path below leads to Wettonmill. The way continues up steepish, grassy slopes.

Beyond more stiles and gates, a road is reached. The stile which provides access to the road has uncovered barbed wire tautly stretched across it and this impediment should be avoided by simply using the gate. From here, continue due N across more meadows before passing Wallacre by making use of more stiles. The way crosses the entrance drive to this establishment and your exit is over a w-stile positioned to the L of a metal gate. The route continues due N, descending as it does so. After the tenth stile/gate combination, be careful to keep first to the L of a wall and then above the hedge leading further N from this, because the next gate, positioned in the far R-hand corner of a field, is somewhat obscure and the way described will best lead you to it. Again, watch out for protruding barbed wire. Then veer L downhill to pass through a stone wall at a gate before crossing the next field by maintaining your diagonal approach. This is to the NNW.

The way then leads down to another tiny brook, the surrounds of which are often muddy and a hassle to cross. Leave this gully through a swing gate and climb up the far grassy slope, this particular one neither too severe nor long. From here, the way leads further N and after another stile-and-gate combination it connects with a farm track before passing Clayton House. More obstacles follow before a minor road is crossed at MR 086575. This is a prelude to descending into another narrow valley. At the bottom of this you have the unaccustomed luxury of using a raised footbridge to cross Warslow Brook but having first run a gauntlet of passing between overgrown thorn bushes. Climb out of the valley to reach a gate in the top R-hand corner of the field above. A more agreeable gradient leads uphill from here; further on, water board installations are passed to your R.

After this feature, the perimeter of Villa Farm is reached. At the time of writing, the public right of way in this vicinity was being diverted and so the recorded directions are designed to take you along the proposed new way. Turn R along the boundary wall and then turn L to pass through a gateway before continuing by veering further L along the walled lane. You return to the established right of way a short distance further on and at this juncture turn sharp R to pass through either a narrow gap or a gateway to reach a path depicted by a symbol representing a walker striding out. Use the stile at the next metal gate, then veer R to pass over or round the subsequent stile directly ahead. The direction here is ENE. More minor obstacles follow, including a very narrow stone G-stile. After this, veer R to pass much more easily through two more of these stiles on either side of a small brook. A similar crossing has to be made at another channel before a wooden step stile provides access to more open grassy slopes.

Now continue NE by veering L between hawthorn hedges. You may encounter more mud hereabouts. Cross the internal farm track by veering L at the gateway ahead and then continue walking NE beside the hawthorn hedge, temporarily on your R. (Some helpful signposting would not go amiss here.) Be particularly vigilant to spot

and then pass through a narrow stone G-stile on your R. Then turn immediately L to continue on the other side of the hawthorn hedge and stone wall, now on your L. Make towards the stone barn ahead. At the end of the field, exit from it by means of the G-stile positioned in the far L-hand corner. Turn L and then almost immediately R to cross the adjacent limestone wall before walking downhill, due E. Lower down and just above the roadway, be careful to bear to the R and then take care to locate and pass through a critical narrow G-stile which is below a supporting post for twin overhead cables. Veer R from here and continue downhill along the diagonal path, now clearly defined, to reach the road below at a wooden stile. Near to your convergence with the road be careful not to tangle with the barbed-wire fence, perilously close on your L!

Veer R along the minor road and use this to cross the River Manifold at Dale Bridge, a short distance ahead. Then turn L down the easily recognized Manifold Way and retrace your outwards steps back to the car park at Hulme End, now less than 1½ km (0.9 miles) away to the NE.

Alternative routes

ESCAPES

The route is in two long parallel sections, the first running N to S along the Manifold Way and the return S to N across higher ground to the W. There are several opportunities for curtailing this route and these are fairly obvious from looking at the OLM. One such possibility is from Wettonmill where the footpath leading SW beside Hoo Brook will re-connect you with the main route at MR 087556.

EXTENSIONS

The obvious extension is to continue further S along the Manifold Way past the entrance to Beeston Tor before circling back along the footpaths to the NW to rejoin the main route at Grindon.

Another possibility is to climb up to Thor's Cave or even as high as the top of the crag above.

159

Route 26: BERESFORD DALE, WOLFSCOTE DALE, THOR'S CAVE and ECTON HILL

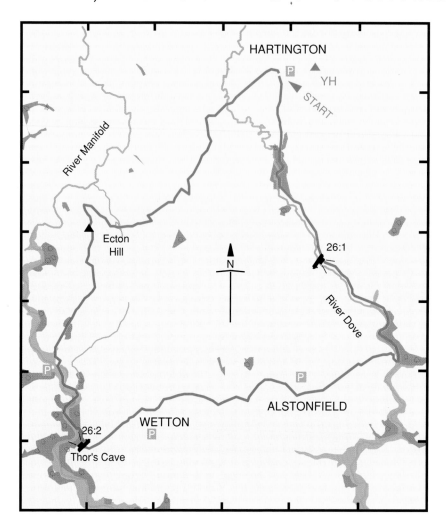

HARTINGTON

YH

START

River Manifold

Ecton
Hill

26:1

N

River Dove

P

ALSTONFIELD

WETTON
P

26:2

Thor's Cave

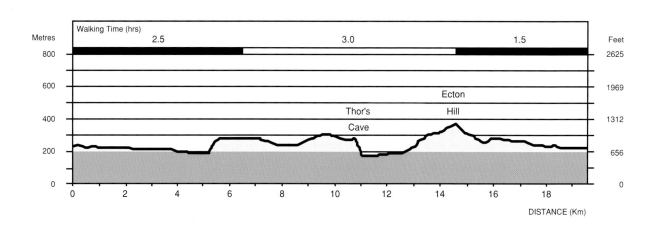

Metres | Walking Time (hrs) | | Feet
2.5 | 3.0 | 1.5
800 | | 2625
600 | | 1969
| Ecton
| Thor's | Hill
400 | Cave | | 1312
200 | | 656
0 | | 0

0   2   4   6   8   10   12   14   16   18

DISTANCE (Km)

ROUTE 26

Beresford Dale, Wolfscote Dale, Thor's Cave and Ecton Hill

•

STARTING LOCATION
Car park at Hartington.
OLM 24: MR 127603.
Large car park, holds over 50 cars.
Toilets across road.
Additional parking in village square.

ALTERNATIVE STARTING POINTS
Alstonefield.
Wetton.
Near Wettonmill.

PUBLIC TRANSPORT
Bus routes 57, 181, 202, 420, 441, 442, 446, 456, 464
    and 901.

OVERVIEW/INTEREST
Mixture of open landscapes and enclosed dales.
Good scenery throughout.
Some spectacular limestone cliffs, tors and columns.
Thor's Cave.
Interesting villages and churches.
Plenty of refreshment facilities.

FOOTPATHS
The refurbished pathways along the dales are
    excellent.
Other paths, bridleways and farm lanes are nearly
    always certain but vary in terms of ease of access.
These, in summer are usually a joy to walk along.
During wet winter weather, sections can become
    quagmires.
Signs adequate to good, apart from in the vicinity of
    Ecton Hill where they are non-existent.

GRADING
Moderate to difficult/severe.

TIME ALLOWANCE
7 hours.

STATISTICS

DISTANCE

Excluding Height	19.5 km	(12.1 miles)
TOTAL HEIGHT GAINED	440 m	(1445 ft)
PRINCIPAL HEIGHTS		
Ecton Hill	369 m	(1210 ft)

The way to Alstonefield   *Allow 2½ hours*

From the car park, cross the road on a L diagonal
and select the footpath leading off by the side of
the toilet block. This is signed to 'Dove Dale via
Beresford and Wolfscote Dales'. Through an iron
gate, the firm, wide path winds uphill to your R
into open country. The direction is to the S. An
enclosed lane is crossed at right angles at a point
where two G-stiles are provided. Continue along
the waysigned path; beyond the next brow ahead,
there are more open views of the rounded, green
hills which are you are now heading towards. The
way veers slightly R downhill along a broad gap
between two stone walls. Then veer L to pass

between stone pillars which mark the remains of a
former G-stile in a tumbled-down stone wall. After
this, the way is downhill, still southwards, to
reach a G-stile to the L of a metal gate. From here,
the path leads slightly uphill to pass round the
pointed hillock of Pennilow. The path leads
through stiles before reaching sparse woodland at
the entrance to Beresford Dale. Then the River
Dove appears at a point where impressive limestone cliffs rise beyond the stream.

The way then winds along the sheltered and
enclosed dale and the first of many weirs is passed.
The stream is crossed by means of a footbridge. A
short distance further on, a particularly impressive
limestone column, jutting out into the water, is

161

passed. The excellent well-drained path continues downstream, following the meandering River Dove. The way passes through a wooded area before the valley widens out, surrendering some of its grandeur. The stream is re-crossed at a narrow footbridge; over this, veer R to continue down the dale along the public footpath across the wide, flat private meadow. Keep to the valley bottom along here, heading towards the jaws of Wolfscote Dale ahead and thus ignoring a wide track leading uphill on your L. Through a G-stile at the S end of the meadow, the dale narrows and deepens to take on gorge-like characteristics. A small tributary stream is crossed and a second G-stile provides an entrance into Wolfscote Dale. After this, bypass another bridge across the stream by keeping to the L-hand bank.

In walking further down the dale the formidable limestone outcrops are softened by the appearance of gentler, interlacing grassy slopes which begin to enclose the dale. Progress downstream is enjoyably uneventful, apart from the

26:1 Springtime in Wolfscote Dale

odd gate and stile. The views progressively become more spectacular and limestone cliffs, tors and columns of every conceivable shape and size rear up vertically beyond the stream with triangular areas of loose scree beneath. These features are named as Drabber Tor and Peaseland Rocks. At MR 142569, ignore the path leading off to your L up the side valley of Biggin Dale and continue through a G-stile, before crossing a stone causeway ahead. The route then passes below a cave up on your L and, still trekking southwards beside the River Dove, walk past stepping stones over the stream, which are often submerged when the river is in spate. (When these stones are exposed, they may be used to reach Alstonefield along an alternative series of pathways to the NW. These provide a slightly shorter alternative route to the more secure, all-weather way next described.) The advocated main route leads further downstream along the dale to pass through a clump of Scots pines.

The way then leads to another footbridge which is used to re-cross the river. This is at Coldeaton Bridge and is located at MR 146561, just before a small, disused stone building is reached. From the W bank of the stream, the continuation way zigzags up steep, grassy slopes which are often very slippery when wet. A short, sharp climb to the NW up the slopes of Gipsy Bank provides a quick exit from the confines of the narrow dale. At the top of the brow, the path leads to a waysigned stile and wooden gate. Over the stile, veer L to follow a walled track which heads WSW, further uphill. Over the crest of the brow ahead, there are extensive views of neat, walled pastures against a backcloth of protective, rolling hillsides. The cart-track veers L towards SW before it zigzags to the R as a prelude to passing between two stone barns. The going along here can be likened to a mud bath after prolonged wet weather. The path continues to track SW and eventually reaches the outskirts of Alstonefield. Some distance further on, the church tower of the village may be spotted ahead on the L. The narrow lane leads down to a minor road. Veer R along this to reach the centre of the village, passing Chapel Cottage en route. Then bear R, to walk to the R of one of several grassed triangles located in Alstonefield. Cross over the road ahead, bearing further R to pass the car park and toilets and leave the village along the road signed to 'Hulme End and Hartington'.

The way to Top of Ecton   *Allow 3 hours*

Past Rose Cottage, veer L down the public foot-path, leaving the road at MR 129558. The route then leads NW past Plum Tree Cottage. From here, the way continues down into a shallow, sheltered valley. Another stile and gate are reached and after these the way continues to bend L beside a stone wall. This continues beyond a further waysigned G-stile as the route leads along a grassy sward further down into the shallow valley. Over the next G-stile, a wall is on your R and a short distance further on the path leads to a narrow lane at which another G-stile has been positioned. Turn R up the lane to pass the residence of Hope Marsh, having ignored a footpath off to your L. Ahead, the lane turns sharp L to go round Brook Lodge; at this point, turn off R to pass through a particularly narrow G-stile next to a metal gate. From here, proceed along a walled, grassy way, initially NW and then more westwards as the way curves round to your L. Be careful now to locate and use a S-stile over the stone wall on your L. This important turning is at a point where the walled way bends to your R. Over the wall, continue to head W beside a wire fence to cross another stone wall ahead by means of a L-stile.

Continue uphill across the next meadow beside the wire fence, before bearing L to pass through a gap in the stone wall ahead. The way continues to rise steadily to reach the minor road at Town End Farm ahead, passing through another gap in a stone wall to your R to do so. Through the G-stile at the road, veer L down the road, crossing the T junction of a side lane to your L. Walk SW into the centre of the tiny village of Wetton. From the central triangle, cross the road and continue W along the public footpath which starts by passing through the church cemetery. This is entered and left by means of K-gates. Then veer L along the lane ahead to pass Croft Cottage Café. Ignore several side paths off and continue downhill,

passing first cottages and then New House Farm. Beyond these, bear R along the road signed to 'Wettonmill (Manifold Valley) and Butterton', ignoring a path directly ahead over a stone wall. Within about 30 paces, veer L down a lane signed to 'Thor's Cave'. This is a concession footpath and it is made clear that walkers use it at their own risk.

Soon the deep scar which marks the irregular shape of the Manifold Valley can be made out ahead on the R and to the W, as the cart-track leads pleasantly downhill. The way along the track terminates and at this juncture the escape, aided by a S-stile, is over a stone wall on your R. The directions here are quite clear: 'No footpath along lane' and 'Footpath to Thor's Cave over stile'. Then continue W down the grassy slope towards the pointed hill rising beyond the shallow hause directly ahead. A narrow but clear path leads to a S-stile near a solitary large tree. Now veer L to climb up the steepish slopes to the crest of the hill. The view from the top is breathtaking, encompassing the craggy, limestone configurations of the most fantastic shapes and sizes rearing up vertically from the valley far below, and beyond to the far-off meanders of the River Manifold snaking away lazily to the north. There is the most awesome sheer drop on the far side of the summit ridge: do exercise the utmost care whilst standing on this exposed spot, particularly when the rocks are slippery after rain.

Afterwards, carefully retrace your steps down the steep, grassy slopes to return to the stile beneath the tree. This time, veer L to continue your descent towards the Manifold Valley. A narrow, exposed and often muddy path leads round the steep slopes to Thor's Cave. This is an exceptionally large, elliptically shaped cavern and hanging from the roof of this void are the lingering remains of some climbing gear which, it is reputed, were placed there by the acclaimed climber, Joe Brown. From just below the cave entrance, a renovated stepped path winds steeply down into the depths of the Manifold Valley below. There is a conveniently positioned foot-bridge at the bottom which you cross. On the far bank of the River Manifold turn R, heading N

163

26:2 A bird's-eye view of the curvaceous Manifold Way

upstream along a macadam way. The route re-crosses the river; after this, veer L along the lane nearest to the stream. This is the quieter of two parallel roads leading northwards along the valley. The river is then crossed once more at Dafar Bridge. A short distance further on, the lane reaches a ford across a gushing side stream. This crossing can be formidable when the stream is in flood but fortunately there is a footbridge round to your L over the watercourse.

Turn back R on the far side and cross the River Manifold by means of the vehicular bridge. Wettonmill café is on the far side. From here, walk uphill along a wide surfaced lane which bends progressively to the R to then head NNE towards Dale Farm. Pass between the farm buildings, following the public footpath signed to 'Back of Ecton'. A metal swing gate is used to exit from the farm – and be careful here because there is an overhead gantry with a clearance height of only 5 ft 8 in. From here, a clear path winds uphill. After prolonged rain this section of the route becomes a muddy watercourse. Keep walking uphill, heading N and making towards a prom-

inent limestone outcrop ahead named the Sugar Loaf. The signed route veers to the L round this formidable obstacle, climbing more steeply along a stony path beside a wire fence. The way leads to a gap in a stone wall at which point there is a footpath sign. Then be vigilant to pass over another stile located ahead to your L in a gap in the hawthorn hedge. Walk along the edge of the adjacent field near to the hedge and its retaining wire fence. Pass through a gap ahead and continue along the gently rising path leading up grassy slopes. Through the next gap, the adjacent fence reverts to being on your L. After crossing the next wooden stile, which is at a gate, the continuation route bears L and flattens off.

From here, the way leads directly towards Broad Ecton Farm. This is at MR 101575. The route passes over another stile located at a farm lane. Veer to the L along this lane, walking NNW uphill. At the entrance and boundary wall of the farm, pass through a metal gate to the R of the approach lane and then veer R beside a wall and walk past the L-stile over this wall to your R. Continue uphill along the signed public footpath, passing through two w-stiles. Your direction here is NE. At the crest of the brow, twin G-stiles provide access to the main ridge path leading to Ecton Hill. Pass through these and head directly towards the trig point on the horizon, walking slightly uphill to the NNW. Pleasant grassy slopes lead to the summit area of Ecton Hill. The views from here on a clear day are superb: go past the trig point to the pronounced rim of the hill directly below in order to observe the best of these, which are down below in the winding Manifold Valley. Radcliffe's Folly stands out in all its foolish fame.

The way back to Hartington   *Allow 1½ hours*

Turn R along the rim and commence your descent to the NNE along a grassy ledge. Ahead, a gap in the stone wall allows you to descend down the steeper slopes to reach a stile over a stone wall. Your way re-connects with the main path down at this point; from here continue down the crest of the spur, keeping a stone wall directly on your R.

Lower down, several deep and dangerous disused mine-shafts are passed; always keep to the safe side of the fenced-off areas surrounding these! Before you reach the stone barn below, turn R through the narrow G-stile in the corner of the stone wall, thus avoiding the other stile to the L of this and more directly ahead. From here, your direction changes abruptly to SE as you veer R along a wide and often muddy farm track.

The route then descends along a straight diagonal towards the green valley on your L. The way leads to a narrow lane accessed at a metal gate. Turn L down this lane and a short distance below, where the lane bends sharp L, continue straight ahead following the signed footpath by passing round a wooden entrance gate. Further on, the route leads over two stiles, on either side of a plank bridge over a small stream. Continue up the far grassy bank beside a wire fence. This direction is to the E. The gradient levels off and then another stile is crossed before a stone barn is passed on your R. Veer R at this barn and cross the adjacent meadow to reach another stile to the R of a wooden gate. This provides access to a lane which you turn L along. Within 100 paces, at the end of a copse, turn full R to walk E down the farm track. Pass over the G-stile positioned at the wooden gate ahead and then veer slightly to the L in order to locate a gate stile positioned in the hedge ahead and to the L of holly and hawthorn bushes. Keep to your established diagonal to thread through a gap between the ends of a stone wall and a wire fence. Then wade through the waterlogged ground beyond to reach another G-stile. From here, a better defined route passes round Archford Moor Farm but it does entail making use of more stiles. The continuation way then leads gently downhill, over another s-stile, across an open field and through a narrow G-stile to reach the road opposite Harecops Farm. This is at MR 114586.

Turn R along the road and then L at the crossroads just ahead to continue down the lane signed to 'Hartington 1'. A short distance further on, bear R along the public footpath located at a G-stile next to a metal gate. Head across the field to reach a stile in stone walling within the hedge to the NE. Keep to this direction, making for the trees

directly in front where a waysigned G-stile provides a crossing of the next hedge. After this, continue downhill, walking through a sheltered glade and then veer slightly to the R to reach the next stile. The now obvious way leads round Lower Hurst Farm where two further stiles have to be contended with. The parkland beyond is crossed on a L diagonal walking NNE. This leads to yet another s-stile at the hedge ahead. From here, walk downhill making for the L of the boundary fence around the building in front, in order to reach and pass through the next G-stile, after passing over a minor watercourse. From here, grassy slopes lead to the road into Hartington which you turn R along, having passed over another stile. Pass by Raikes Farm and at the bottom of the hill, across the River Dove and immediately past the stone house, cross the road and select the footpath leading off to the L. This leads diagonally across meadows back into the village of Hartington, less than 1 km (0.6 miles) away. However, it does involve passing over or through five more wall stiles, the first of which is relatively awkward. Then at the farm area, keep to the clearly indicated passageway which leads to the road into the village. Turn R along this road to return to the car park.

Alternative routes

ESCAPES
The area to the SW of Hartington contains an abundance of footpaths and minor roads which may be conveniently linked together to provide a variety of shorter alternative routes. These possibilities may easily be worked out from studying the OLM. In particular there is no need to climb up to either Thor's Cave or Ecton Hill and the footpath leading northwards from the village of Wetton avoids these.

EXTENSIONS
A much longer circuit is to continue further S along the course of the River Dove into Mill Dale before striking off westwards through Stanshope to rejoin the main route at Wetton.

Route 27: DOVE DALE, WETTON, ECTON HILL, ALSTONEFIELD and WOLFSCOTE DALE

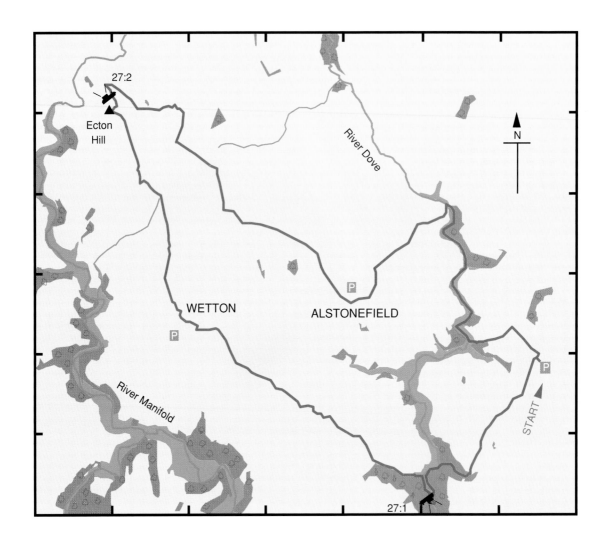

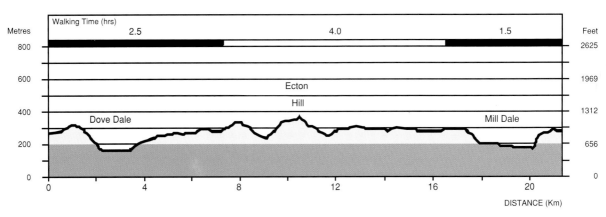

ROUTE 27

Dove Dale, Wetton, Ecton Hill, Alstonefield and Wolfscote Dale

●

STARTING LOCATION
Car park off main A515 road near Alsop-en-le-Dale.
OLM 24: MR 156549.
Large car park holds up to 50 cars.

ALTERNATIVE STARTING POINTS
Wetton.
Alstonefield.

PUBLIC TRANSPORT
Bus routes 202, 415, 420, 426, 441, 442 and 443.

OVERVIEW/INTEREST
Varied walking including dales and open landscapes.
Spectacular limestone tors, caves and rock faces.
Attractive villages and hamlets.
Parts of route beside meandering rivers.
Suitable for family groups.

FOOTPATHS
For the most part very good.
Terrain usually well-drained.

Much of route either across meadows or along clear paths in deep-sided dales.
Route reasonably well signed although vigilance is required.
Footpaths above Paddock House Farm and at Gateham Farm have been re-routed.
Numerous stiles are a frustrating feature!

GRADING
Moderate.

TIME ALLOWANCE
8 hours.

STATISTICS

DISTANCE

Excluding Height	21.4 km	(13.3 miles)
TOTAL HEIGHT GAINED	580 m	(1905 ft)
PRINCIPAL HEIGHTS		
Ecton Hill	369 m	(1210 ft)

The way to Wetton   *Allow 2½ hours*

Carefully cross the main A515 road and pass through the stile in a stone wall to the L of the branch lane opposite, signed to 'Milldale and Alstonefield'. Walk diagonally L across the field, ssw, to reach the iron gate in the opposite corner. A stile provides access to the adjacent minor road. Cross over and continue across the cattle grid and along the farm lane signed to 'New Hanson Grange and Hanson Grange'. The route is now to the sw, marginally uphill, through undulating, open countryside. The gradient steepens and the buildings of New Hanson Grange are passed to your R. At the top of the brow there is a stile and another cattle grid. After this descend along the main surfaced lane, ignoring ways off to both L and R. Towards the farm shippens, veer L and cut

across the corner of the field, following the signed way, then use the stile ahead to cross a stone wall. Bear R towards the next stone wall and rely on the stile below, near the farm buildings of Hanson Grange, to regain the main pathway below. Turn L along this and then immediately R to descend more steeply into the recesses of the narrowing, shaded, tree-fringed dale circling The Nabs. A stile and a gate await ahead.

Towards the bottom of the cleft, veer L (wsw) and then L again to follow the wide path beside the tranquil and splendid River Dove flowing demurely over a series of weirs, down on your R. The river is reached at Dove Holes, situated at MR 143536, and the caves featured here are passed to your L. The deep limestone gorge is quite magnificent, with near-vertical white rock faces blending perfectly with the generously wooded valley (Upper Taylor's Wood). After walking southwards along the dale for a spell, cross the River Dove at the footbridge beneath Ilam Rock and near the fantastic limestone columns of Pickering Tor. Turn immediately R to reverse, temporarily, your direction of travel, now walking NNW along the opposite bank upstream.

After crossing the next W-stile, turn L into Hall Dale which branches off to the NW. This is another attractive dale composed of limestone bluffs and loose screes but it does not contain a watercourse. The way is relentlessly upwards beside the northern flank of Hurt's Wood. Stiles have to be negotiated during the longish climb and at the second of these ignore a narrow path off to the L which leads to Ilam. The gradient eases as the more open mouth of the dale is reached and the way then meanders along a wider, springy grass path. Several more stiles of various forms then have to be crossed in walking diagonally over flatter terrain to the NW, before the tiny village of Stanshope is reached. Helpful yellow waymarkers sign the route along this section and a wide lane is crossed at right angles in your approach to the hamlet. Past a final stile near a shed, turn L down a gravel track and then L again along a surfaced lane. This way then veers R to connect with the minor road that goes past Stanshope Hall.

Continue heading NW past the hall, following the road uphill as it swings to the R. Then select the public footpath off on the L by passing through a stile in the stone wall. This is at MR 126543. Cross the adjacent field on a diagonal to your R, walking W. Make for the next stile just beyond the power lines. Then keep to the line of a stone wall on your L to cross the following field; ahead to the NNW are the rounded slopes that end in the tumuli to the NE of Wetton Hill. Another stile is used at the far corner of the field. This pattern of crossing successive pastures keeping to a NW diagonal is repeated several times. Further stiles signal a crossing at right angles of a narrow surfaced lane. Beyond this, take a L-hand diagonal and be careful then to locate and use another, almost concealed, low stile. Following this, make for the protruding corner of the next field and then veer round this to the R near the boundary hedge to your R. The

continuation way then leads northwards across yet more stiles and fields and the fifth of these access points provides entry to a narrow lane. Watch out for barbed wire here! Turn L and walk uphill into the attractive village of Wetton. Keep to the road and follow this round Yew Tree Farm into the centre of the village.

The way to Alstonefield   *Allow 4 hours*

Leave the village along the road signed to 'Wetton Mill (Manifold Valley) and Butterton'. Bear R round Manor House Farm and walk up the lane signed 'Back of Ecton'. Further on, a car park area is crossed and beyond this pass through a stile in a wall to access a narrow public footpath. Your direction is northwards. Another stile provides access to the route along the lower ground that separates Wetton Hill on your L from the higher escarpment and tumuli to your R rising to a height of 371 m (1220 ft). Keep walking northwards along the valley through a landscape of rounded hills. At MR 107564 bear R along the higher of two paths to continue northwards across grassy slopes heading towards Ecton Hill, now silhouetted on the skyline ahead. Then a tiny watercourse is crossed before a double stile is encountered. Beyond these, the way continues up rising ground to the L and two closely positioned stiles have to be negotiated. The route then climbs up steeper ground to reach a narrow lane above. Turn R to walk further uphill along this and at the intersection ahead keep gaining height by selecting the L-hand branch, then proceeding NNW. Part way up the following slope, turn off to the R through a gateway to engage a wide, grassy path.

The path continues to rise alongside a stone wall and another stile is reached. Continue walking uphill to the NNW and make a slight detour from the path to reach the trig point and summit of Ecton Hill, set in an expansive landscape of rounded, grassy slopes. These features mark the highest point of the route at 369 m (1210 ft) and are located at MR 100580. From this fine vantage

27:1 The bridge over the River Dove at Ilam Rock

27:2 The Manifold Way and Radcliffe's Folly from Ecton Hill

point, the valley of Ecton with its steep-sided slopes is revealed down below to the NW. Thereafter, a descent of no more than a few paces to the high-level rim of the ridge will provide a view of the extensive Manifold Valley snaking away to the W. Following this, turn sharp R and locate a grassy path leading NNE down the hillside. Use a gap to breach the stone wall ahead and a short distance further down the slope turn L to cross another stile. From here, a better established path leads down towards the valley below. During this pleasant descent beware of several dangerous disused mine shafts; these are fenced off but two of them are quite close to your path. Turn R at the next set of stiles, ignoring the one directly ahead near a renovated building.

Continue along the wide cart-track on the far side of the stile and follow this round as it progressively bends to the R to lead you SE down a long traverse. At the far end a gate provides entry to a surfaced lane. Turn L along the lane descending into the steep-sided valley below. When the lane bends sharply to the L, continue ahead by means of the public footpath reached beyond a stile. A small stream and more stiles are crossed before the continuation way leads E uphill at the side of a wire fence. Continue climbing further

uphill beyond the next stile (be careful here — more barbed wire!) then veer to the R between stone posts. A short distance further on the way reaches another stile, near a building. Farm outbuildings are then passed on your L and the indistinct path passes beneath a mature sycamore tree.

Beyond a clearly located wooden stile, bear R along a narrow path and use this to skirt the slopes of the next grassy hillside, on a fairly level traverse. Approaching the second of two sets of twin gates ahead, veer to the L before reaching them in order to keep above this barrier. A plank bridge affords a crossing of a waterlogged area ahead and after this be vigilant to veer L uphill in order to locate a single stile to the R of a gate. (The footpath has been re-routed hereabouts so avoid crossing the twin stiles that you pass just before reaching the single stile.) On the far side of the stile, walk diagonally L to reach the newly erected wire fences flanking the farm road. Cross this at right angles, making use of the two stiles provided.

Continue on a SE diagonal across the next field to reach another twin gate and stile. Bear slightly to the R beyond these to converge with the line of an intermittent boundary wall further to your R. With the road in sight ahead, veer L on a diagonal towards it. However, before reaching it use the stiles to your R to cross, first, an electric fence and then a stone wall which provides entry to the next meadow. Cross this on a diagonal to your R, now walking S. The way converges on another stone wall to your R and this is crossed at a stile. Another R diagonal leads towards the crest of the next field; continue by passing through a stile in the stone wall ahead on your R. Just a few paces further on select another stile on the L. These features are located below the steep slopes of the tumuli rising to the W.

Cross the next field on a SE diagonal, which will bring you to an exit stile to the narrow road beyond. Turn R along the road and continue walking slightly downhill. Take the next turning to your L and then follow the re-routed way round Gateham Farm. Cross the field beyond and then a surfaced lane, passing over two more stiles. Beyond this, keep to your established SE diagonal to pass through, or over, a succession of eight stiles to reach another minor road at MR 127562. Turn R and follow the road into the charming village of Alstonefield less than 1 km (0.6 miles) further on. On approaching the village, bear R along the road signed to 'Wetton, Ilam and Dovedale'. The Memorial Hall is then passed and, following this, an immediate L turn will bring you to the post office, at which refreshments may be obtained. This is next to Jean Goodwin's Cottage Studio (oil paintings and watercolours). Turn L to reach the George Inn and refreshments of a different kind.

The way back to the car park *Allow 1½ hours*

Beyond the George, continue past the opening signed to 'The Smithy caravan site' and then turn R along the road indicated to 'Lodemill and Ashbourne'. An oak furniture store and Wesleyan House are passed before a L turning is taken down an enclosed footpath alley cum track. Further on, fork R to follow the track signed to 'Gipsy Bank'. A pleasant way leads NE past more gates and stiles. A farm building is passed on your L; cross the next field and then, through a particularly awkward G-stile, veer L to pass between two large ash trees. The route from here is waysigned and is along the established diagonal, across fields and over more

stiles. Thereafter, the way descends quite dramatically into Wolfscote Dale, crossing another path as it does so to the N of Gipsy bank. Beyond another gate it commences down a diagonal to the L.

There are fine views from here down into and along the impressive, steep-sided valley, the slopes of which are a mass of yellow when the gorse is in bloom in May. The path drops very steeply, partly by means of wooden steps, to the valley floor. The River Dove is crossed by means of the large stepping stones. Following this, turn R along the footpath on the far bank. There follows a delightful 2 km (1.2 miles) stretch following the course of the Dove towards Mill Dale. Gates, stiles and bridges come almost unnoticed along this section as the scenery is so enchanting. Just before reaching a bank of trees on your L and with the buildings located beneath Shining Tor clearly visible ahead, be vigilant in locating and following a faint path which leads steeply uphill on the L. Towards the top of the stiff climb up Fish Pond Bank ignore a L-stile to your R and instead use the stile ahead to reach the final, less severe gradients of the slope. After another stile, cross the field ahead on an ENE diagonal to reach a final double stile that provides entry to the Tissington Trail. This runs along the former railway line. Turn R and use this trail to reach the car park about ½ km (⅓ mile) away.

Alternative routes

ESCAPES

The elliptical route can be cut short at several points and these are obvious from consulting the OLM. One of the more apparent ones is to use the convenient combination of roads and footpaths running E from Wetton to reach Alstonefield across a direct distance of no more than a couple of kilometres.

EXTENSIONS

From Wetton it is feasible to head westwards and loop in part of the Manifold Valley before heading northwards to follow the path leading round the Sugar Loaf to rejoin the main route to Ecton Hill.

171

Route 28: HIGH PEAK and TISSINGTON TRAILS from FRIDEN

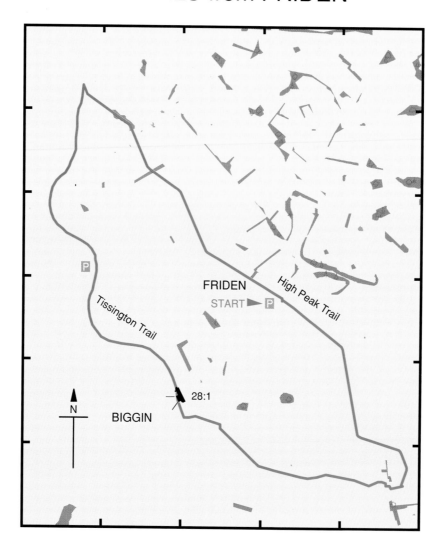

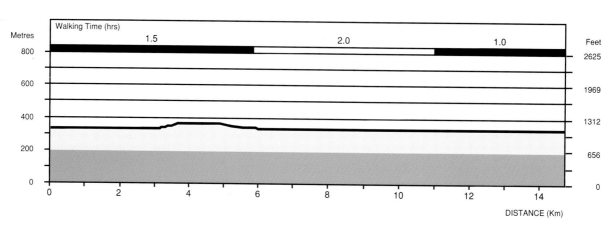

ROUTE 28

High Peak and Tissington Trails from Friden

STARTING LOCATION
Car park at Friden.
OLM 24: MR 173607.
Relatively large car park beside High Peak Trail.
Holds up to 30 cars; picnic area.

ALTERNATIVE STARTING POINT
Tissington Trail (at former station for Hartington).

PUBLIC TRANSPORT
Bus routes 177 and 181.

OVERVIEW/INTEREST
A pleasant stroll along parts of two former railway lines.
Virtually no climbing involved.
A walk eminently suitable for families.
Beware of a small minority of inconsiderate cyclists!
Gentle, rolling countryside but somewhat lacking in dramatic physical features.
Interesting limestone faces in several cuttings.

FOOTPATHS
Along the trails these are excellent with a virtual absence of waterlogged areas.
Patches of the southerly crossing between the two trails are more demanding and mud does feature after prolonged wet spells.
Signs on and near the trails are very adequate but the connecting route across open country is neglected.

GRADING
Easy.

TIME ALLOWANCE
4½ hours.

STATISTICS

DISTANCE		
Excluding Height	14.7 km	(9.2 miles)
TOTAL HEIGHT GAINED	30 m	(100 ft)
PRINCIPAL HEIGHTS		
HIGHEST POINT	364 m	(1195 ft)

The way to the Tissington Trail

Allow 1½ hours

Depart from the far end of the picnic area, walking SE along the High Peak Trail. The way is signed to 'Minninglow and Gotham'. At an immediate swing gate, more precise directions are provided which read 'Minninglow 2½ miles – Middleton Top 9 – High Peak Junction 11½'. Your route does not continue s that far! From here a wide path leads through a cutting between grassy banks and stone retaining walls. After a short distance the cutting levels off and extensive views of pleasant, rolling countryside open up on either side.

The trail leads SE in a dead straight line extending as far as the eye can see and a short distance further on a second cutting is entered. The trail then bisects the A5012 road at Newhaven Crossing. Continue s from here and further on

pass a footpath signed to 'Biggin'. It also marks the point where waysigned walk number 1 parts company with your route. Passing an extensive piggery down to your L you will come across a multitude of paths and tracks leading off to both L and R and again you must avoid these.

The next feature of note is that the trail curves effortlessly through 90 degrees to the R. When you reach Gotham you bid a fond farewell to the trail for the time being. This act is performed at MR 188585 by turning off to the R and then walking up the slight gradient to reach Gotham Granges Farm. You may obtain drinks, sandwiches, scones, cakes, ice cream and sweets at this enterprising establishment. These goodies are reached by walking w, crossing over a s-stile to the R of a cattle grid and then following the surfaced farm lane uphill to the farm buildings.

The next part of the route across country from

Gotham Granges Farm is relatively tricky, so carefully follow the directions provided. First a wide track coming in from the L has to be avoided as the correct way continues above the farm across an area which may be muddy. From here, proceed up a walled track which leads w; further on, near a metal gate, ignore a public footpath leading off at an angle to the R, northwards. Just beyond this, the wide track bends sharp L to wind below a tiny outcrop of inclined limestone. This interesting edge outcrops again further along on the L of the track where it supports a solitary tree which has dared to take root within its inhospitable rocky ledges. The clearly defined track winds further uphill to pass through a gap in limestone walling which crosses your approach route at right angles. Beyond this gap, do not continue to follow the clear tractor way round to the R as this loops back downhill a short distance further on. Instead, strike off across the meadowland directly ahead to maintain direct progress to the w. Towards the crest of the hill in front, pass through a gap in the limestone walling directly ahead.

From here, continue w across the next meadow and pass through the metal gate on the far side. (A directional sign would be helpful hereabouts.) This gate provides access to a broad, enclosed grassy way at MR 172587 which you veer R along, changing your direction to NW. Almost immediately you have to pass through another gateway and on the gatepost here is a waysign informing you that you are now treading along walking route 3. From here, continue walking NW along a deeply rutted track, sometimes filled with water. Along this stretch a series of fairly straight diagonals will eventually lead you down to the main A515 road at MR 165592. This is just to the s of Ivy House and the final approach to the highway can be unpleasantly boggy. Cross this busy road on a diagonal to your R, exercising care. Then turn off down the side road signed to 'Biggin ½'. Cross over in order to make use of the adjacent surfaced footpath on the far side. From here, the road dips down to reach the Tissington Trail as it passes the outskirts of Biggin further away to the w. Turn R through the gate and climb the embankment to join the trail.

The way to rejoin the High Peak Trail

Allow 2 hours

Bear R down the Tissington Trail to walk NW along another exceedingly well-maintained path. This one is particularly well used by walkers, horse riders and cyclists. Be particularly vigilant when a strong wind is blowing towards you because in these conditions it is difficult to detect the sound of bikes approaching fast from your rear. The next part of the route is north westwards along the Tissington Trail until it connects at MR 148633 with the High Peak Trail.

A feature of the Tissington Trail is that, following prolonged wet weather, you do occasionally come across some surface water. However, this minor inconvenience is offset by interesting vegetation lining the trail. Further on, a shallow valley is crossed by an elevated section of the trail and beyond this the way passes beneath an arched bridge in a sheltered cutting. This provides a good spot to stop for refreshments.

The pleasant, undemanding way curves to both L and R as it continues northwards. Further along the trail, avoid the footpaths leading off up stone steps to both L and R. Along this stretch the gently rounded hillock dominating the landscape to the sw is Wolfscote Hill, lying beyond Biggin Dale. Past this, you arrive at a most delightful picnic area off to the R. This is located at Ruby Wood, not marked on some OLMs.

The trail continues northwards and features which are encountered in the following section include another cutting, the passing beneath a further stone bridge, the temptation to peel off along walking route number 2 in the direction of Heathcote, a sectioned-off quarry area, and yet another cutting (this one tree-lined), before you reach an extensive and much-used car parking area at the former station serving Hartington. Further footpaths lead off from here which you again avoid.

The trail then crosses above the valley and road leading down to Hartington village as you continue further NW along an elevated section. Then an interesting rock-faced cutting, deeper than the previous ones, is entered and in places the exposed rocks are covered with some unusual leaching of mineral salts. A not dissimilar cutting features further along the trail and provides more open aspects as it curves gracefully and uniformly round to the R. After passing through this, more fine rural landscapes appear. Another elevated embankment follows and this leads to yet another cutting, this one spanned by a slanted bridge.

Along here, the top of the deep chink exposed across the fields on your L to the WNW is the northerly tip of Long Dale. Further on, a rectangular brick shelter is passed just before the trail enters Parsley Hay Nature Reserve (maintained by Derbyshire Wildlife Trust.) The next cutting is impressively deep with almost perpendicular rock faces rising high above you. The passage through this signals that you are nearing your rendezvous with the High Peak Trail and this intersection is reached immediately after passing out of the cutting. At this point turn acutely R and follow the lighter-coloured surfaced trail which converges from the SSE.

The way back to Friden   *Allow 1 hour*

Your abruptly changed direction of travel is now back southwards. The High Peak Trail, after curving to the L and to the SE, soon establishes long, straight diagonal stretches which lead away into the distance. Then the trail penetrates another nature reserve; this one is Blake Moor. After this, the way passes beneath the A515 road by means of a tunnel, skillfully engineered by Jos Jessop. The cutting on the far side of this contains a group of larch trees. Another bridge of more normal proportions is reached and beyond this the width of the trail narrows. Then a series of twin gates which flank a number of farm crossings of the trail have to be negotiated. These are separated by further fairly straight sections. During this section, walking route number 2 bears off to the R. A penultimate straight section leads through another shallow cutting, after which the chimney and outline of the brickworks located at Friden come into view on the skyline to your L across the intervening dip.

28:1 The outline of Biggin viewed from the Tissington Trail

One further set of gates flanking the approach lane to Brundcliffe Farm needs to be negotiated before the trail passes the extensive, dusty buildings housing the brickworks. Another gate provides access to this passage. The car parking area is just beyond these long sheds of humming activity, on the R, after crossing the bridge over the road connecting Friden with Youlgreave.

Alternative routes

ESCAPES
The route is roughly triangular in shape and there are numerous paths and minor roads which may be used to connect and at the same time curtail the route within the area covered by the triangle. The various possibilities are obvious from the OLM.

EXTENSIONS
Should walkers wish to extend the route, it is suggested that they venture further up or down either of the trails at one or both of the far ends of the prescribed route. This does, however, necessitate retracing your footsteps back to the point where you departed from the main route.

Route 29: ALSTONEFIELD, MANIFOLD VALLEY ILAM and DOVE DALE

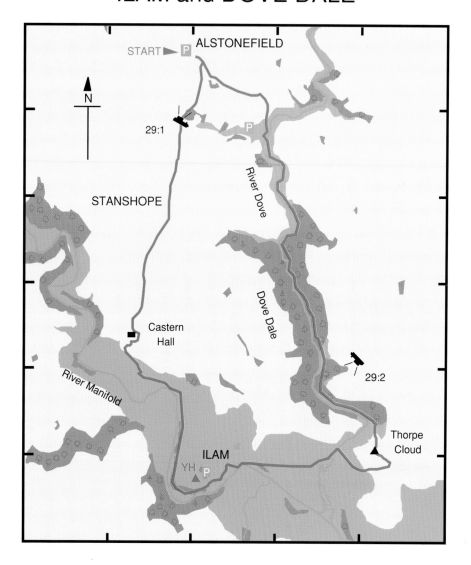

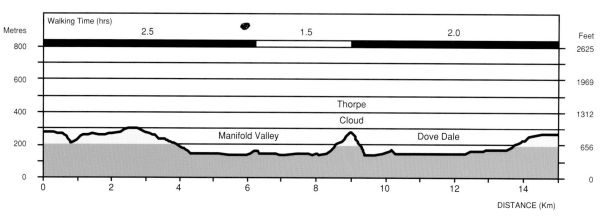

ROUTE 29

Alstonefield, Manifold Valley, Ilam and Dove Dale

●

STARTING LOCATION
Car park at Alstonefield.
OLM 24: MR 131556.
Tiny car park, holds up to 12 cars, with separate
   provision for coaches; toilet facilities.

ALTERNATIVE STARTING POINTS
Ilam Hall.
Dove Dale, at both s and n extremities.

PUBLIC TRANSPORT
Bus routes 57A, 202, 441, 442 and 450.

OVERVIEW/INTEREST
Good views and plenty of variety.
Many highlights including Manifold Valley, Ilam
   Hall, Thorpe Cloud and Dove Dale.
Interesting picturesque villages.
Both open landscapes and enclosed gorges.
Fantastic limestone features along Dove Dale
   including pillars, tors, caves and natural bridges.
Part of route beside rivers Manifold and Dove.
Older more adventurous children should thoroughly
   enjoy this walk.

FOOTPATHS
For most of the way, footpaths and signs are
   extremely good and clear.
Few problems with route finding; biggest single
   difficulty is getting out of Alstonefield.
Some muddy areas after prolonged rain in wet
   winter months.
Erosion control restrictions on part of Thorpe Cloud.

GRADING
Easy/straightforward to moderate.

TIME ALLOWANCE
6 hours.

STATISTICS
DISTANCE

Excluding Height	15.0 km	(9.3 miles)
TOTAL HEIGHT GAINED	440 m	(1445 ft)
PRINCIPAL HEIGHTS		
Thorpe Cloud	287 m	(940 ft)

The way to Ilam Hall   *Allow 2½ hours*

Turn r out of the car park and pass the toilet block. Then bear r along a narrow track, walking s. At the road veer r to pass a grassed triangular area on your l and continue to a second such feature. Past this, veer l and then turn l along a signed public footpath, the lettering arranged vertically on the post shaft. Continue walking s along an enclosed, walled way, passing the distinctive towered church which is some distance away across the fields on your l. The most difficult part of the entire route finding is now behind you! When the track bends sharply to the r, keep walking straight ahead and pass through a stile/gate to maintain your s direction, now walking beside a stone wall. The route leads downhill through meadows and a short distance further on an enclosed area is reached which contains a solitary mature tree. Bear progressively r from here down a steep slope which can become muddy and slippery after prolonged rain. The descent brings you to a minor road at a stone stile in a locality known as Dale Bottom. This is at MR 129549 and is close to an attractive cottage, the surrounds of which in February are covered in white by the tiny, delicate flowers of hundreds of snowdrops.

Cross the road and proceed up the broad track opposite. This is along a steepish incline between stone walls. Further up, a stone barn signifies flatter ground and from the brow of the hill here there are good views to the rear across the intervening valley with Alstonefield church still visible in the distance. The route passes Grove

29:1 Cottage at Dale Bottom

Farm before leading pleasantly downhill towards trees and the tiny village of Stanshope. On the way down, Hall Dale appears to your L in the SE. Veer L along the road, still walking S, and ignoring a track off to the L signed as a public footpath.

About ½ km (⅓ mile) further on, turn off the lane to your R, using the G-stile to follow a public footpath. Cross the adjacent meadow on a diagonal line to your L, walking SW and to the L of a prominent barn featured on the skyline and heading towards the far corner of the field. Across the G-stile in the next stone wall, keep to your esablished diagonal to reach an intersection of signposted paths. There is a S-stile to the L of this crossing. Continue ahead, walking slightly uphill to the SW beside a wall on your R. Cross another stone wall by a stile and then follow the wall as it bends to the L. Another waysigned stile is crossed at the brow of the hill and from here a clear path leads gently downhill beside another guiding wall on your R. During the descent good views open up of the wide Manifold Valley and of the gentle landscape of rounded hills rising on the far side of the valley. These hillsides are well sprinkled with trees.

More waymarked stiles are encountered and past the second of these the descent steepens appreciably as the way veers slightly R following the line of yet another stone wall. In this section the route crosses beneath electricity power lines. Just beyond an iron gate, bear R to pass over another S-stile in a stone wall, after which veer further to the R to follow the narrow footpath across the slopes of the grassy hillside. Your direction of travel is still to the SW. Then Castern Hall comes into view down to your L, but before you reach this impressive building you have to go round the farm of that name in a rather complicated way. The route leads down to an unusual G-stile fashioned from metal girders, to the L of a gate. Through this stile veer R uphill away from the farm along a surfaced way. When this strip of concrete bends to your R, bear off L to cross another metal stile between a stone wall and a water tank. Then keep to the L alongside the wall before turning L to pass through a narrow stone G-stile just before the corner of the enclosure. Drop down the steep slope ahead, circling back to your R to reach a G-stile below partly obscured by a large tree.

Turn R down the narrow surfaced lane and walk s to pass the residence named Paddock House. Follow the lane as it first swings to the L to go round Castern Hall and then zigzags down the steepish hillside beyond. A cattle grid has to be crossed, then a footpath off to the R signed to Wetton is ignored. Further along there is a path off to the L, but as this alternative route down is more difficult to follow than the surfaced lane, keep to the lane. Further down still pass by a farm track off to your R as the dominant shape of Bunster Hill with its twin peaks comes into view, rising to the ESE on your L. Following more twists, the lane bends L to provide from here onwards a predominantly SE direction of travel towards Bunster Hill. A more substantial lane is reached at a grass triangle; veer L here to pass by Riverlodge cottage after crossing a cattle grid. This is at MR 129518. Veer R at the cottage to pass through a gate at which a toll box has been placed, the latter presumably intended to induce an instantaneous search for coins. Having forked out, pass over the G-stile beyond to reach the meandering Manifold River a short distance further on.

Follow the river downstream along the shaded, grassy way. The next wooden stile marks the boundary of the extensive grounds of Ilam Country Park, protected by the National Trust. For the time being keep steadfastly to the riverside path passing through more stiles and ignoring alternative ways, both across the bridge spanning the river on your R and uphill to your L. The route curves elegantly to the L on a long, broad sweep as you approach Hinkley Wood. Much nearer, on the slopes to your L, dense shrubbery appears containing a mixture of rhododendrons, beech, western hemlock and yew. Eventually, a fenced-off shaft of a cross is reached. This was taken from the foundations of a cottage during the rebuilding of Ilam village in about 1840. It is known traditionally as the 'Battle Stone' and is associated with the struggle between the Saxons and the Danes. Veer L at the shaft and walk up the gently rising incline, leaving the main valley path down below on your R. The way then leads pleasantly beneath trees and through shrubbery to reach Ilam Hall at the top of the brow.

The way to Thorpe Cloud

Allow 1½ hours

Pass by the Manifold Tea Room and bear R to walk through the ornamental terraced gardens. As you do this the pointed peak of Thorpe Cloud comes into view across the valley to the E. The fine buildings of Ilam Hall deserve some attention and the turrets, castellated walling and arched doorways and open passages impress most casual observers. Continue eastwards down to the church, passing through the car park and by the National Trust Shop and Information Centre. The beautifully proportioned St Bertram's Chapel, dedicated to the Holy Cross, is well worth visiting, especially for its narrow stained-glass lancet windows. Inside the church you will find a modestly priced and interesting guide to 'The Church and Village of Ilam'.

From the church, walk into the pretty village of Ilam, keeping to the path as instructed. Beyond the K-gate at Dovedale House, turn R along the road to pass the village green and then a group of charming cottages with the most immaculate gardens. This will bring you to the impressive monument at the road junction ahead. This intricately carved cross incorporates six figures in its unusual hexagonal shape and there is more information about it in the guide that you may have purchased in the church. Veer L along the road signed to 'Dove Dale and Thorpe'. A short distance further on, turn off L through a gate to use the footpath round the lower slopes of Bunster Hill, now climbing to the E. The initially narrow path soon merges with a wide track above, along which you veer R. More stiles and gates have to be negotiated as you make your way across fields around and to the L of, first, farm buildings and then the celebrated hostelry of the Izaak Walton Hotel, still walking due E. The obvious path then veers L and NE down the hillside directly towards the inviting jaws of Dove Dale. The way drops down to a very large and popular car park, where there are toilets and a refreshment stall.

Veer L along the traffic-prohibited lane to enter Dove Dale and then turn R to cross the River Dove at the wooden footbridge before resuming your way up the dale on the far side of the stream. At

179

the fenced-off area protecting the much-trodden and eroded slopes leading directly to the top of Thorpe Cloud, veer R along the broad track and climb eastwards to reach the top of the brow ahead near a barn and animal pens. From here, climb directly to the summit of Thorpe Cloud up the permissible route by veering L and scaling the steep, grassy slopes rising to the WNW along the obvious but narrow path of compacted earth. Near the top the ground becomes quite craggy with exposed limestone rock and a steadying hand is called for as you scramble up the final sections.

The top ridge, although exposed, is a joy to tread along but do this with great care as the rocks here have been smoothed down through constant use and when wet they can become extremely slippery. The views from the top, in clear weather, are superb and two of the highlights must be those along Dove Dale and towards Bunster Hill. There is a morer complete description of this summit area as a feature for Route 30 (see p. 187).

The way back to Alstonefield   *Allow 2 hours*

Descend by the equally steep and even more adventurous slopes leading N towards Lin Dale. This descent requires constant alertness and a head for heights as the footing is precarious in places. The most challenging sections are at the top and towards the bottom where some elementary scrambling is demanded. The route veers away from Lin Dale and back into Dove Dale in its lower levels and the River Dove is again reached at a spot where there are stepping stones and a pool. Turn R and pass between either of two narrow stone G-stiles to continue northwards along Dove Dale. There is now a fascinating journey of some 4 km (2.5 miles) beside the River Dove within the breathtaking limestone gorge. The route is an obvious one along a wide refurbished way, not entirely favoured by some traditional walkers but firm, dry, safe and durable. The planners of this refurbished way also deserve praise for the safe elevated way along duckboards round the narrowest part of the gorge, the previous passage through which could be a night-

mare when the river was swollen after heavy rain.

Apart from the delights of the merrily gurgling clear waters as they pass over countless weirs, the dale contains the following interesting features (amongst many others), listed in approach sequence:

- Dovedale Castle – a spectacular limestone column.

- Lover's Leap – a craggy hillside with a precipitous cliff towering above the river. This is accessed by flights of steps.

- Twelve Apostles – outcrops of limestone on the far side of the stream opposite Lover's Leap. See if you can spot all twelve.

- Tissington Spires – jagged, tooth-like, narrow columns of limestone rising spectacularly and almost vertically to your R.

- Jacob's Ladder – imposing limestone feature on far side of stream almost opposite Tissington Spires.

- Natural Arch – a rock arch, the size of which is impressively large.

- Pickering Tor, Caves and Ilam Rock – a concentration of limestone pinnacles and large caves straddling both banks of the stream. There is a footbridge here which you do not use.

A short distance after passing the last of the splendid features listed above, a side dale leading towards and signed to Alsop-en-le-Dale is passed. After passing through another K-gate, the upper reaches of the dale become less spectacular as the valley widens out and the cliffs above decline in height and are replaced by rounded, grassy hillsides. More stiles and gates follow as the dale widens and flat, grassy areas appear beside the river. Eventually the Dove is crossed by means of a particularly attractive arched stone bridge, Viators Bridge. This is at MR 139547 and it signifies your departure from the delightful dale.

At the huddle of buildings ahead, veer L and then turn immediately R to walk up the lane which passes Polly's Cottage shop and further

29:2 Peeping down on Lover's Leap in Dove Dale

along a real, red telephone kiosk! From here, a narrow lane winds pleasantly uphill passing the Methodist church. Follow this lane into Alstone-field about 1 km (0.6 miles) to the NW. Towards the village the impressive, squat-towered church with its ornate mausoleum is passed again, on this occasion much nearer on your L. Immediately beyond this, the village is reached; walk past the triangular green and the George Inn, bear L and then turn R and the car park is to your L a short distance ahead.

Alternative routes

ESCAPES
For those who do not enjoy steep climbs or dizzy heights, the obvious short-cut is to avoid scaling Thorpe Cloud. This is easily achieved by walking round it to the W, keeping to the footpath which skirts the River Dove.

A much more severe curtailment is to walk SE from Stanshope down the steep-sided dry valley of Hall Dale and then proceed S along the banks of the River Dove, before crossing it by the footbridge at MR 142531 to re-connect with the main route along the E bank of the stream.

EXTENSIONS
A feasible and attractive extension is to continue northwards at the end of Dove Dale along Mill Dale into Wolfscote Dale for about 2 km (1.2 miles) before returning to Alstonefield by making use of the footpaths then leading SW.

Route 30: TISSINGTON, PARWICH, FENNY BENTLEY and THORPE CLOUD

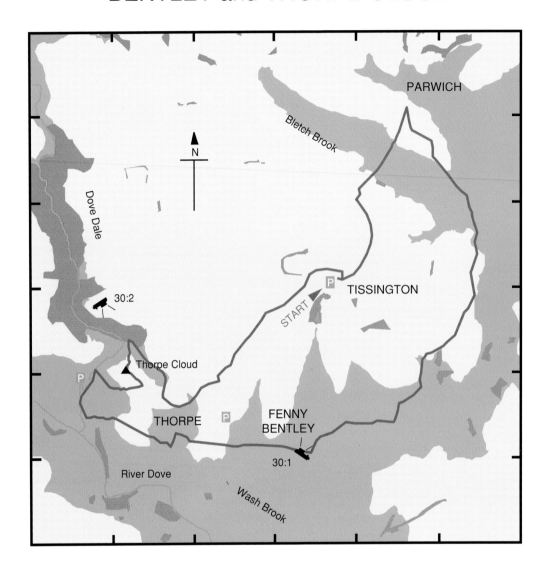

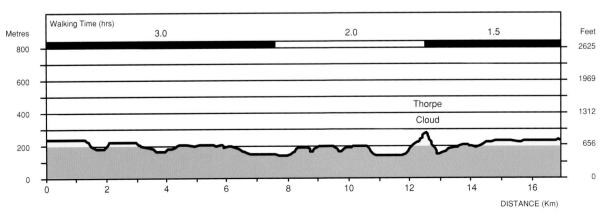

ROUTE 30

Tissington, Parwich, Fenny Bentley and Thorpe Cloud

●

STARTING LOCATION
Car park at Tissington, on Tissington Trail.
OLM 24: MR 178521.
Large car park with toilets and adjacent picnic area.

ALTERNATIVE STARTING POINTS
Parwich.
Near Thorpe Cloud.

PUBLIC TRANSPORT
Bus route to village 441.
(More extensive service to nearby Tissington Gates.)

OVERVIEW/INTEREST
Superb starting location from Tissington with its
     several wells and other attractions.
Route a mixture of farmlands and more open rugged
     countryside.
Peep into the limestone gorge of Dove Dale.
The highlight must be standing on top of Thorpe
     Cloud.
Pleasant villages and attractive churches.
A challenging route, one for dedicated walkers.

FOOTPATHS
Good and clearly defined at the start and in other
     sections.
Indistinct and confusing in several places.
The steep, crag-like slopes of Thorpe Cloud are
     challenging.
Several nasty, boggy areas in wet winter conditions.
Route signing is also mixed and ranges from
     acceptable to non-existent.

GRADING
Moderate to difficult/severe.

TIME ALLOWANCE
6½ hours.

STATISTICS
DISTANCE
Excluding Height   16.9 km (10.5 miles)
TOTAL HEIGHT GAINED   480 m   (1575 ft)
PRINCIPAL HEIGHTS
Thorpe Cloud   287 m   (940 ft)

The way to Fenny Bentley   *Allow 3 hours*

Leave the car park to the NE walking along the Tissington Trail towards Alsop-en-le-dale and immediately passing beneath a road bridge. A Nature Reserve needs to be respected just past the bridge. Walk first past the paths opposite each other, the L one leading back to Tissington and that to the R going to Bradbourne. The trail emerges from a cutting and as more open land-scapes appear reaches another stone road bridge. Just before reaching the bridge, climb the steps to your L and follow the footpath signed to 'Tissington & Parwich'. After crossing a stile, turn R over the bridge and avoid using the cattle grid ahead by clambering over the s-stile. This is at the entrance track to Shaws Farm.

The way curves pleasantly downhill to the NE. A short distance further on, maintain this bearing by veering off to the R across the meadowland, keeping to the direction of the sign pointing to 'Parwich 1½'. The way leads more steeply down towards Bletch Brook, which is crossed at MR 184536, after passing over and through a number of obstacles on the way. The crossing is by means of a wooden footbridge. On the other side climb up the grassy hill ahead. The obvious way continues along a well-trodden grassy path and another footbridge is crossed towards the top of the brow. This is over a (more often than not) dried-up stream bed adjacent to a hedge contain-ing holly and to your R. Veer L across the plank and then maintain a route close to the L-hand side of the next two fields. You will then sight a stone

183

barn in the far corner of the adjacent field further to your L and at the next hedge ahead the buildings of Parwich appear below to the NE. These are seen through a convenient gap, which you pass through. Veer L again after this, continuing to hug the L-hand side of the following field. As the ground falls ahead of you there is a most unexpected and delightful view of the village and setting of Parwich and it is seen to perfection from just beyond the next G-stile. This position at MR 186541 marks the most northerly extremity of the route.

Turn about and, having passed back through the G-stile, cross the field on a s diagonal covering ground where there is no distinct path. One marker is that you pass beneath overhead electricity lines. Your diagonal converges with a hedge to your L fortified by two strands of barbed wire. Be vigilant to locate the obscure G-stile at the far end of this hedge, near the corner of the field. Having passed through this, follow a SSE diagonal to reach an even more obscure wooden stile in the far corner of the adjacent field. This stile leans awkwardly away from you so turn about to cross it and be careful where you place each foot. (Some route signing and refurbishing of the stiles and other crossings in this area is needed.) On the far side of the stile veer slightly L to walk SE following the line of mature deciduous trees to your L. Pass through a conveniently positioned gap in the hedge ahead and repeat this at the following one; at the second be careful to avoid the worst of a deepish, boggy morass. Then take care in locating another obscure G-stile in the next wall, between a disused gateway to its L and a hedge of trees to the R. After this, be particularly careful to keep beside the boundary fence on your R and be extra vigilant in finding and passing over an extremely obscure wooden stile in a low stone wall on your R. Watch out here as the stile is loose! Continue across the next meadow on a SE diagonal, surrendering height in the process.

The route then leads to another hedge, this time to your L, and from here a more distinct path leads round the brow of the hill to your L, still leading SE. Your confidence should become fully restored on reaching the next certain wooden G-stile ahead

but it is another awkward one. Following this another, less clear, stile has to be crossed in the far R-hand corner of the next field. Again exercise care here, avoiding the loop of barbed wire. Keep beside the hedge on your R as you descend further, crossing a number of more obviously positioned stiles. There are three of these and at the middle one again avoid the barbed wire. Further down, the outline of Gorsehill Farm comes into view ahead and lower down still the route leads through a gateway, the surrounds of which are often muddy after prolonged rain. Beyond this, veer slightly to your R to re-cross Bletch Brook by a wooden footbridge in the R-hand far corner of the next field. This is at MR 194529 and from here your continuation way is to the s. The ground rises ahead and the correct line up is to the R, towards the trees near the top of the hill. A formidable wire fence is reached; there is an excellent wooden s-stile available to cross over this but it is half hidden behind the thick trunk of a large tree. Safely over, continue uphill following a diagonal line to your L to pass above and parallel to Gorsehill Farm, still progressing s.

The way leads through another gap and then dips to cross a shallow depression. The approach to this is through another hedge in which a further stile has been concealed. From the dell continue s, veering R up a grassy slope. Further up the slope you need to pass over another s-stile in order to cross a stone wall by a metal gate. Veer R across the next meadow and then cross a narrow macadam road at which – surprise, surprise – there are signposts! The one pointing along your continuation route is only marginally helpful; it says 'Public Footpath'.

The way leads to Lea Cottage Farm, just ahead and further s. Beware of a yapping dog here which, according to the farmer, has had a go at several commercial callers but fortunately, so far, at no walkers! Veer L towards the farm house but before reaching it bear to the R to pass between the extensive farm outbuildings. Exit from these along a concrete track designed for tractors. The way continues uphill through a gateway. At the second gateway use the stile to cross the fence and bear R, away from the continuation of the tractor track, and follow the line of a stone wall on your R. Continue slightly downhill to the sw where two more stiles are reached, the second of these being somewhat redundant. Keep to your established diagonal and cross the stream to your R at the copse ahead. This is achieved by passing through two gateways, the second much narrower than the first. The crossing is quite a challenge as there is no bridging assistance and the ground here, after heavy rain, is covered in deep mud. The steep and sometimes muddy bank on the opposite side can be even harder to scale. Continue sw up the hillside, making for the higher ground as quickly as possible. There is one further hardship just ahead and this is the crossing of a narrow ravine to your L through which a small stream flows, sometimes again through waterlogged ground. The best crossing is up above the official footpath route and is by means of a concrete bridging which the farmer from Woodeaves Farm has installed. (I have spoken to the farmer and he has informed me that he does not object to walkers using the route I have described.)

From this permissive concrete crossing of the culvert, head s directly to Woodeaves Farm, walking down over firmer ground and following tractor tracks that lead to a hay store and beyond this to the farm buildings. Bear L to walk below the farmhouse, passing to the R of a recently constructed large barn. Continue along the farm drive to reach The Priory below, crossing over a cattle grid in your approach. At the entrance to Lees Farm located just beyond, use the stile to the L of another cattle grid to access a path which crosses the next field and bypasses the farm. This is achieved on a westwards diagonal. The route passes beneath electricity lines at an acute angle as the buildings of Fenny Bentley appear ahead. Continue sw towards these.

To reach the hamlet you will have to negotiate further stiles and a small watercourse. Your line of approach is guided by the electricity lines and your final steps are along the side of a hedge and then down across an open meadow to a stile at a metal gate. The way leads past cottages to reach the A515 road through Fenny Bentley, almost opposite the church.

30:1 *Looking back towards Fenny Bentley*

The way to Thorpe Cloud   *Allow 2 hours*

Cross the road on a diagonal to your R and almost immediately turn L up the public footpath which passes by the attractive church with its unusually narrow spire. The next section passes through the graveyard and this is reached by means of stone steps, positioned on the L-hand side of the church gates. Two tiny G-stiles lead to the enclosed area behind the school further on. The exit from this is by means of similar stile and through this the route immediately bridges a small watercourse. Follow the rectangular perimeter of the fence to your R by making a full turn to the R part-way along. The way leads across a surfaced track, reached and left by passing through further stiles. The second of these is somewhat difficult to squeeze through but your efforts are rewarded by the subsequent path being signed to 'Thorpe'. The route leads westwards uphill to reach another stile and culvert. From here, a clearer path leads further uphill and the way passes through a gap in a hedge at the top. Continue further w beside a

185

hawthorn hedge on your L. The view improves as you do this and soon the conical shape of Thorpe Cloud appears away to the NW.

After the next G-stile, the continuation way dips to cross a wide valley through which Wash Brook meanders. This is crossed by means of a concrete beam at MR 167502. Again it can be quite muddy here. On the far side, bear slightly L up the slope. Immediately ahead, K-gates provide an entrance and exit for crossing the Tissington Trail. The path beyond is signed to 'Thorpe and Dovedale'. Continue W up the brow of the hill ahead to reach and cross the minor road at a point where more stiles are provided. Continue W along the surfaced lane directly opposite. Some distance on, the farm at Broadlowash is passed as your route snakes downhill to the R of it, towards a huddle of attractive buildings below. The first residence passed is Stoney Cottage. Before you reach any others, turn L along the footpath marked by a venerable sign, to walk SSW down a shallow grassy dell. The way crosses a boggy watercourse where an unusual sign is passed which reads 'Footpath here 4 feet wide – Danger –'. The 'danger' is deep,

30:2 The long spur of Thorpe Cloud separating Lin Dale from Dove Dale

boggy ground on either side. The way continues uphill along a broad, shaded path. When the path bends further R, be extremely careful to locate and to turn sharply back along a narrower path leading off to the R. From here, the continuation way passes to the R of Thorpe's parish church. On reaching the lane ahead, veer R away from the church to walk W along the higher of two roads, avoiding the one bearing off downhill to your R. When the road bends sharply to the R, select the public footpath on the L and immediately pass through a narrow G-stile, followed in quick succession by a wooden K-gate and another stile.

Cross the lush meadows ahead walking WNW to negotiate three more stiles, the last of which is to the R of a neat bungalow which you then pass along a wide track. When this track bends L, abandon it by passing through another narrow G-stile next to a metal gate on your R. Continue walking across the fields, with the shape of Thorpe Cloud away on your R. The way descends, first gently and then more steeply in line with the Izaak Walton Hotel, far away across the valley of the River Dove. Be careful part way down in negotiating another G-stile in a dry-stone wall, for the rake is awkward and there is new barbed wire tied round the R-hand post. The final descent is to the minor road just to the R of Thorpe Mill Farm. Turn L down the road and immediately cross over a cattle grid. Before reaching the first of two low arched bridges, turn off R to cross over another stile. The adjacent field is crossed on a diagonal to your L to reach a stile on which there is a waysign. From here, follow the course of the River Dove northwards upstream towards the limestone gorge of Dove Dale immediately ahead.

Further on, past another stile, keep to the L and on the river side of a fenced-off clump of trees. Further stiles follow and the last of these provides access to the touristy southern end of Dove Dale. Unfortunately, the interesting direct climb to the summit of Thorpe Cloud from here is at present fenced off as part of an erosion control programme. Therefore, veer R along the broad track with the fenced-off slopes of the hill rising to your L. The way climbs to the E along a narrow path to reach the top of the brow some distance on, near a barn and animal pens. From this point it is permissible to climb Thorpe Cloud and this is achieved by veering L and scaling the steep, grassy slopes rising to the WNW along a narrow, compacted path. The climb is a challenge and the final approach takes on the characteristics of a minor scramble. The reward is the narrow top ridge which is surprisingly elongated and has features more in keeping with a Borrowdale volcanic plug than a limestone tor. Walk northwards with caution along the exposed ridge, as its polished rock can be surprisingly slippery. The views from the far end are terrific, taking in part of Dove Dale with its interlocking limestone spurs, and Bunster Hill on the far side of the deep gorge rising to a height similar to your present precarious position.

The way back to Tissington   *Allow 1½ hours*

Descend via the equally steep slopes leading N towards the side valley of Lin Dale. The way down is slippery and the worst sections are near the top and then again towards the bottom, where minor scrambling is required. The way down does in fact lead back into Dove Dale and the river is reached at a particularly attractive spot often frequented by exuberant school parties. Your continuation route is along Lin Dale and this is entered by turning R and using the K-gate. A clearly defined path leads uphill to the SE along a comfortable gradient. Further up, veer round and below the craggy, steeper hillsides on your L, following what has now become a much less obvious path. The route leads through grassy hillocks before reaching a col to the R of higher, craggy limestone outcrops. In your approach to this col be careful to maintain a southwards bearing. Thorpe Pastures and Hamston Hill Quarry are then passed to your L and in this vicinity ignore the track leading downhill on your R by continuing to walk SE round the grassy slopes of Hamston Hill, passing just above the Peveril of the Peak Hotel. Continue by circling beside a stone wall on your R and ignore a G-stile in this wall. A short distance further on, veer R to pass through a waysigned G-stile followed by a S-stile over a stone wall.

A grassy path then leads uphill, bending L to follow the line of a hawthorn hedge. Keep walking uphill to the NE without passing through an opening on your R. Turn R at the next stone wall to pass through another narrow G-stile and then veer L to locate and pass through a second such obstacle to the L of a metal gate in the wall directly ahead. Following this, a field is crossed adjacent to a hedge which gives way to a stone wall and then another G-stile provides entrance to a narrow lane at MR 163509. Turn L here in the direction of Pike House but, before reaching it, branch off R through another G-stile to follow the footpath signed to Tissington. Continue NE through pastures where in quick succession five more G-stiles have to be negotiated. The last stile provides access to a lane at the entrance to Hollington End Farm.

Immediately cross over this lane to join the footpath towards Tissington, once again entered through a G-stile. Walk downhill beside the stone wall and further on rejoin the lane at another G-stile, just before crossing Wash Brook. Turn R along the lane to reach and cross the main A515 road at Tissington Gates. From here, continue down the lane leading through Tissington Estate parkland to return to Tissington. The car park is at the far end of the village, beyond the village green, church and pond and is reached by veering R and passing between these features.

Alternative routes

ESCAPES
To shorten the route (in order of increasing length): use the minor road just to the N of Lea Cottage Farm to walk back W directly into Tissington; use the Tissington Trail crossed at MR 165502 to walk back north eastwards; cut out the Thorpe Cloud climb.

EXTENSIONS
The walk is quite exacting in physical terms and the route finding is very demanding. For these reasons no extensions are either recommended or suggested.

187

Appendix 1: Relevant Addresses

Introduction

There are many reference books that provide comprehensive facts and general information about the Peak District. This appendix is therefore confined to presenting a list of relevant contact addresses and telephone numbers that may be useful to walkers.

It is perhaps worth mentioning that the Peak National Park publish a comprehensive series of Educational Fact Sheets. Copies of these Fact Sheets may be obtained from the Peak National Park Study Centre at Losehill Hall. Other relevant publications include the informative free newspaper *Peakland Post*. Also available is a modestly priced timetable covering bus and train services within the Peak District.

Contact addresses and telephone numbers

COUNCIL FOR THE PROTECTION OF   01742 665822
RURAL ENGLAND (CPRE)
SHEFFIELD AND PEAK BRANCH
22 Endcliffe Crescent
Ranmoor
Sheffield S10 3EF

DERBYSHIRE COUNTY COUNCIL   01629 580000
Planning Department
County Offices
Matlock DE4 3AG

ENGLISH HERITAGE   01604 730350
(East Midlands and East Anglia)
Hazelrigg House
33 Marefair
Northampton NN1 15R

ENGLISH NATURE   01629 815095
Peak and Derbyshire Region
Manor Barn
Over Haddon
Bakewell DE4S 1JE

FORESTRY COMMISSION   01623 822447
Sherwood Forest Office
Forestry Enterprises
Edwinstowe
Mansfield
Notts NG21 9JL

INFORMATION CENTRES
Bakewell	01629 813227
Castleton	01433 620679
Edale	01433 670207
Fairholmes (Derwent Valley)	01433 650953
Hartington	
Langsett (Near Sheffield)	} Open at weekends
Torside (Longendale Valley)	

Mobile Information Centre: The Board's Caravan will be at various summer events, including well-dressings.

MOUNTAIN RESCUE SERVICE   999 EMERGENCY

NATIONAL TRUST   01909 486411
East Midlands Region
The Stables
Clumber Park
Worksop
Notts S80 3BE

PEAK NATIONAL PARK
   NATIONAL PARK OFFICE   01629 814321
   Aldern House
   Baslow Road
   Bakewell
   Derbyshire DE45 1AE

   PEAK NATIONAL PARK STUDY CENTRE   01433 620373
   Losehill Hall
   Castleton
   Sheffield S30 2WB

TOURIST BOARD 01522 531521
East Midlands Tourist Board
Exchequergate
Lincoln LN2 1PZ

TOURIST INFORMATION CENTRES
  Ashbourne   01335 343666
  Buxton   01298 25106
  Glossop   01457 855920
  Holmfirth   01484 687603
  Leek   01538 381000
  Matlock   01629 55082

WATER AUTHORITIES
  NORTH WEST WATER   01629 825850
  PO Box 30
  New Town House
  Buttermarket Street
  Warrington WA1 2QG

SEVERN TRENT WATER   0121-722 4000
Abelson House
Sheldon Road
Birmingham B26 3PR

YORKSHIRE WATER   01532 448301
West Riding House
Albion Street
Leeds LS1 5AA

YOUTH HOSTELS ASSOCIATION   01629 825850
Central Regional Office
PO Box 11
Matlock
Derbyshire DE4 2XA

Appendix 2: Statistical Summary

This appendix provides a concise statistical summary of the 30 routes listed in numerical sequence within the separate regions of the Dark Peak and the White Peak.

THE DARK PEAK

Route	Description	Walking time	Walking distance (excluding height)		Total height gained		Highest peak	
		Hours	Km	Miles	Metres	Feet	Metres	Feet
1	Dove Stone Reservoir, Ashway Rocks and Chew Reservoir	5.5	13.8	8.6	360	1180	480	1575
2	Crowden, Black Hill and Laddow Rocks	5.5	12.8	7.9	430	1410	582	1910
3	Old Glossop, Shelf Stones and Bleaklow Head	5.5	12.7	7.9	470	1540	633	2075
4	Glossop, Cown Edge, William Clough and Doctor's Gate	8.5	23.4	14.5	570	1870	544	1785
5	Hayfield, Snake Path and Kinder Edges	9.5	28.7	17.9	960	3150	633	2075
6	The Derwent Edges, Derwent and Ladybower Reservoirs	6.0	17.4	10.8	400	1310	538	1765
7	Higher Poynton, Lyme Park and Bow Stones	4.0	10.8	6.7	260	855	390	1280
8	Chinley, South Head and Chestnut Centre	5.5	15.8	9.8	450	1475	494	1620
9	Hayfield, Rushup Edge, Edale and Jacob's Ladder	8.0	24.9	15.5	940	3085	541	1775
10	Hope, Jaggers Clough, Edale and Lose Hill	6.5	17.2	10.7	480	1575	560	1840
11	Hope, Win Hill and Ladybower Reservoir	5.0	13.4	8.3	480	1575	462	1515
12	Mam Tor, Lose Hill, Castleton and the Winnats	4.5	10.4	6.5	460	1510	517	1695
13	Shining Tor, Goyt Valley and Windgather Rocks	6.0	14.4	8.9	480	1575	559	1835
14	Curbar, Froggatt and Baslow Edges and River Derwent	4.5	12.6	7.8	250	820	340	1115
15	Macclesfield Forest, Shutlingsloe and Wildboarclough	5.0	11.9	7.4	430	1410	506	1660
16	The Roaches, Hanging Stone and Lud's Church	5.5	13.3	8.3	360	1180	505	1660
		95.0	253.5	157.5	7780	25520	8284	27180

THE WHITE PEAK

Route	Description	Walking time	Walking distance (excluding height)		Total height gained		Highest peak	
		Hours	Km	Miles	Metres	Feet	Metres	Feet
17	Eyam, Highlow, River Derwent and Stoney Middleton	6.5	16.8	10.4	410	1345	381	1250
18	Tideswell, Chee Dale and Miller's Dale	6.5	18.5	11.5	420	1380	330	1085
19	Miller's Dale, Chee Dale, Chelmorton and Taddington	4.5	12.3	7.6	320	1050	438	1440
20	Ashford in the Water, Longstone Villages and Monsal Dale	4.0	10.5	6.5	200	655	235	770
21	Baslow, Chatsworth Park and Edensor	4.5	12.7	7.9	260	855	240	785
22	Longnor, Earl Sterndale, Chrome Hill and Hollinsclough	6.0	15.4	9.6	460	1510	430	1410
23	Lathkill Dale, Bradford Dale and Cales Dale	6.0	17.3	10.8	320	1050	310	1015
24	Elton, Birchover, Stanton Moor and Winster	5.0	13.4	8.3	350	1150	323	1060
25	Manifold Way, Wettonmill and Grindon	5.0	13.4	8.3	300	985	320	1050
26	Beresford Dale, Wolfscote Dale, Thor's Cave and Ecton Hill	7.0	19.5	12.1	440	1445	369	1210
27	Dove Dale, Wetton, Ecton Hill, Alstonefield and Wolfscote Dale	8.0	21.4	13.3	580	1905	369	1210
28	High Peak and Tissington Trails from Friden	4.5	14.7	9.2	30	100	364	1195
29	Alstonefield, Manifold Valley, Ilam and Dove Dale	6.0	15.0	9.3	440	1445	287	940
30	Tissington, Parwich, Fenny Bentley and Thorpe Cloud	6.5	16.9	10.5	480	1575	287	940
		80.0	217.8	135.3	5010	16450	4683	15360

Description	Walking time	Walking distance (excluding height)		Total height gained		Highest peak	
	Hours	Km	Miles	Metres	Feet	Metres	Feet
16 Walks in the Dark Peak	95.0	253.5	157.5	7780	25520	8284	27180
14 Walks in the White Peak	80.0	217.8	135.3	5010	16450	4683	15360
	175.0	471.3	292.8	12790	41970	12967	42540

The plans included in the route diagrams are based on information extracted from Ordnance Survey Outdoor Leisure Maps, with the permission of Her Majesty's Stationery Office © Crown copyright.

INDEX

Page numbers in *italic* refer to the illustrations